A Working Bibliography on

# THE NEGRO IN THE UNITED STATES

Compiled by

Dorothy B. Porter

## XEROX

University Microfilms

A Xerox Company

1969

# CONTENTS

# Introduction

The great outpouring of recent literature reflects widespread consciousness of the Negro in American life. Some of this writing has been prompted by such events as the 1954 Supreme Court ruling that outlawed segregation. Other elements of the current flood of written material emphasize the history of Negro Americans and their African heritage.

Perhaps the major portion of this literature reflects the dynamic personalities and politics of the Negro movement. Much has been written about evolving ideology and methodology of such organizations as The Congress of Racial Equality, the Student Non-Violent Coordinating Committee and the National Urban League. Leaders of social and political movements have contributed memoirs to the mass of writing about Negro life in the United States, and many authors have focussed on the lives of such public figures as the late Martin Luther King, Jr., Malcolm X; Adam Clayton Powell and Stokely Carmichael.

Unless order is brought to this literary outpouring, the flood will overwhelm those who are most in need of this literature. Selective, authoritative bibliographies are essential in improving access to Negro literature.

This working bibliography — which has the virtue of brevity, is a continuing attempt to establish order and facilitate book selection. It is designed to guide persons interested in acquiring printed books for public, private and university collections of Afro-Americana. While it is comprised primarily of English-language monographs, a few periodical article references are included in the bibliography section because of their significance.

The first step towards publishing this bibliography was the preparation of a short, general list of sources on the Negro in the United States for use in a summer workshop on bibliography held at Howard University, July 22-26, 1968, sponsored by the National Endowment for the Humanities. Participants in the workshop expressed their immediate need for a general bibliography of works on the Negro. They also indicated an important, though less urgent, need for annotated bibliographies on specific subjects. Hopefully, some of these special lists are now in preparation.

The compiler expresses her sincere appreciation to participants of the 1968 bibliographic workshop who contributed titles to this bibliography:

John W. Blassingame, assistant editor of the Booker T. Washington Papers and lecturer in History, University of Maryland; Miss Sheila R. Herstein, librarian, City College of the City University of New York; Miss

Carol Jopling, Librarian, Goodell Library, The University of Massachusetts; Mrs. A Mordine Mallory, Queens College, New Jersey; Mrs. Louise J. Still, Bibliographer, Honnold Library, Claremont Graduate School, California; Miss Margaret Thrasher, Librarian, Sojourner ? Truth Collection, Prince Georges County, Oxon Hill, Maryland; and Mrs. Jean Fagan Yellin, Assistant Professor, Pace College, New York.

Finally, special gratitude is expressed to University Microfilms, which has made possible the publication of this bibliography.


Dorothy B. Porter

# REFERENCE TOOLS

## BIBLIOGRAPHY

1    ADGER, Robert M. *Catalogue of Rare Books on Slavery and Negro Authors in Science, History, Religion, Biography, etc.* Philadelphia, Privately printed, 1906. 14 p. Out of print. One of the few catalogues of a Negro collector.

2    AMOS, Preston E. *One Hundred Years of Freedom: a Selected Bibliography of Books about the American Negro.* Washington, D.C., Association for the Study of Negro Life and History, 1963. 53 p. $1.50.

3    CLEAVES, Mary W. and Alma L. Gray. *A Bibliography of Negro History and Culture for Young Readers,* Miles M. Jackson, Jr., ed. Pittsburgh, University of Pittsburgh Press, 1968. Paperback. $2.50.

4    THE NEGRO BIBLIOGRAPHIC AND RESEARCH CENTER, INC. *Bibliographic Survey: The Negro in Print.* Washington, D.C. Vol. 1 no. 1, May 1965, Vol. 4 no. 3, Sept. 1968. $7.50 per year. Published every other month. Includes books for young and older adults.

5    DuBOIS, William Edward Burghardt. *A Select Bibliography of the Negro American. A Compilation made under the Direction of Atlanta University; together with the Proceedings of the Tenth Conference for the Study of the Negro Problems, held at Atlanta University, on May 30, 1905.* Atlanta, Atlanta University Press, 1905. 71 p. Out of print.

6    ELLIS, Ethel M. Vaughan. *The American Negro: A Selected Checklist of Books. Including a List of Periodicals, Films and Filmstrips, Recordings and Agencies that distribute Free and Inexpensive Material.* Washington, D.C., Negro Collection, Howard University, 1968. 46 p. $1.00. A good basic list for any library. Includes current titles published before 1967.

7    FILLER, Louis. *Negro Materials in the 1960's. Choice,* 6:161-70, April 1968.

8    FOREMAN, Paul B. and Mozell C. Hill. *The Negro in the United States: a Bibliography; a Select Reference and Minimum College Library Resources List.* Stillwater, Oklahoma, Oklahoma A. & M. College, 1947. 24 p.

9    GRINSTEAD, Scott. *A Select, Classified and Annotated List of Two Hundred Fifty Books by or about the Negro, published during the past ten years.* Nashville, Tennessee, Fisk University Library, 1939. 42 unnumbered leaves.

10  HOMER, Dorothy R. and Ann M. Swartout. *Books About the Negro: an Annotated Bibliography. New York, Praeger, 1966.*

11  HUSSEY, Edith, Mary Henderson and Barbara Marx. *The Negro American: a Reading List.* New York, The Department of Racial and Cultural Relations, National Council of Churches of Christ in the USA, 1957. 40 p. $1.68.

12  LOCKE, Alain LeRoy. *A Decade of Negro Self-Expression.* Charlottesville, Va. 1928. 20 p. (Trustees of the John F. Slater Fund. Occasional papers no. 26). Annotated. Out of print.

13  LOCKE, Alain LeRoy. *The Negro in America.* Chicago, American Library Association, 1933. 64 p. (Reading with a purpose, no. 68). Out of print.

14  MILES, Louella. *One World in School, a Bibliography.* Montgomery, Alabama, The American Teachers Association, 1946.

15  MILLER, Elizabeth W. *The Negro in America: a Bibliography* compiled for the American Academy of Arts and Sciences. With a foreword by Thomas F. Pettigrew. Cambridge, Harvard University Press, 1966. 190 p. $6.95. Annotated. Lists over 3,500 books, documents, articles, and pamphlets written since 1954.

16  MURRAY, Daniel Alexander Payne. *Preliminary List of Books and Pamphlets, by Negro Authors, for Paris Exposition and Library of Congress.* Washington, D.C., U.S. Commission to the Paris Exposition, 1900. 8 p. Out of print.

17  NATIONAL URBAN LEAGUE. Department of Research. *Selected Bibliography on the Negro.* 4th ed. New York, 1951. 124 p.

18  NEW YORK PUBLIC LIBRARY. *The Negro in the United States; a List of Significant Books.* 9th rev. ed. New York, New York Public Library, 1965. 24 p. $0.50.

19  PENN, Joseph E., Elaine C. Brooks and Mollie L. Beech. *The Negro American in Paperback; a Selected List of Paperbound Books.* Compiled and Annotated for Secondary School Students. Washington, D.C., National Education Association, 1967. 28 p. $0.35.

20  PIER, Helen Louis and Mary Louisa Spalding. *Negro; a Selected Bibliography.* In: *Monthly Labour Review,* Vol. 22, Jan. 1926, pp. 216-44.

21  PORTER, Dorothy B. *A Selected List of Books by and about the Negro.* Washington, D.C., U.S. Government Printing Office, 1936. 19 p. Out of print.

22  RICHARD B. HARRISON PUBLIC LIBRARY. Raleigh, North Carolina. *A Selected List of Books by and about the Negro, 1950-1956.* Raleigh, North Carolina, Richard B. Harrison Public Library, 1957. 26 p.

23  THE RISE OF THE AMERICAN NEGRO. *Saluting a Century of Negro Progress 100th Anniversary of the Emancipation Proclamation, January 1, 1863-January 1, 1963,* pp. 37-52. (Special issue of the *Open Shelf,* Cleveland Public Library, Nos. 9-10, 11-12, Sept.-Oct., Nov.-Dec., 1962).

24  ROLLINS, Charlemae Hill. *We Build Together; a Reader's Guide to Negro Life and Literature for Elementary and High School Use.* Prepared for the National Council of Teachers of English, 1967. 71 p. $1.50.

25  SCHOMBURG, Arthur A. and Robert T. Browne. *Exhibition Catalogue. First Annual Exhibition of Books, Manuscripts, Paintings, Engravings, Sculptures, et cetera.* By The Negro Library Association at the Carlton Avenue Young Men's Christian Association, 405 Carlton Avenue, Brooklyn, August 7 to 16, 1918. New York, The Pool Press Association Printers, 1917. 23 p. One of the first lists of works by Negro authors designed by the compilers to serve as a "guide" for the acquisition of important items and the building of libraries. Includes 377 titles.

26  SHERMAN, Caroline B. *New Books by and about Negroes.* Reprinted from *Rural Sociology,* Vol. 9, No. 2, pp. 161-69, June 1944. Abstracts.

27  TENNESSEE. Department of Education. Division of School Libraries. *The Negro; a Selected List for School Libraries of Books by or about the Negro in Africa and America,* compiled by the Division of School Libraries. Revised and reprinted through the courtesy of the Julius Rosenwald Fund. Nashville, Tennessee, State Department of Education, 1941. 48 p. Classified and annotated, with author and title index.

28   U.S. LIBRARY OF CONGRESS. Division of Bibliography. *Select List of References on the Negro Question;* compiled under direction of A.P.C. Griffin. Washington, D.C., U.S. Government Printing Office, 1903. 61 p. Out of print.

29   WELSCH, Erwin K. *The Negro in the United States; a Research Guide.* Bloomington, Indiana, Indiana University Press, 1965. 142 p. $5.00. Annotated.

30   WORK, Monroe N. *A Bibliography of the Negro in Africa and America.* New York, Octagon Books, 1966. 698 p. $22.50. Reprint of Work's monumental list of 17,000 references issued before 1928. First published in 1928.

### Subject

31   AMERICAN COUNCIL ON RACE RELATIONS. *Inventory of Research in Racial and Cultural Relations.* Chicago, Illinois, Committee on Education, Training and Research in Race Relations of the University of Chicago, 1948-53. Vols. 1-2, 1948-50; Vol. 3, 1950; Vols. 4-5, 1951-53. Abstracts of literature in the field.

32   AMERICAN JEWISH COMMITTEE. *Negro-Jewish Relations; a Selected Bibliography.* The American Jewish Committee, 1963. 4 p. $10.00.

33   ARCHIBALD, Helen A. *Negro History and Culture: Selected Material for Use with Children.* Chicago, Chicago City Missionary Society, 1965.

34   BAKER, Augusta. *Books about Negro Life for Children.* Rev. ed. New York, New York Public Library, 1963. 33 p. $0.35.

35   BOLIVAR, William Carl. *Library of William C. Bolivar, Philadelphia, Pennsylvania. Together with Printed Tracts, Magazines, Articles, Reports, Addresses and Miscellaneous not enumerated; Americana, Negroana, Manuscripts, Autograph Letters, Lincolniana, Rare Pamphlets, Travels, Africana, etc.* Philadelphia, 1914. 32 p. Out of print. One of the two known catalogues of private Negro collectors, prepared for sale.

36   *Books, Films, Recordings By and About the American Negro, 1968 edition.* Selected by Young Adult Librarians, The New York Public Library, North Manhattan Project, Countee Cullen Regional Branch, 1968. 23 p. Gratis.

37    BROOKS, Alexander D. *Civil Rights and Liberties in the United States, an Annotated Bibliography. With a Selected List of Fiction and Audio-Visual Materials* collected by Albert A. Alexander and Virginia H. Ellison. New York, Civil Liberties Educational Foundation, 1962. 151 p. $1.95.

38    BROWN, Warren. *Check List of Negro Newspapers in the United States (1827-1946).* Jefferson City, Missouri, Lincoln University School of Journalism, 1946. 37 p. Out of print.

39    CALIVER, Ambrose. *Education of Negroes.* A five-year bibliography, 1931-35. Washington, D.C., U.S. Government Printing Office, 1937. 63 p. Out of print.

40    CALIVER, Ambrose. *Sources of Instructional Materials on Negroes.* Revised by Theresa B. Wilkins. Washington, D.C., National Education Association of the United States, 1946. 23 p.

41    CAREY, Elizabeth L. and Corienne K. Robinson. *A Selected List of References on Housing for Negroes.* Washington, D.C., Federal Housing Authority Library, 1945. 17 p.

42    CONNECTICUT. Inter-racial Commission. *Selected Bibliography for Inter-racial Understanding.* Hartford, Connecticut, 1944. 36 p.

43    THE COUNCIL ON HUMAN RELATIONS. *Resource Handbook in Human Relations.* Cleveland, Ohio, 1959. 75 p.

44    CROSBY, Muriel. *Reading Ladders for Human Relations.* 4th ed. Washington, D.C., American Council on Education, 1963. 242 p. $4.00. Annotated list of more than 1,000 books for reading by children and young people to help them utilize the experiences stored in books for growth in human understanding.

45    DICKINSON, Donald C. *A Bio-Bibliography of Langston Hughes, 1902-1967.* With a preface by Arna Bontemps. Hamden, Connecticut, Archon Books, 1967. 267 p. $10.00. Portrait.

46    DUMOND, Dwight Lowell. *A Bibliography of Antislavery in America.* Ann Arbor, Michigan, University of Michigan Press, 1961. 119 p. $10.00. See no. 1287 - companion volume.

47 EDUCATION OF THE COLORED RACE IN INDUSTRY. *In Report of the Commissioner of Education for the Year 1893-94,* Vol. 1, Part 1, pp. 1038-61. One of the earliest lists of books and periodicals. Includes Negro authors.

48 EVANS, James C. *Integration in the Armed Forces; Pertinent Readings and Related Background Information.* n.p., 1963. 8 p. Mimeographed.

49 FARBE, Michel and Edward Margolies. *Richard Wright (1908-1960): Bibliography.* In *Bulletin of Bibliography,* Vol. 24, Jan.-April 1965. pp. 131-33, 137.

50 FELDMAN, Eugene P. R. *Negro History Educational Materials Bulletin.* Chicago, Ill., Museum of Negro History and Art, 1966. $2.00.

51 FISCHER, Russell G. *James Baldwin: A Bibliography, 1947-1962.* In *Bulletin of Bibliography,* Vol. 24, Jan.-April 1965, pp. 127-30.

52 FLANDERS, T. *Equal Employment Opportunity; a Selected Bibliography.* In *ALA Library Service Labor Newsletter,* Fall 1964. pp. 1-5.

53 FURTHER READING ON STUDENT MOVEMENT; *a Selected Bibliography.* In *New South,* Vol. 15, No. 10, Oct. 1960, pp. 13-14.

54 GARDINER, George L. *A Bibliography of Charles S. Johnson's Published Writings.* With an introductory note by Arna Bontemps. Nashville, Tennessee, The Fisk University Library, 1960. 41 p.

55 GILMER, Gertrude Cordelia. *Checklist of Southern Periodicals to 1861.* Boston, F.W. Faxon Company, 1934. 128 p. Titles are arranged alphabetically, chronologically, and by states.

56 GRAYSHON, Matthew Clifford and Vincent Paul Houghton. *Initial Bibliography of Immigration and Race.* Institute of Education, Nottingham University, 1966. 38 p. (Education Papers, No. 6)

57 GREENE, Harry Washington. *Two Decades of Research and Creative Writings at West Virginia State College.* Institute, W. Va., West Virginia State College, 1939. 24 p. Includes unpublished articles and monographs.

58 GRIFFIN, Appleton Prentiss Clark. *List of Discussions of the Fourteenth and Fifteenth Amendments with Special Reference to Negro Suffrage.* Washington, D.C., U.S. Government Printing Office, 1906. 18 p. List is annotated. Griffin was Chief Bibliographer in the Library of Congress when this list was compiled.

59 GUZMAN, Jessie Parkhurst. *Civil Rights and the Negro, a List of References Relating to Present Day Discussions.* Revised. Tuskegee Institute, Alabama, Department of Records and Research, 1950. 28 p. $0.30.

60 GUZMAN, Jessie Parkhurst. *George Washington Carver: A Classified Bibliography.* In *Bulletin of Bibliography,* Vol. 21, No. 1, May-Aug. 1953, pp. 13-16; Vol. 21, No. 2, Sept.-Dec. 1953, pp. 34-38.

61 HALL, Woodrow Wadsworth. *A Bibliography of the Tuskegee Gerrymander Protest; Pamphlets, Magazine and Newspaper Articles Chronologically Arranged.* Tuskegee Institute, Alabama, Department of Records and Research, 1960. 54 p.

62 HAYWOOD, Charles. *A Bibliography of North American Folklore and Folksong.* Vol. 1: The American People North of Mexico, including Canada. 2d rev. ed. New York, Dover Publications, Inc., 1961. 748 p. Section on the Negro pp. 430-560.

63 HEARTMAN, Charles Frederick. *Phillis Wheatley (Phillis Peters); a Critical Attempt and a Bibliography of Her Writings.* New York, Charles F. Heartman, 1915. 4 p. Portrait. Out of print.

64 JACKSON, Miles M., Jr. *A Bibliography of Materials by and About Negro Americans for Young Readers.* Washington, D.C., U.S. Office of Education, 1967. 92 p. $3.76.

65 JOHNSON, Preston C. and Julia O. Saunders. *The Education of Negroes in Virginia: an Annotated Bibliography.* 16 p. Reprinted from *Virginia State College Gazette,* Vol. 50, No. 1, Feb. 1944.

66 JONES, J. Alvin. *A Selected Bibliography of Current Literature and Visual Aids on Employment of Minority Group Workers.* Washington, D.C., Minority Groups Conference, 1956. 16 p. Mimeographed.

67 KAISER, Ernest. *The History of Negro History.* Negro Digest, Vol. 17, Feb. 1968, pp. 10-15, 64-80. Running commentary of titles with brief identification of authors.

68    KAISER, Ernest. *A Selected Bibliography of the Published Writings of W.E.B. DuBois. Freedomways,* Vol. 5, Winter, 1965. first quarter pp. 207-13.

69    KAPLAN, Louis, in association with James Tyler Cook, Clinton C. Colby, Jr., and Daniel C. Haskell. *A Bibliography of American Autobiographies.* Madison, University of Wisconsin Press, 1961. 372 p. The subject index refers to a number of autobiographies relating to the Negro.

70    KESSLER, S. H. *American Negro Literature; a Bibliographical Guide.* In *Bulletin of Bibliography,* Vol. 21, Sept. 1955, pp. 181-85.

71    KINDT, Kathleen A. *James Baldwin; a Checklist; 1947-1962.* In *Bulletin of Bibliography,* Vol. 24, Jan.-April 1965, pp. 123-26.

72    LASH, John S. *The American Negro and American Literature: A Check List of Significant Commentaries.* In *Bulletin of Bibliography,* Vol. 19, Sept.-Dec., 1946, pp. 12-15; Vol. 19, Jan.-Apr., 1947, pp. 33-36.

73    LAWSON, Hilda Josephine. *The Negro in American Drama* (Bibliography of Contemporary Negro Drama). An abstract of a thesis submitted in partial fulfillment of the requirements for the degree of Doctor of Philosophy in English in the Graduate School of the University of Illinois, 1939. Urbana, Illinois, 1939. 13 p.

74    LOGGINS, Vernon. *The Negro Author: His Development in America to 1900.* New York, Columbia University Press, 1931. 480 p. $12.50. Reprinted, New York, Kennikat, 1964. An excellent work of literary history and criticism with an especially valuable bibliography.

75    LONG, Margaret. *The Book Explosion of 1964: Authors Assess Negro Protest, Poverty and Personality; a Year's Books.* Atlanta, New South, Southern Regional Council, 1964. 24 p.

76    LOS ANGELES. Public Library. Municipal Reference Library. *The Prevention and Control of Race Riots: a Bibliography for Police Officers.* Los Angeles, 1944. 12 p. Mimeographed.

77    MARTIN, Robert E. *Bibliography of the Writings of Alain LeRoy Locke.* In *The New Negro Thirty Years Afterward.* Papers Contributed to the Sixteenth Annual Spring Conference of the

Division of the Social Sciences, April 20, 21, and 22, 1955. (Washington, D.C., the Howard University Press, The Graduate School, Washington, D.C., 1955) pp. 89-96. Lists 157 titles: Books, Booklets, Essays, Articles, Book Reviews, and Miscellany.

78    MAY, Samuel Joseph. *Catalogue of Anti-Slavery Publications in America.* In *Proceedings of the American Anti-Slavery Society,* at its Third Decade, held in the city of Philadelphia, Dec. 3d and 4th, 1863. With an Appendix and a Catalogue of the Anti-Slavery Publications in America, from 1750-1863. (New York, American Anti-Slavery Society, 1864) pp. 157-75. Out of print. The May Anti-Slavery Collection was acquired by Cornell University.

79    MERRIAM, Alan P. with the assistance of Robert J. Benford. *A Bibliography of Jazz.* Philadelphia, The American Folklore Society, 1954. 145 p.

80    MIDGETTE, Lillian Avon. *A Bio-Bibliography of Alain LeRoy Locke.* A thesis submitted to the faculty of Atlanta University in partial fulfillment of the requirements for the Degree of Master of Science in Library Science. Atlanta, Atlanta University School of Library Science, 1963. 48 leaves. Unpublished.

81    MILLS, Clarence Harvey. *Selective Annotated Bibliography on the Negro and Foreign Languages.* Reprinted from the *Journal of Negro Education,* Vol. 8, April 1939, pp. 170-76.

82    NATIONAL ASSOCIATION FOR THE ADVANCEMENT OF COLORED PEOPLE. Education Department. *Integrated School Books; A Descriptive Bibliography of 399 Pre-School and Elementary School Texts and Story Books Prepared by the NAACP Education Department.* New York, NAACP, 1967. 55 p. $1.00.

83    NATIONAL CLEARINGHOUSE FOR MENTAL HEALTH INFORMATION OFFICE OF COMMUNICATIONS, NIMH AND THE PLANNING BRANCH OFFICE OF PROGRAM PLANNING AND EVALUATION, NIMH. *Bibliography on the Urban Crisis. The Behaviorial, Psychological, and Sociological Aspects of the Urban Crisis.* U.S. Department of Health, Education, and Welfare — Public Health Services and Mental Health Administration, National Institute of Mental Health, Maryland. 156 p.

84    NEVINS, Allan, James I. Robertson, Jr. and Bell Wiley. *Civil War Books; a Critical Bibliography.* Baton Rouge, Louisiana State University Press, 1968. 278 p. 2 vols. $11.50 each.

85 NEW JERSEY LIBRARY ASSOCIATION. *New Jersey and the Negro: A Bibliography, 1715-1966.* Compiled by the Bibliography Committee of the New Jersey Library Association. Trenton, N.J., Trenton Free Public Library, 120 Academy Street, 1967. 196 p. $6.75.

86 NEW YORK PUBLIC LIBRARY. *Catalogues.* List of Works Relating to the American Colonization Society, Liberia, Negro Colonization, etc., in the New York Public Library. In *New York City Public Library Bulletin,* Vol. 6, 1902, pp. 265-69.

87 *NOT JUST SOME OF US; a Limited Bibliography on Minority Group Relations.* Washington, D.C., U.S. Department of Health, Education, and Welfare, 1963. 29 p.

88 OAKLAND, CALIFORNIA. Public Schools. *Cultural Diversity: Library and Audio Visual Materials for In-service Education,* prepared by Helen Cyr, Barbara Baker, and George Noone. Oakland, 1964. 39 p.

89 PAGENSTECHER, Ann. *Martin Luther King, Jr.: an Annotated Checklist.* In *Bulletin of Bibliography,* Vol. 24, Jan.-April 1965. pp. 201-7.

90 PARKER, Franklin. *Negro Education in the U.S.A.: A Partial Bibliography of Doctoral Dissertations.* In *Negro History Bulletin.,* Vol. 24, No. 8, May 1961. pp. 190-92.

91 PARKER, Franklin. *Public School Desegregation: a Partial Bibliography of 113 Doctoral Dissertations.* In *Negro History Bulletin,* Vol. 26, No. 7, April 1963. pp. 225-28.

92 PARKER, John W. *A Bibliography of the Published Writings of Benjamin Griffith Brawley.* In *The North Carolina Historical Review,* Vol. 34, No. 2, April 1957. pp. 165-78.

93 PORTER, Dorothy B. *Early American Negro Writings: a Bibliographical Study.* In *Bibliographical Society of American Papers,* Vol. 39, third quarter, 1945, pp. 192-268.

94 PORTER, Dorothy B. and Betty Jo Lanier. *Howard University: a Selected List of References.* Washington, D.C., Howard University Library, 1965. 9 p. Mimeographed.

95    PORTER, Dorothy B. *North American Negro Poets: a Bibliographical Checklist of their Writings, 1760-1944.* Hattiesburg, Mississippi, Book Farm, 1945. 90 p. Out of print. Revised edition in process.

96    PORTER, Dorothy B. *Selected List of Books with Negro Characters for Young Children.* National Educational Outlook among Negroes. Vol. 1, Dec. 1937, pp. 33-35; Jan. 1938, pp. 27-29.

97    PORTER, Dorothy B. *Selected References on the American Negro in World War I and World War II.* In *Journal of Negro Education,* Vol. 12, Summer 1943. pp. 579-85.

98    PROFESSIONAL RIGHTS AND RESPONSIBILITIES COMMITTEE ON CIVIL AND HUMAN RIGHTS OF EDUCATORS. National Education Association. *A Bibliography of Multi-Ethnic Textbooks and Supplementary Materials.* Washington, D.C., National Educational Association, 1966. 14 p. Paperback. Gratis. Arranged by subject, with brief but accurate annotations. Reading level and age group often given for titles listed.

99    RECORD, Wilson and Jane Cassels Record, Eds. *Little Rock, U.S.A.* San Francisco, Chandler Publishing Company, 1960. 338 p.

100   REID, Ira DeAugustine. *Negro Youth. Their Social and Economic Backgrounds; a Selected Bibliography of Unpublished Studies, 1900-1938.* Washington, D.C. The American Youth Commission of the American Council on Education, 1939. 71 p. Out of print.

101   REISNER, Robert George. *The Literature of Jazz; a Selective Bibliography.* With an introduction by Marshall W. Stearns. New York, New York Public Library, 1959. 63 p.

102   ROSS, Frank Alexander and Louise Venable Kennedy. *A Bibliography of Negro Migration.* New York, Columbia University Press, 1934. 251 p.

103   ROUNTREE, Louise M. *An Index to Biographical Sketches and Publications of the Bishops of the A.M.E. Zion Church.* Salisbury, North Carolina, Livingstone College, Carnegie Library, 1963. 34 p.

104   RUSSEL SAGE FOUNDATION, LIBRARY. *The Negro in Industry.* New York, 1924. Bulletin No. 66, Aug., 1924.

105  SCHOMBURG, Arthur A. *A Bibliographical Checklist of American Negro Poetry.* New York, Charles F. Heartman, 1916. 57 p. Out of print.

106  SELECTED ANNOTATED BIBLIOGRAPHY FOR STUDENT READING. In *Journal of Education,* Vol. 147, Dec. 1964, pp. 103-9.

107  SIEG, Vera. *The Negro Problem: a Bibliography.* Madison, Wisconsin, Wisconsin Library School, 1908. 22 p. Out of print.

108  SMITH, Benjamin F. *Racial Integration in Public Education: an Annotated Bibliography:* Parts IV-VIII. In *The Negro Educational Review,* Part IV, Vol. 13, No. 1, Jan. 1962; Part V, Vol. 14, No. 1, Jan. 1963; Part VI, Vol. 15, No. 1, Jan. 1964; Part VII, Vol. 16, Nos. 1 & 2, Jan.-April 1965; pp. 4-18, Part VIII, Vol. 17, No. 2, April 1966, pp. 52-64.

109  SNOWDEN, George. *Negro Political Behavior; a Bibliography.* Bloomington, Indiana, Indiana University, 1941. 19 p.

110  SPANGLER, Earl. *Bibliography of Negro History: Selected and Annotated Entries, General and Minnesota.* Minneapolis, Ross and Haines, 1963. 101 p. $7.50.

111  SPRAGUE, M.D. *Richard Wright: a Bibliography.* In *Bulletin of Bibliography,* Vol. 21, No. 2, Sept.-Dec., 1953. 39 p.

112  STANDLEY, Fred L. *James Baldwin, 1963-1967.* In *Bulletin of Bibliography,* Vol. 25, May-Aug. 1968, pp. 135-37, 160.

113  STERLING, Philip. *Laughing on the Outside; the Intelligent White Reader's Guide to Negro Tales and Humor;* Introductory Essay by Saunders Redding. New York, Grosset, 1965, pp. 251-54.

114  STETLER, Henry G. *Inter-group Relations Bibliography; a Selected List of Books, Periodicals, and Resource Agencies in Inter-group Relations, including a Special Section devoted to Connecticut Studies.* Hartford, Connecticut, Connecticut State Inter-Racial Commission, 1947. 82 p.

115  THOMPSON, Edgar Tristam and Alma Macy. *Race and Region; a Descriptive Bibliography compiled with Special Reference to the Relations Between Whites and Negroes in the United States.* Chapel Hill, University of North Carolina Press, 1949. 194 p. Out of print.

116  TINKER, Edward Larocque. *Les Écrits de Langue Française en Louisiane au XIXe Siècle;* Essais Biographiques et Bibliographiques. Paris, Librairie Ancienne Honoré Champion, 1932. 502 p. Includes sketches on 21 "Hommes de couleur libre."

117  TINKER, Edward Larocque. *Gombo; the Creole Dialect of Louisiana, with a Bibliography.* In *Proceedings of the American Antiquarian Society at the Semi-Annual meeting held in Boston, April 17, 1935* (Worcester, Mass., Published by the Society, 1935), pp. 101-42.

118  TOLSON, Ruth M. *Hampton Institute Press Publications; a Bibliography.* Hampton, Virginia, Hampton Institute, 1959. 6 p. Mimeographed.

119  TUSKEGEE INSTITUTE. Department of Records and Research. *A Bibliography of the Student Movement Protesting Segregation and Discrimination, 1960.* Tuskegee Institute, Alabama, Department of Records and Research, 1961. 10 p. Introductory statement by Jessie P. Guzman, Director.

120  TUSKEGEE INSTITUTE. Department of Records and Research. *Civil Rights and the Negro.* A List of References Relating to Present Day Discussions. Tuskegee, Alabama, Tuskegee Institute, 1949. 19 p. Mimeographed.

121  TUSKEGEE INSTITUTE. Department of Records and Research. *A Selected List of References Relating to the Negro Teacher 1949 to June 1955.* Tuskegee Institute, Alabama, Department of Records and Research, 1955. 3 p.

122  U.S. CONGRESS. Committee on Education and Labor. House of Representatives, 89th Congress, 2d Session. *Books for Schools and the Treatment of Minorities.* Washington, D.C., U.S. Government Printing Office, 1966. 828 p. Paperback $2.50. Selection criteria as stated by educators, publishers, librarians and authors. The Appendix, pp. 642-828, contains critical bibliographies of children's books and textbooks.

123  U.S. DEPARTMENT OF COMMERCE. Negro Affairs Division. *The Negro in Business; a Bibliography, 1935.* Washington, D.C., Department of Commerce, 1935. 9 p.

124 U.S. DEPARTMENT OF HOUSING AND URBAN DEVELOPMENT, LIBRARY. *Bibliography of Published Works* by Robert C. Weaver, Secretary U.S. Dept. of Housing and Urban Development. Washington, D.C., 1967. 12 p.

125 U.S. WORKS PROGRESS ADMINISTRATION. *Subject Index to Literature on Negro Art* Selected from the *Union Catalog of Printed Materials on the Negro in the Chicago Libraries.* Chicago, Chicago Public Library Omnibus Project, 1941. 49 p.

126 WATT, Lois B., Myra H. Thomas and Harriet L. Horne. *The Education of Disadvantaged Children: a Bibliography.* Washington, D.C., U.S. Government Printing Office, 1966.

127 WAXMAN, Julia. *Race Relations, a Selected List of Readings on Racial and Cultural Minorities in the United States with Special Emphasis on Negroes.* Chicago, Julius Rosenwald Fund, 1945. 47 p.

128 WEGELIN, Oscar. *Jupiter Hammon. American Negro Poet; Selections from His Writings and a Bibliography.* New York, Charles F. Heartman, 1915. 51 p. Out of print.

129 WEINBERG, Meyer, ed. *School Integration: a Comprehensive Classified Bibliography of 3,100 References.* Chicago, Integrated Education Associates, 1967. 137 p. $3.95.

130 WEST, Earle H. *Summary of Research During 1963 Related to the Negro and Negro Education.* In *Journal of Negro Education,* Vol. 34, No. 1, Winter 1965, pp. 30-38, Vol. 35, No. 1, Winter 1966, pp. 62-72; Vol. 36, No. 1, Winter 1967. pp. 58-69.

131 WHEATLEY, Phillis. *Phillis Wheatley: Poems and Letters.* Edited by Charles F. Heartman. New York, Charles F. Heartman, 1915. 111 p. Out of print.

132 WHITEMAN, Maxwell. *A Century of Fiction by American Negroes, 1853-1952, a Descriptive Bibliography.* Philadelphia, Albert Saifer, 1955. 64 p. $7.50.

133 WILLIAMS, Daniel T. and Carolyn L. Redden. *The Black Muslims in the United States: a Selected Bibliography.* Tuskegee Institute, Alabama, Hollis Burke Frissel Library, 1964. 19 p.

134 WILLIAMS, Daniel T. *Freedom Rides: A Bibliography, 1961;*

*Periodicals and Pamphlets, Selected Newspapers.* Tuskegee Institute, Hollis Burke Frissell Library, 1962. 17 p.

135  WILLIAMS, Daniel T. *University of Mississippi and James H. Meredith; a Bibliography.* Tuskegee Institute, Hollis Burke Frissell Library, 1963. 9 p.

136  (WINSTON, Michael R.) *Writings of E. Franklin Frazier.* In (Program of) a Lecture Series in Honor of Edward Franklin Frazier. March 13, 14, 15, 1962, Cramton Auditorium, Howard University, Washington, D.C. pp. 9-16. Lists 117 titles: books, articles, chapters in books, and 5 unpublished manuscripts. An example of a bibliography of a well-known sociologist listed in an obscure source.

## CATALOGUE, CALENDARS AND BIBLIOGRAPHIES OF COLLECTIONS IN INSTITUTIONS

137  BENNETT, Elaine C. *Calendar of Negro-related Documents in the Records of the Committee for Congested Production Areas in the National Archives.* Prepared by Elaine C. Bennett for the Committee on Negro Studies of the American Council of Learned Societies. Washington, D.C., American Council of Learned Societies, 1949. 100 leaves.

138  BETHEL, Elizabeth, Sarah Dunlap and Lucille Pendell. *Preliminary Checklist of the Records of the Bureau of Refugees, Freedmen, and Abandoned Lands, 1865-1872.* Washington, D.C., National Archives, War Records Office, 1946. 64 p.

139  DeWITT, Josephine. *The Black Man's Point of View; a List of References to Material in the Oakland Free Library,* compiled by Josephine DeWitt at a suggestion from Delilah L. Beasley. Oakland, California, Oakland Free Library, 1930. 30 p.

140  FISK UNIVERSITY. Nashville, Tennessee. *A List of Manuscripts, Published Works and Related Items in the Charles Waddell Chesnutt Collection of the Erastus Milo Cravath Memorial Library, Fisk University.* Nashville, Tennessee, Fisk University, 1954. 32 p.

141  HAMPTON, Virginia. Normal and Agricultural Institute. Collis P. Huntington Library. *A Classified Catalogue of the Negro Collection in the Collis P. Huntington Library, Hampton Institute.* Compiled by Workers of the Writers' Program of the Works Projects Administration in the State of Virginia. Sponsored by Hampton Institute, 1940. 225 p.

142 HEARTMAN NEGRO COLLECTION. *Catalogue*, Texas Southern University. Houston, Texas, Texas Southern University, 1957. 325 p.

143 HISTORICAL RECORDS SURVEY. District of Columbia. *Calendar of the Writings of Frederick Douglass in the Frederic Douglass Memorial Home, Anacostia, D.C.* Prepared by District of Columbia Historical Records Survey, Division of Professional and Service Projects, Work Projects Administration. Sponsored by the Board of Commissioners of the District of Columbia. Washington, D.C., District of Columbia Historical Records Survey, 1940. 93 p. Out of print.

144 HOWARD UNIVERSITY, FOUNDERS LIBRARY, MOORLAND FOUNDATION. *A Catalogue of Books in the Moorland Foundation*, compiled by Workers on Projects 271 and 328 of the Works Progress Administration, Margaret R. Hunton and Ethel Williams, Supervisors, Dorothy B. Porter, Director. Washington, D.C., Howard University, 1939. 499 leaves. Mimeographed. Out of print.

145 HUBBARD, Geraldine Hopkins, comp. Julian S. Fowler, ed. *A Classified Catalogue of the Collection of Anti-Slavery Propaganda in the Oberlin College Library.* Oberlin, Ohio, Oberlin College, 1932. 84 p. *Oberlin College Library Bulletin*, Vol. 2, No. 3.

146 JORDAN, Casper LeRoy. *The Levi Jenkins Coppin Collection at Carnegie Library, Wilberforce University, Wilberforce, Ohio.* Wilberforce, Ohio, Wilberforce University, 1957. 17 p. Mimeographed.

147 LEWINSON, Paul. *A Guide to Documents in the National Archives: for Negro Studies.* Washington, D.C., American Council of Learned Societies Executive Offices, 1947. 28 p.

148 McCONNELL, Roland C. *Preliminary Inventory of the Papers of the Emmett J. Scott Collection in Morgan State College, 1916-1951.* Baltimore, Soper Library, Morgan State College, 1959. 8 p.

149 McLIN, Velma E. *The Charles Eaton Burch Collection in Founders Library, Howard University.* Washington, D.C., Howard University, 1962. 67 p. Mimeographed.

150 MICHIGAN STATE UNIVERSITY, EAST LANSING. Library. *Partial Bibliography on the American Negro: Books and Their Call*

*Numbers in the Library, as of September 1, 1962, by J.F. Thaden and Walter E. Freeman. Institute for Community Development and Services, 1962. (Bibliography Series, No. 1). 12 p.*

151 *NEW YORK PUBLIC LIBRARY. SCHOMBURG COLLECTION. Dictionary Catalog of the Schomburg Collection of Negro Literature and History.* Boston, G.K. Hall, 1962. 9 vols. $605.00. Supplement, 1968. 2 vols. $95.00.

152 OAKLAND FREE LIBRARY. *The Negro Literature Collection: Books of Negro Authorship to be Found in the Oakland Free Library.* Rev. Oakland, California, 1937. 11 p.

153 RUTGERS UNIVERSITY LIBRARY. *The Negro in New Jersey: a Checklist of Books, Pamphlets, Official Publications, Broadsides, and Dissertations, 1754-1964, in the Rutgers University Library.* Compiled by Donald A. Sinclair, Curator of Special Collections. New Brunswick, 1965. 56 p.

154 U.S. LIBRARY OF CONGRESS. Manuscript Division. *Booker T. Washington: a Register of his Papers in the Library of Congress.* Washington, D.C. Manuscript Division, Reference Department, Library of Congress, 1958. 105 p. $0.80.

155 U.S. WORKS PROGRESS ADMINISTRATION. Historical Records Survey. Division of Community Service Programs. *Calendar of the Gerrit Smith Papers in the Syracuse University Library, General Correspondence, Volume 1, 1819-1846,* prepared by the Historical Records Survey, Division of Community Service Programs, Works Progress Administration. Albany, New York, 1941. 290 p.

156 U.S. WORKS PROGRESS ADMINISTRATION. Historical Records Survey. Division of Community Service Programs. *Guide to Manuscripts and Source Material Relating to the Negro in Massachusetts.* Prefaced by The Historical Records Survey, Division of Service Programs, Works Projects Administration. Boston, Mass., The Historical Records Survey, 1942. 129 p. Manuscripts indexed are located in the Boston Public Library and cover the period 1827-65.

157 UNIVERSITY OF NORTH CAROLINA. Chapel Hill, North Carolina. *Lists of Books by and About Negroes Available in the Libraries of the University of North Carolina and Duke University.* Chapel Hill, North Carolina, University of North Carolina (n.d.) 88 p.

## HANDBOOKS, YEARBOOKS AND ENCYCLOPEDIAS

158 AMERICAN OIL COMPANY. *American Traveler's Guide to Negro History*. Chicago, American Oil Company, 1956. 58 p. Illustrations. Paperback, Gratis. Monuments, museums, historic sites of Negro America, listed by state and city. Revised and expanded version available. See: Drotning, Phillip T., p. 9.

159 BICKNELL, Marguerite Elizabeth and Margaret C. McCulloch. *Guide to Information about the Negro and Negro-White Adjustment*. Memphis, Brunner Printing Co., 1943. 39 p.

160 CULP, D.W. *Twentieth Century Negro Literature: or, A Cyclopedia of Thought on the Vital Topics Relating to the American Negro by One Hundred of America's Greatest Negroes*. Copiously Illustrated with One Hundred Five Photo Engravings. Naperville, Ill., J. L. Nichols Co., 1902. 472 p. Illustrations. Out of print.

161 DAVIS, John P. *The American Negro Reference Book*. Englewood Cliffs, N.J., Prentice-Hall, 1966. 969 p. $22.50. This volume, sponsored by the Phelps-Stokes Fund, is the first title in the projected series — *The American Negro Reference Shelf*. Twenty-four scholars have contributed articles on all facets of Negro experience in the United States. Footnotes and bibliographical references accompany the articles.

162 *DIRECTORY OF U.S. NEGRO NEWSPAPERS, MAGAZINES AND PERIODICALS, 1966*. New York U.S. Negro World, 1966. 31 leaves. $7.50.

163 DROTNING, Philip T. *A Guide to Negro History in America*. Garden City, N.Y., Doubleday, 1968. 247 p. $4.95. An expanded version of the American Oil Company pamphlet, *American Traveler's Guide to Negro History*. Author is a member of the public relations staff, American Oil Company.

164 *ENCYCLOPEDIA OF THE NEGRO*. Preparatory Volume with Reference Lists and Reports by W.E.B. DuBois and Guy B. Johnson. Prepared with the cooperation of E. Irene Diggs, Agnes C.L. Donohugh, Guion Johnson and others. Introduction by Anson Phelps Stokes. Rev. and enl. ed. New York, The Phelps-Stokes Fund, Inc., 1946. 215 p.

165  GAY, Joseph R. *Life Lines of Success: A Practical Manual of Self-Help for the Future Development of the Ambitious Colored American. The Whole Embracing an Inspiring Symposium on Our Present Day Opportunities. Lessons from the Ancient and Glorious History of the Race and the Wonderful Civilization of Our Ancestors as an Example to the Rising Generation. Words of Wisdom from the Wiseman's Philosophy as a Guide to a Happy and Successful Life. To Which is added Life Lines of Knowledge Presenting a Series of Valuable Instructions for the Self-Improvement of those of Desire to Keep Step with the Progress and Prosperity of a Rising Race as Told by the Camera.* Chicago, Ill., W.R. Vansant & Co., 1913. 512 p. Illustrations. Out of print.

166  (GIBSON, John William). *Progress of a Race; or, The Remarkable Advancement of the American Negro, from the Bondage of Slavery, Ignorance, and Poverty to the Freedom of Citizenship, Intelligence, Affluence, Honor and Trust.* Rev. and enl. by J.L. Nichols and William H. Crogman with Special Articles by well known authorities, Mrs. Booker T. Washington, Charles Melden, M.W. Dogan, Albon Holsey and an introduction by Robert R. Moton. Naperville, Ill., J.L. Nichols & Company, c1920. 480 p. Illustrations. Reprint, New York, Arno Press, $12.00.

167  HALEY, James T. *Afro-American Encyclopedia: or, The Thoughts, Doings and Sayings of the Race, Embracing Addresses, Lectures, Biographical Sketches, Sermons, Poems, Names of Universities, Colleges, Seminaries, Newspapers, Books and a History of the Denominations, giving the Numerical Strength of Each. In fact it teaches every subject of interest to the Colored People, as discussed by more than one hundred of their wisest and best men and women.* Illustrated with beautiful half-tone engravings. Nashville, Tenn., Haley and Florida, 1895. 639 p.

168  HARLAN, Louis R. *The Negro in American History.* Washington, D.C., Service Center for Teachers of History, 1965. 29 p. $0.50. Designed for teachers in high schools.

169  HARTSHORN, W.N. *An Era of Progress and Promise, 1863-1910. The Religious, Moral, and Educational Development of the American Negro Since His Emancipation.* Boston, Mass., The Priscilla Publishing Co., 1910. 576 p. Illustrations.

170  *INTERNATIONAL LIBRARY OF NEGRO LIFE AND HISTORY.* New York, Publishers Co., 1967. 5 vols. Illustrations. $60.00.

Published under the auspices of the Association for the Study of Negro Life and History, Charles H. Wesley, general editor. Each volume of this set is listed under subject categories of this bibliography. See: Morais, Herbert M. *The History of the Negro in Medicine;* Patterson, Lindsay. *Anthology of the American Negro in the Theatre;* Patterson, Lindsay. *The Negro in Music and Art;* Robinson, Wilhelmena S. *Historical Negro Biographies;* Wesley, Charles H. *Negro Americans in the Civil War.*

171 KATZ, William Loren. *Teachers' Guide to American Negro History.* Chicago, Quadrangle Books, 1968. 192 p. $5.50. Paperback $2.25. Arranged by curriculum units. "A Basic Teacher Reference Library," pp. 21-30. Bibliographies accompany each study unit, some 72 pages in all. Also included: "Sources of Inexpensive or Free Materials"; "Pamphlets on Race"; "Directory of U.S. Libraries with Negro History Book Collections"; "Museums of Negro History."

172 LYLE, Jack and others, eds. *The Black American and the Press.* Los Angeles, Ward Ritchie Press, 1968. 86 p. $3.95. Paperback $1.50. Papers and related comments presented at a symposium during the UCLA Foreign Journalism Awards Program, 1967. Gunnar Myrdal, Charles Evers, residents of Watts, and others discuss "The Racial Crisis," "Coverage in the Domestic Press," "International Reporting," "Negro Reaction to Press Coverage." Crisis reporting and its effect is the common theme.

173 MURRAY, Florence. *The Negro Handbook.* New York, Wendell Malliet and Co., 1942. 269 p.

174 MURRAY, Florence. *The Negro Handbook, 1944; a Manual of Current Facts, Statistics and General Information Concerning Negroes in the United States.* New York, Current Reference Publications, 1944. 283 p.

175 MURRAY, Florence. *The Negro Handbook, 1946-1947.* New York, Current Books, Inc., A.A. Wyn Publisher, 1947. 392 p. Out of print.

176 MURRAY, Florence. *The Negro Handbook, 1949.* New York, Macmillan Co., 1949. 368 p. Out of print.

177 THE NATIONAL REGISTER; Pertinent Facts About Colored Americans. 1st ed. Louisville, Register Publications, 1952, 632 p.

178 *THE NEGRO HANDBOOK,* Compiled by the editors of *Ebony.*

Chicago, Ill., Book Division, Johnson Publishing Co., 1966. 535 p. $12.50. Events and statistics related to all aspects of Negro America, with historical emphasis on the areas of civil rights. educational and employment opportunities, and legal decisions. Biographical and directory sections. Bibliography— "List of Significant Books," pp. 185-201.

179 *THE NEGRO HERITAGE LIBRARY*. Yonkers, New York, Educational Heritage, Inc., 1964-. 20 vols. $250.00. Illustrations. Ten of the contemplated twenty volumes are available. The following volumes are listed under subject categories of this bibliography: Cain, Alfred E., ed. *The Winding Road to Freedom;* Dannett, Sylvia G.L. *Profiles of Negro Womanhood.* Other volumes of this set are: *The American Negro Reference Book;* Evans, Lancelot O. *Emerging African Nations and Their Leaders;* King, Martin Luther. *A Martin Luther King Treasury; Negro Heritage Reader for Young People; The Negro in Public Affairs and Government.*

180 NEW YORK CITY BOARD OF EDUCATION. *The Negro in American History.* Brooklyn, New York, Board of Education of the City of New York, 1964. 166 p. Paperback $1.00. A resource bulletin reprinted, without revision, in 1967. Unlike many curriculum guides which begin the story in 1619, this publication offers three pre-America sections: "slavery in the old world: a background"; "The African heritage"; "The Latin-American Experience." Bibliography, pp. 151-60.

181 NORTHRUP, Henry Davenport, Joseph R. Gay and I. Garland Penn. *The College of Life; or, Practical Self-Educator, A Manual of Self-Improvement for the Colored Race forming an Educational Emancipator and a Guide to Success Giving Examples and Achievements of Successful Men and Women of the Race as an Incentive and Inspiration to the Rising Generation including Afro-American Progress.* Illustrated. Chicago, Illinois, Chicago Publication and Lithograph Co., 1895. 691 p.

182 PARSONS, Talcott, and Kenneth B. Clark, eds. *The Negro American.* Boston, Houghton Mifflin, 1965. 781 p. $9.50. Paperback $3.95 Boston, Beacon, 1968. Originally published as two issues of *Daedalus,* the quarterly journal of the American Academy of Arts and Sciences. Thirty contributors study the current civil rights scene. Reforms are proposed and criticized. The contradiction between social need and political power is the major theme of the collection.

183 PHINAZEE, Annette H. *Materials by and about American Negroes.* Proceedings of the Institute on Materials by and about American Negroes. Atlanta, Atlanta University School of Library Science, 1967. 111 p.

184 PLOSKI, Harry A. and Roscoe Brown, eds. *The Negro Almanac.* New York, Bellwether Pub. Co., 1967. 1012 p. $14.50. History, biography and statistics are the focal points of this volume. Intended for ready reference, maps, tables, charts may be found through an extensive index. Bibliography, pp. 946-65.

185 RICHINGS, G.F. *Evidences of Progress Among Colored People.* Philadelphia, Ferguson, 1905. 595 p. Illustrations. Out of print.

186 SALK, Edwin A. *A Layman's Guide to Negro History.* Chicago, Quadrangle Books, 1966. 170 p. $5.95. Paperback $1.95. Bibliography, pp. 3-169. "A Suggested Basic Library of Negro History," pp. 3-8; "Books on the General History of the Negro in the U.S., " pp. 9-12; "Books for Adults" (sections on biography, cultural contributions, Negro slave revolts, the Negro in American Wars), pp. 13-61; "Books for Children and Young Adults," pp. 64-73; "Paperback Books on Negro History," pp. 85-92; "Phonograph Records, Song Books and Film Strips," pp. 93-98; "Books and Pamphlets on Race," pp. 156-57; "Racial Attitudes in Textbooks," pp. 158-59; "Periodicals," pp. 161-62; "Bibliography of Bibliographies," pp. 163-65; "Visual Materials," pp. 166-67; "Teaching Materials and Guides," pp. 168-69.

187 SAN FRANCISCO UNIFIED SCHOOL DISTRICT. *The Negro in American Life and History.* San Francisco, 1967. 344 p. Paperback $2.00. An example of the type of resource books being produced by curriculum committees of major public school systems. The narrative text is organized on the same chronological and topical lines as most texts. Outstanding individual achievements are included, although the emphasis is upon the collective experience of American Negroes. Bibliography, pp. 335-44.

188 SIMMS, James N. *Simms' Blue Book and National Negro Business and Professional Directory.* Chicago, James N. Simms, 1923. 305 p.

189 SLOAN, Irving. *The American Negro; a Chronology and Fact Book.* Ferry, New York, Oceana Publications, 1965. 84 p. $2.75. Dates and facts from 1442 to 1965. A brief directory section and a two-page bibliography, pp. 67-68.

190 TRUBOWITZ, Sidney. *A Handbook for Teaching in the Ghetto School.* Chicago, Illinois, Quadrangle Books, 1968. 175 p. $4.95. The author is the principal of P.S. 113 in New York City. He gathered his material through teacher and pupil interviews in Harlem and through a questionnaire sent to supervisors working in the Harlem area. The teaching methods evolved are in practice at P.S. 113 and other Harlem elementary schools. "Books for Children," pp. 147-55; "Books for Teachers," pp. 156-62; Bibliography, pp. 163-68.

191 TUMIN, Melvin Marvin and Cathy S. Greenblat, eds. *Research Annual on Intergroup Relations,* 1966. New York, Praeger, 1967. 39 p. $6.00.

192 WATKINS, Sylvestre C. *The Pocketbook of Negro Facts.* Chicago, Illinois, Bookmark Press, 1946. 24 p. Out of print. 160 short paragraphs covering dates, biography, history, literature, etc. Arranged in dictionary form. Bibliography, pp. 21-22.

193 WORK, Monroe N. *Negro Year Book and Annual Encyclopedia of the Negro.* Tuskegee, Ala., Negro Year Book Co., 1912-52. See: *A Select Bibliography of the Negro,* 1912 ed. pp. 302-48; 1914-15 ed. pp. 390-417; 1917 ed. pp. 418-55; 1918-19 ed. pp. 473-93; 1921-22 ed. pp. 426-56; 1925-26 ed. pp. 473-510; 1931-32 ed. pp. 471-518; 1937-38 ed. pp. 501-48; 1947 ed. pp. 635-84; 1952 ed. pp. 384-412. The 1947 and 1952 editions were edited by Jessie Parkhurst Guzman. The titles of the editions vary slightly.

194 WRIGHT, Richard Robert, Jr., assisted by associate editors, W.A. Fountain and others. *The Encyclopaedia of the African Methodist Episcopal Church,* Containing Principally the Biographies of the Men and Women, Both Ministers and Laymen, whose Labors during a Hundred and Sixty years, helped make the AME Church what it is; also Short Historical Sketches of Annual Conferences, Educational Institutions, General Departments, Missionary Societies of the AME Church, and General Information about Historical, Theological, Sociological, Legal and Other Matters concerning African Methodism and the Christian Church in General. Introduction by William A. Fountain, foreword by Reverdy Cassius Ransom. 2d ed. Philadelphia, 1947. 688 p. Portraits.

195 WRIGHT, Richard Robert, comp., assisted by Ernest Smith. *The Philadelphia Colored Directory; a Handbook of the Religious, Social, Political, Professional Business and Other Activities of the Negroes*

*of Philadelphia.* Philadelphia, Philadelphia Colored Directory Co., 1907. 107 p. Portraits.

## INDEXES TO NEWSPAPERS AND PERIODICALS

196  *INDEX TO FACTS ON FILM.* Nashville, Tennessee. Prepared by Southern Education Reporting Service, 1954-58. 172 p. Supplements; July 1958 to June 1959. 83 p.; July 1959 to June 1960. 93 p.; July 1960 to June 1961. 114 p.

197  *INDEX TO SELECTED PERIODICALS RECEIVED IN THE HALLIE Q. BROWN LIBRARY.* Decennial Cumulation 1950-59. Edited by Charlotte W. Lytle. Boston, G.K. Hall & Company, 1961. 501 p.

198  *INDEX TO SELECTED PERIODICALS.* Annual Cumulations, Vols. 11-16, 1960-64. Compiled by the Staffs of the Hallie Q. Brown Library, Central State College Library, Central State College, Wilberforce, Ohio and the Schomburg Collection, the New York Public Library. Boston, G.K. Hall & Company, 1962-65. 5 Vols.

199  *INDEX TO PERIODICAL ARTICLES BY AND ABOUT NEGROES* (formerly, *Index to Selected Periodicals*). Vol. 17, 1966. Compiled by the Staffs of the Hallie Q. Brown Memorial Library, Central State University, Wilberforce, Ohio and the Schomburg Collection, the New York Public Library. Boston, G.K. Hall & Company, 1967. 46 p.

200  JANDA, Kenneth. *Cumulative Index to the American Political Science Review.* Volumes 1-57; 1906-63. Evanston, Illinois, Northwestern University Press, 1964. 225 p.

201  MARSHALL, Albert Prince. *A Guide to Negro Periodical Literature* (Subject and Author). Jefferson City, Missouri, Lincoln University, 1941-46. 4 Vols.

202  McPHEETERS, Annie L. *Negro Progress in Atlanta, Georgia 1950-1960: a Selective Bibliography on Human Relations from Four Atlanta Newspapers.* Atlanta, West Hunter Branch, Atlanta Public Library, 1964. 55 leaves.

203  *NEWS INDEX TO THE JOURNAL AND GUIDE,* Norfolk, Virginia. Prepared by the Staff of Fisk University as a Reliable Source of Information on Contemporary Negro Life and Activities. Norfolk, Virginia, The Guide Publishing Company, Inc., 1935-. Index for 1935 appeared in *Journal and Guide,* April 4, 1936. 1936 Index pamphlet form, 53 p. 1937-38 Index, 71 p.

204 PORTER, Dorothy B. and Ethel M. Ellis, comps. *Index to the Journal of Negro Education.* Volumes 1-31, 1932-62. Washington, D.C., Bureau of Educational Research, Howard University, 1953. 82 p. $5.00.

205 POUNCY, Mitchell Louis. *An Annotated Cumulative Index to Phylon Quarterly from 1950 through 1959.* A thesis submitted to the faculty of Atlanta University in partial fulfillment of the requirements for the Degree of Master of Science in Library Science. Atlanta, Atlanta University School of Library Science, 1961. 205 p. $22.00.

## MASTERS' THESES COMPLETED IN NEGRO INSTITUTIONS

206 BARKSDALE, Gaynelle W. *Graduate Theses of Atlanta University, 1931-1942.* Atlanta, Ga., The Library, Atlanta University, 1944. 71 p. (Atlanta University, Library Publication, No. 1). Titles listed by departments and chronological. Contains author and subject index.

207 BARKSDALE, Gaynelle W. *Graduate Theses of Atlanta University, 1943-1947.* Atlanta, Ga., The Library, Atlanta University, 1948. 58 p. (Atlanta University, Library Publication, No. 2).

208 BARKSDALE, Gaynelle W. and Edward B. Miller. *Graduate Theses of Atlanta University, 1948-1953.* Atlanta, Ga., Trevor Arnett Library, Atlanta University, 1955. 102 p. (Atlanta University, Library Publication, No. 3).

209 BARKSDALE, Gaynelle W. and Edward B. Miller. *Graduate Theses of Atlanta University (1948-1953)* 1954 Departmental Supplement. Atlanta, Ga., Trevor Arnett Library, Atlanta University, 1955. 10 p. (Atlanta University, Library Publication, No. 3). Mimeographed.

210 BARKSDALE, Gaynelle W. *Graduate Theses of Atlanta University, 1954-1959,* with Supplement through 1961. Atlanta, Ga., Trevor Arnett Library, Atlanta University, 1962. 114 p. (Atlanta University, Library Publication, No. 4).

211 FISK UNIVERSITY, Nashville, Tenn. *Masters' Theses of Fisk University, 1912-1958.* Nashville, Tenn., Fisk University, 1958. 62 leaves.

212 JOLLY, David. *Masters' Theses, 1932-1945;* an Annotated List. Hampton, Virginia, Hampton Institute, 1945. 34 p. Mimeographed.

213  KING, Annie Greene. *An Annotated Bibliography of Graduate Theses Completed at Tuskegee Institute, 1945-1953.* Tuskegee, Ala., Hollis Burke Frissell Library, 1954. 30 p.

214  NORTH CAROLINA COLLEGE, Durham, N.C. *Theses Written at North Carolina College, 1940-1949.* 5 p. Mimeographed.

215  PORTER, Dorothy B. *Howard University Masters' Theses,* submitted in partial fulfillment of the requirements for the Masters Degree at Howard University, 1918-45. Washington, D.C., The Graduate School, Howard University, 1946. 44 p.

216  PRAIRIE VIEW STATE COLLEGE, Prairie View, Texas. *Masters' Theses of Prairie View State College, 1938-1944,* compiled by O.J. Baker. Prairie View, Texas, Prairie View University, 1945. 16 p.

217  VIRGINIA STATE COLLEGE, Petersburg, Va. Library. *Bibliography of Masters' Theses, 1937-1962.* Compiled by the Reference Department, Virginia State College Library. Petersburg, Va., 1963. 48 p. (Virginia State College. *Gazette,* Vol. 69, No. 3, Sept. 1963).

218  WALKER, George H. *Masters' Theses Underway in Negro Colleges and Universities, 1960-1961.* In *The Negro Educational Review,* Vol. 12, No. 3, July 1961, pp. 85-95.

219  WALKER, George H. *Masters' Theses Underway in Negro Colleges and Universities, 1961-1962.* In *The Negro Educational Review,* Vol. 13, Nos. 3 & 4, July-Oct. 1962, pp. 127-41.

## DISSERTATIONS

220  McNAMEE, Lawrence F. *Dissertations in English and American Literature;* theses accepted by American, British, and German Universities, 1865-1964. New York, London, R.R. Bowker Co., 1968. 1124 p. $17.50. Chapter thirty-two is on Negro literature.

221  WEST, Earle H. *A Bibliography of Doctoral Research on the Negro, 1933-1966.* Ann Arbor, Michigan, University Microfilms, 1969; 130 p. To be published in 1969.

# BIOGRAPHY
## BIOGRAPHICAL DICTIONARIES

222  *THE BLACK BOOK: Who's Who in Greater Philadelphia in the Negro Community.* Philadelphia, Bricklin Press, 1968. $10.00.

Paperback $4.95. Contains more than 5,000 entries — names, addresses, and telephone numbers of individuals, churches, organizations and action groups, a total of 250,000 black people in the professions.

223 RICHARDSON, Clement. *National Cyclopedia of the Colored Race.* Montgomery, Alabama, National Publishing Co., Inc., 1919. 622 p. Out of print. Contains excellent photographs.

224 SIMMONS, William J. *Men of Mark: Eminent, Progressive and Rising.* With an Introductory Sketch of the author by Rev. Henry M. Turner. Cleveland, Ohio, Geo. M. Rewell & Co., 1887. 1138 p. Portraits. Reprint-Arno Press, Inc. 1968. $39.50.

225 *WHO'S WHO IN COLORED AMERICA; A Biographical Dictionary of Notable Living Persons of Negro Descent in America.* Joseph J. Boris, ed. New York, Who's Who in Colored America Corp., 1927. 333 p. Portraits. Out of print.

226 *WHO'S WHO IN COLORED AMERICA; A Biographical Dictionary of Notable Persons of African Descent in America.* Joseph J. Boris, ed. 1928-29. 2d ed. New York, Who's Who in Colored America Corp., 1929. 470 p. Portraits. Out of print.

227 *WHO'S WHO IN COLORED AMERICA; A Biographical Dictionary of Notable Living Persons of African Descent in America. 1930-1931-1932.* 3d ed. New York, Who's Who in Colored America, Thomas Yenser, ed. and publisher, 1933. 499 p. Portraits. Out of print.

228 *WHO'S WHO IN COLORED AMERICA; A Biographical Dictionary of Notable Living Persons of African Descent in America. 1938-1939-1940.* 5th ed. New York, Who's Who in Colored America, 1940. 608 p. Portraits. Out of print.

229 *WHO'S WHO IN COLORED AMERICA; A Biographical Dictionary of Notable Living Persons of African Descent in America. 1941 to 1944.* 6th ed. New York, Who's Who in Colored America, c1942. 607 p. Portraits. Out of print.

230 *WHO'S WHO IN COLORED AMERICA; An Illustrated Biographical Dictionary of Notable Living Persons of African Descent in the United States.* G. James Fleming and Christian Burckel, eds. 7th ed. New York, Yonkers-on-Hudson, 1950. 684 p. Portraits. Out of print. Supplement — 34 p.

231  *WHO'S WHO OF THE COLORED RACE; A General Biographical Dictionary of Men and Women of African Descent.* Frank Lincoln Mather, ed. Chicago, Memento Edition Half-Century Anniversary of Negro Freedom in the U.S., 1915. 296 p. Out of print.

232  WILLIAMS, Ethel L. *Biographical Directory of Negro Ministers.* New York, Scarecrow Press, 1965. 421 p. $9.00. New edition in progress.

233  WRIGHT, Richard Robert. *Centennial Encyclopaedia of the African Methodist Episcopal Church Containing Principally the Biographies of the Men and Women both Ministers and Laymen, whose Labors during a Hundred Years, helped make the A.M.E. Church what it is...* Philadelphia, Pa., 1916. 390 p. Illustrations. Out of print.

234  WRIGHT, Richard Robert. *The Encyclopaedia of the African Methodist Episcopal Church, Containing Principally the Biographies of the Men and Women both Ministers and Laymen, whose Labors during a Hundred and Sixty Years, helped make the A.M.E. Church what it is...* Philadelphia, Pa., The Book Concern of the A.M.E. Church, 1947. 688 p. Portraits. Out of print. Excludes some of the biographies included in the 1916 edition.

## BIOGRAPHIES IN COLLECTIONS

235  ADAMS, Russell L. *Great Negroes; Past and Present.* 2d. ed. Chicago, Afro-American Pub. Co., 1964. 182 p. $4.95. A thumbnail collection of biographical stories of the lives of 150 outstanding American Negroes and their African antecedents.

236  BARDOLPH, Richard. *The Negro Vanguard.* New York, Rinehart, 1959. 388 p.

237  BARTON, Rebecca Chalmers. *Witnesses for Freedom; Negro Americans in Autobiography.* Foreword by Alain Locke. 1st ed. New York, Harper, 1948. 294 p. Out of print. Studies of the autobiographical writings of twenty-three American Negroes including: Booker T. Washington, Zora Neale Hurston; Frederick Douglass; Era Bell Thompson; W.E.B. DuBois; James Weldon Johnson; Richard Wright.

238  BENNETT, Lerone. *Pioneers in Protest.* Chicago, The Johnson Publishing Co., 1968. $5.50.

239 BONTEMPS, Arna Wendell and Jack Conroy. *Anyplace But Here.* New York, Hill and Wang, 1966. 372 p. A revised and expanded version of *They Seek a City.*

240 BONTEMPS, Arna Wendell. *We Have Tomorrow.* Boston, Houghton Mifflin Co., 1945. 131 p.

241 BRAGG, George F. *Men of Maryland.* Rev. ed., Baltimore, Church Advocate Press, 1925. 160 p.

242 BRAWLEY, Benjamin Griffith. *Negro Builders and Heroes.* Chapel Hill, University of North Carolina Press, 1937. 315 p. $3.50. This book contains thumbnail biographical sketches of prominent Negroes in all lines of endeavor, from slave times to 1937.

243 BRAWLEY, Benjamin Griffith. *Women of Achievement; Written For the Fireside Schools, Under the Auspices of the Women's American Baptist Home Mission Society.* Chicago, Woman's American Baptist Home Mission Society, c1919. 92 p.

244 BREWER, John Mason. *Negro Legislators of Texas and Their Descendants; a History of the Negro in Texas Politics From Reconstruction to Disfranchisement.* Dallas, Texas, Mathis Publishing Co., 1935. 134 p.

245 BROWN, Hallie Quinn, comp. and ed. *Homespun Heroines and Other Women of Distinction.* Foreword by Mrs. Josephine Turpin Washington. Xenia, Ohio, The Aldine Publishing Company, c1926. 248 p.

246 BROWN, William Wells. *The Black Man, His Antecedents, His Genius and His Achievements.* New York, T. Hamilton; Boston, R.F. Wallcut, 1863. 288 p.

247 BROWN, William Wells. *The Rising Son: or, The Antecedents and Advancement of the Colored Race.* Boston, A.G. Brown & Co., 1874. 552 p.

248 BRUCE, John Edward, comp. and ed. *Short Biographical Sketches of Eminent Negro Men and Women in Europe and the United States, With Brief Extracts from Their Writings and Public Utterances.* Vol. 1, Yonkers, N.Y., Gazette Press, 1910-.

249 CHERRY, Gwendolyn and others. *Portraits in Color; the Lives of Colorful Negro Women.* New York, Pageant Press, 1962. 224 p. $4.00. Out of print.

250 CUTHBERT, Marion Vera. *Education and Marginality; a Study of the Negro Woman College Graduate.* New York, N.Y., 1942. 167 p.

251 DABNEY, Wendell P. *Cincinnati's Colored Citizens; Historical, Sociological and Biographical.* Cincinnati, Ohio, The Dabney Publishing Co., 1926. 440 p.

252 DANIEL, Sadie Iola. *Women Builders.* Washington, D.C., The Associated Publishers, Inc., 1931. 187 p.

253 DANNETT, Sylvia G.L. *Profiles of Negro Womanhood.* Yonkers, N.Y., Educational Heritage, 1964-66. 2 vols. $10.00. Vol. 1, 1619-1900; Vol. 2, 20th Century.

254 DAVID, Jay, ed. *Growing Up Black.* New York, Morrow, 1968. $6.95. "The stories of 19 Negro children raised in America during the past two centuries. Included are Ethel Waters, Booker T. Washington, Richard Wright, and Dick Gregory."

255 DAVIS, Elizabeth Lindsay. *Lifting as They Climb.* Chicago, Ill., 1933. 424 p.

256 DESDUNES, Rodolphe L. *Nos Hommes et Notre Histoire; Notices Biographiques Accompagnées de Réflexions et de Souvenirs Personnels, Hommage à la Population Créole, en Souvenir des Grands Hommes Qu'elle a Produits et des Bonnes Choses Qu'elle a Accomplies.* Montreal, Arbour & Dupont 1911. 196 p. (Louisiana Negroes are included).

257 DOBLER, Lavinia G. and Edgar A. Toppin. *Pioneers and Patriots: the Lives of Six Negroes of the Revolutionary Era.* Garden City, N.Y., Doubleday, 1965. 118 p.

258 DUNBAR, Ernest. *Black Expatriates, a Study of American Negroes in Exile.* New York, Dutton, 1968. $4.95. Seventeen black Americans who, for a variety of reasons have gone abroad to live tell what it means to be black in Europe.

259 DURHAM, Philip and Everett L. Jones. *The Negro Cowboys.* New York, Dodd, Mead & Co., 1965. 278 p. $5.00. Among the cowboys

who rode the ranges from Texas to Montana, driving cattle to market, were more than 5,000 Negroes. This startling fact was uncovered by University of California professors who studied 300 memoirs and histories in search of references to Negro cowboys.

260 EMBREE, Edwin R. *Thirteen Against the Odds.* Port Washington, N.Y., Kennikat Press, 1967 (c1944). 261 p. $9.00. A collection of biographies of thirteen black Americans who overcame the odds. Among the thirteen are such figures as Paul Robeson, Mordecai Johnson, Richard Wright, William Grant Still, Walter White, Mary McLeod Bethune, and Charles S. Johnson.

261 FABER, Harold and Doris. *American Heroes of the 20th Century.* New York, Random House, 1967. 179 p.

262 FAUSET, Arthur Huff. *For Freedom; a Biographical Story of the American Negro.* Philadelphia, Franklin Publishing and Supply Co., 1927. 200 p.

263 FERRIS, William Henry. *The African Abroad; or, His Evolution in Western Civilization, Tracing His Development Under Caucasian Milieu.* New Haven, Conn., The Tuttle, Morehouse & Taylor Press, 1913. 2 vols.

264 FISK UNIVERSITY, Nashville. Social Science Institute. *Unwritten History of Slavery, Autobiographical Account of Negro Ex-slaves.* Nashville, Tenn., Social Science Institute, Fisk University, 1945. 322 p. The interviews with these ex-slaves were conducted during 1929 and 1930.

265 FOLEY, Albert Sidney. *God's Men of Color; the Colored Catholic Priests of the United States, 1854-1954.* New York, Farrar, Straus, 1955. 322 p.

266 GREENE, Harry Washington. *Holders of Doctorates Among American Negroes; an Educational and Social Study of Negroes who have earned Doctoral Degrees in course, 1876-1943.* Boston, Meador Publishing Co., 1946. 275 p.

267 HANDY, James A. *Scraps of American Methodist Episcopal History.* Philadelphia, Pa., A.M.E. Book Concern, n.d. 421 p.

268 HARTSHORN, William Newton, ed. *An Era of Progress and Promise, 1863-1910; the Religious, Moral, and Educational Develop-*

*ment of the American Negro Since His Emancipation.* Boston, Mass., The Priscilla Publishing Co., 1910. 576 p.

269  *HAYNES, Elizabeth R. Unsung Heroes.* New York, DuBois and Dill, 1921. 279 p.

270  HILL, Roy L. *Who's Who in the American Negro Press.* Dallas, Royal Publishing Co., 1960. 80 p. $3.95. Out of print. Biographical sketches were compiled from a questionnaire. The respondents included their views on the strengths and weaknesses of the American Negro press. Methods for improvement are given. These statements are tabulated. Respondents are classified by political affiliation, religious affiliation, educational background, etc.

271  HUGHES, Langston. *Famous American Negroes.* New York, Dodd, Mead, 1954. 147 p.

272  HUGHES, Langston. *Famous Negro Heroes of America.* New York, Dodd, Mead, 1958. 202 p.

273  HUGHES, Langston. *Famous Negro Music Makers.* New York, Dodd, Mead, 1955. 179 p.

274  KEENE, Josephine Bond. *National Directory; Negro Business and Professional Women.* Philadelphia, Josephine Bond Keene, 1942. 19 p.

275  KING, John T. and Mariet H. King. *Famous Negro Americans; Stories of Twenty-three.* Texas, Stock-Vaughn Co., 1967. 120 p. $1.65.

276  LERNER, Gerda. *The Grimke Sisters from South Carolina; Rebels against Slavery.* Boston, Houghton Mifflin Co., 1967. 479 p. $6.95. A biography of two sisters, Charleston-born aristocrats who deserted the church of their youth, the land of their birth, and the political beliefs of their family, and who were outstanding abolitionists. The author describes the leaders of various movements, political, religious, and dietary, who influenced the sisters, and gives an account of the sisters' pioneering efforts for woman's rights.

277  MAJORS, Monroe Alphus. *Noted Negro Women, Their Triumphs and Activities.* Chicago, Donohue & Henneberry Printers, 1893. 365 p. Portraits. Out of print.

278 METCALF, George R. *Black Profiles.* New York, McGraw-Hill, 1968. 341 p. $6.95. "Biographies of eleven prominent Americans from Harriet Tubman to Dr. King."

279 MOSSELL, Gertrude E.H. Bustill. *The Work of the Afro-American Woman.* 2d ed. Philadelphia, G.S. Ferguson Co., 1908 (c1894). 178 p. Out of print.

280 MOTT, Abigail F., comp. *Narratives of Colored Americans.* New York, Browne & Co., 1872. 276 p.

281 NELL, William Cooper. *The Colored Patriots of the American Revolution with Sketches of Several Distinguished Colored Persons: To Which is Added a Brief Survey of the Condition and Prospects of Colored Americans.* With an Introduction by Harriet Beecher Stowe. Boston, R.F. Wallcut, 1855. 396 p.

282 *NEWBOLD, Nathan Carter. Five North Carolina Negro Educators.* Chapel Hill, The University of North Carolina Press, 1939. 142 p.

283 OVINGTON, Mary White. *Portraits in Color.* New York, Harper, 1927. 241 p. Out of print. Thumbnail biographical sketches of the life work of twenty interesting Negro personalities. It is an honest and moving piece of work, opinionated and definite, but always frank and clear.

284 PERKINS, A.E., ed. *Who's Who in Colored Louisiana.* Baton Rouge, Louisiana, Douglas Loan Co., Inc., 1930. 153 p.

285 PETERSON, Frank Loris. *Climbing High Mountains.* Washington, Review and Herald Pub. Association, 1962. 144 p.

286 REDDING, Jay Saunders. *The Lonesome Road, the Story of the Negro's Part in America.* New York, Doubleday & Co., Inc., 1958. 355 p. $5.95. Paperback (Dolphin) $1.45. The difficult struggle of the Negro; from slavery to equal rights, is traced through the lives of twelve Negro men and one woman. While a fundamental and understandable sympathy with the author's own race seeps through, this is a work of considerable scholarship.

287 RICHARDSON, Ben. *Great American Negroes,* revised by William A. Fahey. New York, Thomas Y. Crowell Co., 1956. 339 p. Contains 26 biographies of Negroes who have achieved success in various fields.

288   ROBINSON, Wilhelmena S. *Historical Negro Biographies.* 1st ed. New York, Publishers Co., 1967. (International Library of Negro Life and History). 291 p.

289   ROGERS, Joel Augustus. *World's Great Men of Color.* New York, J.A. Rogers, 1946. 2 vols.

290   ROGERS, Joel Augustus. *World's Greatest Men and Women of African Descent.* New York, J.A. Rogers Publications, 1935. 71 p.

291   ROLLINS, Charlemae Hill. *Famous American Negro Poets.* New York, Dodd, Mead & Co., 1965. 95 p. $3.25. One or two of the careers chosen are perhaps too slight, but the cumulative effect is impressive. The style is straight-forward, relaxed, and anecdotal. Childhood and the discovery of poetry are emphasized, and wherever the story touches on the old sufferings of the Negro people, or their twentieth century struggles for true emancipation, these are quietly clarified.

292   ROLLINS, Charlemae Hill. *They Showed the Way; Forty American Negro Leaders.* New York, Thomas Crowell Co., 1964. 166 p. $3.00. Biographical accounts of Negroes successful in a variety of careers, ranging from the creative arts to the professions of law and medicine, from exploration and invention to publishing and religion. Well written, highly recommended.

293   SCRUGGS, Lawson Andrew. *Women of Distinction, Remarkable in Works and Invincible in Character.* Introduction by Mrs. Josephine Turpin Washington. Special Contributions by T. Thomas Fortune, William Still. Raleigh, L.A. Scruggs, 1893. 382 p. Portraits. Out of print.

294   SIMMONS, William J. *Men of Mark: Eminent, Progressive and Rising.* Cleveland, G.M. Rewell & Co., 1887. 1138.

295   SMITH, S.D. *The Negro in Congress, 1870-1901.* New York, Kennikat, 1940. $6.00.

296   STEWARD, S. Maria. *Women in Medicine; A Paper Read Before the National Association of Colored Women's Clubs at Wilberforce, Ohio, August 6, 1914.* Wilberforce, Ohio, S. Maria Steward, 1914. 24 p.

297   TERRELL, Mary Church. *The Progress of Colored Women, an*

*Address Delivered Before the National American Women's Suffrage Association at the Columbia Theater.* Washington, D.C., February 18, 1898, on the Occasion of its Fiftieth Anniversary. Washington, D.C., Smith Brothers, 1898. 15 p.

298  THOMAS, Adah B., comp. *Pathfinders, a History of Progress of Colored Graduate Nurses.* With biographies of many prominent nurses. New York, Kay Printing House, Inc., 1929. 240 p.

299  THORPE, Earl E. *Negro Historians in the United States.* Baton Rouge, Louisiana, Fraternal Press, 1958. 188 p.

300  TROUP, Cornelius V. *Distinguished Negro Georgians.* Dallas, Royal Pub. Co., 1962. 203 p.

301  WHEADON, Augusta Austin. *The Negro From 1863-1963.* New York, Vantage Press, 1963-64. 99 p. $2.50. A listing of prominent Negroes during a hundred years.

302  WRIGHT, Richard Robert. *The Bishops of the African Methodist Episcopal Church.* Nashville, A.M.E. Sunday School Union, 1962. 389 p.

303  YOUNG, Andrew Sturgen Nash. *Negro Firsts in Sports,* by A.S. "Doc" Young. With illustrations by Herbert Temple. Chicago, Johnson Pub. Co., 1963. 301 p.

## INDIVIDUAL BIOGRAPHIES AND AUTOBIOGRAPHIES

304  ALBERT, Octavia Victoria Rogers. *The House of Bondage; or, Charlotte Brooks and Other Slaves,* Original and Life-Like, as They Appeared in Their Old Plantations and City Slave Life; Together with Pen-Pictures of the Peculiar Institution, with Sights and Insights into Their New Relations as Freedmen, Freemen, and Citizens. With an Introduction by Rev. Bishop Willard F. Mallalieu. New York, Hunt & Eaton; Cincinnati, Cranston & Slowe, 1890. 161 p. Portrait.

305  ALLEN, Walter C. and Brian A.L. Rust. *King Joe Oliver.* London, Sidgwick and Jackson, 1958. 224 p.

306  ANDERSON, Marian. *My Lord What a Morning; an Autobiography.* New York, The Viking Press, 1956. 312 p. $5.00. Paperback (Avon, 1964). $0.60. Autobiography of one of America's greatest twentieth-century singers.

307 APTHEKER, Herbert. *Nat Turner's Slave Rebellion.* Together With the Full Text of the So-called "Confessions" of Nat Turner Made in Prison in 1831. New York, Humanities Press, Inc., 1966. 152 p. $4.00. Paperback, (Humanities.) $1.95. The author of *American Negro Slave Revolts* has written a full length study of the slave uprising, led by Nat Turner in Virginia in 1831.

308 ASHE, Arthur. *Advantage Ashe,* as told to Clifford George Gewecke, Jr. New York, Coward-McCann, Inc., 1967. 192 p. $4.95.

309 ATKINS, James A. *The Age of Jim Crow.* New York, Vantage Press, 1965-66. 300 p. $3.95. Autobiography detailing the author's handicaps and attainments as educator, civil servant, and stalwart fighter for civil rights.

310 *AUNT SALLY; or, The Cross the Way to Freedom. A Narrative of the Slave-Life and Purchase of the Mother of Rev. Isaac Williams of Detroit, Michigan.* Cincinnati, American Reform Tract and Book Society, 1862. 216 p. Portrait.

311 BAILEY, Pearl. *The Raw Pearl.* New York, Harcourt, Brace & World, Inc., 1968. 206 p. $5.75.

312 BALL, Charles. *Fifty Years in Chains, or, The Life of an American Slave.* New York, H. Dayton; Indianapolis, Ind., Dayton & Asher, 1859. 430 p.

313 BALL, Charles. *Slavery in the United States; a Narrative of the Life and Adventures of Charles Ball, a Black Man, who Lived Forty Years in Maryland, South Carolina and Georgia as a Slave.* Lewiston, Pa., J.W. Shugert, 1836. 400 p.

314 BANKETT, Lelia W. *A Testimonial of Love Tendered Mrs. Maggie L. Walker, Twenty-five Years of Service.* (Addresses of Various People). Richmond, Va., St. Luke Press, 1925. 60 p.

315 BANKS, J.H. *A Narrative of Events of the Life of J.H. Banks, an Escaped Slave, from the Cotton State, Alabama, in America.* Written with Introduction, by J.W.C. Pennington. Liverpool, M. Rouke, 1861. 93 p.

316 BATES, Daisy. *The Long Shadow of Little Rock; a Memoir.* New York, David McKay Co., 1962. 234 p. $5.50. The author, co-publisher with her husband of an Arkansas Negro newspaper,

relates her role in the Little Rock integration fight.

317   BAYLEY, Solomon. *A Narrative of Some Remarkable Incidents in the Life of Solomon Bayley, Formerly a Slave in the State of Delaware, North America; Written by Himself, and Published for His Benefit; To Which are Prefixed a Few Remarks by Robert Hurnardt.* 2d ed. London, Harvey and Darton, 1825. 48 p.

318   BENNETT, Lerone. *What Manner of Man; a Biography of Martin Luther King, Jr.* Chicago, Johnson Publishing Co., 1964. 227 p. $4.95. Paperback (Simon and Schuster). $1.00. An in-depth biographical study of the well-known Negro civil rights leader.

319   BERNARD, Jacqueline. *Journey Toward Freedom, the Story of Sojourner Truth.* New York, Norton, 1967. 265 p. $4.50. A biography of Sojourner Truth, born Isabelle Hardenberg, a Negro slave in New York state thirty years before the local laws freed slaves. She became famous both as an abolitionist and as an early champion of women's rights.

320   BIBB, Henry. *Narrative of the Life and Adventures of Henry Bibb, an American Slave, Written by Himself.* With an Introduction by Lucius C. Matlack. New York, Henry Bibb, 1849. 204 p. Portrait.

321   BRADFORD, Sarah. *Harriet Tubman, the Moses of Her People.* New York, Corinth Books, 1961. 149 p. $3.25. Paperback $1.25. A reprint of the 2d ed. of 1886. Describes the former slave's heroic struggle for her people on the underground railroad and in the Civil War.

322   BRANCH, Hettye Wallace. *The Story of "80 John," a Biography of One of the Most Respected Negro Ranchmen in the Old West.* 1st ed. New York, Greenwich Book Publishers, 1960. 59 p.

323   BRAWLEY, Benjamin Griffith. *Paul Laurence Dunbar, Poet of His People.* Chapel Hill, University of North Carolina Press; Port Washington, N.Y., Kennikat Press, 1936. 159 p. $6.00. Biography of the poet, first published by the University of North Carolina, who rose from a Dayton, Ohio, elevator operator to a position as the most celebrated of Negro writers.

324   BREITMAN, George. *The Last Year of Malcolm X: the Evolution of a Revolutionary.* New York, Merit Pubs., 1967. 169 p. Illustrations. $4.50. Paperback (Schocken Books, 1968). $1.95. The author has

more than adequately documented speeches, interviews, and writings of this leader to document the fact that Malcolm X did change his philosophy and position on black nationalism a year or so before his assassination. This book will serve as a companion to the *Autobiography of Malcolm X,* and *Malcolm X Speaks.*

325 BRODERICK, Francis L. *W.E.B. DuBois, Negro Leader in a Time of Crisis.* Stanford, California, Stanford University Press, 1959. 259 p. $5.00. Paperback $2.95. An evaluation of the Negro American who was one of the founders of the NAACP, editor of *Crisis,* educator, writer, and chief spokesman for his race for many years.

326 BROWN, Claude. *Manchild in the Promised Land.* New York, Macmillan, 1965. 415 p. $5.95. Paperback (New American Library, 1966). $0.95. The autobiography of a young man who grew up in Harlem, this book recounts the realities of the author's childhood and youth during the 1940's and 1950's, a world of drugs and gang fights that could, with persistence, be escaped.

327 BROWN, H. Rap. *H. Rap Brown Autobiography.* New York, Delacorte Press, 1968. $4.95. An ideological autobiography by the former chairman of SNCC.

328 BROWN, John. *Slave Life in Georgia: a Narrative of the Life, Sufferings, and Escape of John Brown, a Fugitive Slave, now in England.* Edited by L.A. Chamerovzow. London, W.M. Watts, 1855. 250 p. Portrait.

329 BROWN, Josephine. *Biography of an American Bondman, by his Daughter.* Boston, R.F. Wallcut, 1855. 104 p. Biography of William Wells Brown by his daughter.

330 BROWN, William Wells. *Clotel; or, The President's Daughter: a Narrative of Slave Life in the United States.* With a sketch of the author's life. London, Patridge & Oakey, 1853. 245 p. Illustrations.

331 BUCKLER, Helen. *Doctor Dan, Pioneer in American Surgery.* 1st ed. Boston, Little, Brown, 1954. 381 p. New ed. Pitman, 1968. $6.95.

332 CADE, John Brother. *Holsey, The Incomparable.* New York, Pageant Press, Inc., 1964. 221 p. $4.00. The biography of Lucius Henry Holsey, founder of the Colored Methodist Episcopal Church in America. Holsey was born a slave and he educated himself in the

face of seeming insurmountable odds, becoming a bishop at the age of 31.

333  CHESNUTT, Helen M. *Charles Waddell Chesnutt, Pioneer of the Color Line.* Chapel Hill, University of North Carolina Press, 1952. 324 p. $1.30. Biography of a self-taught teacher, stenographer, and lawyer, Charles W. Chesnutt, who is usually called the most competent Negro writer of fiction before the 1920's. Works such as *The Conjure Woman, The Wife of His Youth and Other Stories of the Color Line* won him high praise from William Dean Howells and other critics. His professional literary career ended in disillusionment and he spent the last twenty-seven years of his life fighting prejudice.

334  CLARK, Septima Poinsette, with Legette Blythe. *Echo in My Soul.* Foreword by Harry Golden. New York, E.P. Dutton, 1962. 243 p. $4.50. Autobiography of a Negro woman who as a young girl went out to Johns Island, South Carolina, as a school teacher and has devoted most of her years since to educational work among Negroes.

335  CLEAVER, Eldridge. *Soul On Ice.* With an Introduction by Maxwell Geismar. New York, McGraw-Hill, 1968. 210 p. $5.95. Paperback, (Delta) $1.95. In a collection of essays and open letters written from California's Folsom State Prison, the author, an Afro-American now on the staff of *Ramparts*, writes about the forces which shaped his life.

336  CONRAD, Earl. *Harriet Tubman.* Washington, D.C., The Associated Publishers, Inc., 1943. 248 p.

337  CRONON, Edmund David. *Black Moses; the Story of Marcus Garvey and the Universal Negro Improvement Association.* Madison, Wisconsin, University of Wisconsin Press, 1955. 278 p. Illustrations. $5.00. Paperback $1.95. The first full-length biography of the Jamaica-born Negro, who created a back to Africa movement about three decades ago. An interesting and serious portrayal of a Negro leader who was perhaps the most controversial, loved, mocked, and criticized personality of the turbulent twenties.

338  DALY, John Jay. *A Song in His Heart.* Philadelphia, John C. Winston Co., 1951. 102 p. $3.00. Out of print. A slight, fictionalized story built around the few known facts of the life of the popular Negro minstrel, James Bland, composer of "Carry Me Back to Old Virginia" and other favorites. Includes eight songs and reproductions of handbills.

339  DAVIS, Benjamin Jefferson. *Communist Councilman From Harlem: an Autobiography.* New York, International Publishers, 1958. $5.95. Paperback $1.95.

340  DAVIS, Edwin Adams and Williams Ransom Hogan. *The Barber of Natchez, Wherein a Slave is Freed and Rises to a Very High Standing; Wherein the Former Slave Writes a Two-Thousand-Page Journal About His Town and Himself; Wherein the Free Negro Diarist is Appraised in Terms of His Friends, His Code, and His Community's Reaction to His Wanton Murder.* Baton Rouge, Louisiana State University Press, 1954. 272 p. $4.00. See also — Johnson, William.

341  DAVIS, Sammy and Jane and Burt Boyar. *Yes I Can; the Story of Sammy Davis, Jr.* New York, Farrar, Straus and Giroux, 1965. 612 p. $6.95. Paperback (Pocket Books, 1966). $1.95. Beginning with his life in vaudeville, learning his craft, Sammy Davis, Jr. writes of the conflict and events which shaped his life.

342  DOUGLASS, Frederick. *Frederick Douglass.* Edited by Benjamin Quarles. New York, Prentice-Hall, 1968. 378 p. $4.95.

343  DOUGLASS, Frederick. *Life and Times of Frederick Douglass: His Early Life as a Slave, His Escape From Bondage, and His Complete History, Written by Himself.* With a New Introduction by Rayford W. Logan. Reprinted from the revised edition of 1892. New York, Collier Books; London, Collier-Macmillan, Ltd., c1962. 640 p. 2d ptg. 1967. $2.45. One of the great classics of American biographical writing. Originally published in 1881, this work provides insight into the personality of the famous abolitionist, writer, and statesman who was born a slave.

344  DOUGLASS, Frederick. *Narrative of the Life of Frederick Douglass, an American Slave.* Edited by Benjamin Quarles. Cambridge, Mass. The Belknap Press of Harvard University Press, 1967. 163 p. $3.50. Paperback $1.45.

345  DOUTY, Esther M. *Forten, the Sailmaker; Pioneer Champion of Negro Rights.* Chicago. New York, San Francisco, Rand McNally and Co., 1968. 208 p. $4.95.

346  DuBOIS, William Edward Burghardt. *The Autobiography of W.E.B. DuBois; a Soliloquy of Viewing My Life From the Last Decade of Its First Century.* New York, International Publishers, 1968. 448 p.

$10.00. See no. 61. This is the third autobiographical volume by the late Dr. DuBois, a leader in the movement for black liberation. Completed in 1960 when DuBois was past ninety, the book gives an account of his life in the Negro movement and includes sections on his travels in Russia and China and his harassment as a political suspect during the McCarthy years. Previous volumes were entitled *Darkwater; Voices From Within the Veil,* and *Dusk of Dawn; an Essay Toward an Autobiography of a Race Concept.*

347 DuBOIS, William Edward Burghardt. *John Brown.* Centennial ed. New York, International Publishers, 1962. 414 p. $5.50.

348 ELLIOTT, Lawrence. *George Washington Carver; the Man Who Overcame.* Englewood Cliffs, N.J., Prentice-Hall, 1966. 256 p. $5.95. This is a very well researched and well written biography. While Carver's dedication to science is well known, through this volume readers will also come to understand his grasp of the theory of science as well as its practical aspects.

349 EMANUEL, James Andrew. *Langston Hughes.* New York, Twayne Publishers, 1967. 192 p. $3.95. The first full length critical study of the late Negro writer's works.

350 EVERS, Myrlie with William Petes. *For Us the Living.* Garden City, New York, Doubleday, 1967. 378 p. $5.95. The widow of the NAACP leader slain in 1963 gives a picture of the childhood and youth of her husband, of his parents, and of the life of sharecroppers. She then goes on to recount the awakening of Medgar Evers to the conviction that freedom has to be won, that it is worth fighting for, and devotes the rest of the book to his work with the National Association for the Advancement of Colored People. The book is to some considerable extent her own autobiography as well, and reveals the tragic role of Negro woman in the deep south.

351 FARR, Finis. *Black Champion: the Life and Times of Jack Johnson.* New York, Charles Scribner's Sons, 1964. 245 p. $4.95. Out of print. A study of the career of the first Negro heavyweight champion. Analyzes Johnson's career as boxer and his problems as an individual. Mr. Farr shows Johnson as a product of his time.

352 FELDMAN, Eugene Pieter Romayn. *Black Power in Old Alabama; the Life and Stirring Times of James T. Rapier, Afro-American Congressman From Alabama, 1839-1883.* Illustrated by Margaret T. Burroughs and Jennie Washington. (Chicago) Museum of African-

American History, 1968. 69 p.

353 FERGUSON, Blanche E. *Countee Cullen and the Negro Renaissance.* New York, Dodd, Mead, 1966. 213 p. Illustrations. $5.00. This biography is about an American Negro poet who was active during the 1920's in the Harlem-centered Negro Renaissance.

354 FOLEY, Albert Sidney. *Bishop Healy: Beloved Outcaste; the Story of a Great Man Whose Life has Become a Legend; Negro Catholic Bishop.* New York, Farrar, Straus and Young, 1954. 243 p. Out of print. Story of Bishop James Augustine Healy, D.C., Second Bishop of Portland, Maine, 1875-1900.

355 FONER, Philip Sheldon. *Frederick Douglass, a Biography.* New York, Citadel Press, 1964. 444 p. $6.00. Paperback $2.45. An excellent, up-to-date study by a distinguished scholar which should be read together with Douglass' own autobiography.

356 GARVEY, A. Jacques. *Garvey and Garveyism.* Kingston, Jamaica, A. Jacques Garvey, 1963. 287 p. $6.00. A biography of Marcus Garvey by his widow.

357 GIBSON, Althea. *I Always Wanted to be Somebody.* Edited by Ed Fitzgerald. New York, Harper and Brothers, 1958. 176 p. $4.95. The story of an American Negro from Harlem who tells of her childhood and adolescent experiences until her success as an international woman tennis player.

358 GILBERT, Olive. *Narrative of Sojourner Truth, a Northern Slave, Emancipated from Bodily Servitude by the State of New York, in 1828.* With a Portrait. Boston, Olive Gilbert, 1850. 144 p.

359 GRAHAM, Shirley. *Jean Baptiste Pointe de Sable, Founder of Chicago.* New York, J. Messner, 1953. 180 p. $3.34.

360 GRAHAM, Shirley. *Paul Robeson, Citizen of the World.* Foreword by Carl Van Doren. New York, J. Messner, Inc., 1946. 264 p.

361 GRAHAM, Shirley. *Your Most Humble Servant; the Story of Benjamin Banneker.* New York, J. Messner, 1949. 235 p. $3.34. Biography of a Negro who was a scientist, an assistant in the planning of the city of Washington, D.C., publisher of an almanac, inventor of a clock and author of a letter to Thomas Jefferson that was a sharp reminder of the human rights of Negroes.

# BIOGRAPHY

362 GREEN, Ely. *Ely; an Autobiography*. New York, The Seabury Press, 1966. 236 p. $4.95.

363 GREEN, Jacob D. *Narrative of the Life of J.D. Green, a Runaway Slave from Kentucky Containing an Account of His Three Escapes in 1839, 1846, and 1848*. Huddersfield, Henry Fielding, 1864. 43 p.

364 GREGORY, Dick with Robert Lipsyte. *Nigger; an Autobiography*. New York, E.P. Dutton, 1964. 224 p. $4.95. Gregory tells of growing up black in America. His autobiography is free of self-pity and is propelled by cauterizing candor and some wit.

365 HARDWICK, Richard. *Charles Richard Drew, Pioneer in Blood Research*. New York, Scribner's Sons, 1967. 144 p. $3.63. A biography of the Negro doctor and scientist whose work led to the establishment of a blood plasma bank which served as a model for the system used by the American Red Cross in World War II.

366 HAWKINS, Hugh, ed. *Booker T. Washington and His Critics*. Boston, D.C. Heath, 1962. 113 p.

367 HAWKINS, William George. *Lunsford Lane; or, Another Helper from North Carolina*, Boston, Crosby & Nichols, 1863. 305 p.

368 HAYDEN, William. *Narrative of William Hayden, Containing a Faithful Account of His Travels for a Number of Years, Whilst a Slave, in the South. Written by Himself*. Cincinnati, Ohio, William Hayden, 1846. 156 p.

369 HEDGEMAN, Anna Arnold. *The Trumpet Sounds; a Memoir of Negro Leadership*. New York, Holt, Rinehart & Winston, 1964. 202 p. $4.95. From a sheltered background in Anoka, Minnesota, where hers was the only Negro family, Anna Arnold Hedgeman went in 1922 to teach at all-Negro Rust College in Holly Springs, Mississippi, and discovered abruptly the essence of being a Negro in America. Ever since, she has been fighting for Negro rights. This is not a straight autobiography, but a memoir of the author's years as a Negro leader from 1922 up through the 1963 Freedom March on Washington.

370 HENSON, Josiah. *Father Henson's Story of His Own Life*. A Complete Reissue of the 1858 Edition. Magnolia, Mass., Peter Smith. $3.50. Paperback (Corinth-Citadel, 1962). $1.50.

371 HENSON, Josiah. *The Life of Josiah Henson: Formerly a Slave, Now an Inhabitant of Canada, as Narrated by Himself.* Boston, A.D. Phelps, 1849. Out of print. Narrative of a Negro generally believed to be the prototype of Stowe's Uncle Tom.

372 HICKEY, Neil and Ed Edwin. *Adam Clayton Powell and the Politics of Race.* New York, Fleet Pub. Corp., 1965. 308 p. $6.50. In this biography, two newsmen review Adam Clayton Powell's still unfinished career. The authors cover his early successes in the 1930's; his 1958 primary triumph over Carmine DiSapio's attempts to deny him renomination as a Democrat; his forays into Puerto Rico and his disputes with the Presidents from Roosevelt on; his three marriages and his gloriously high living; his income tax and libel troubles. Interspersed are brief sketches of Harlem and such figures as Marcus Garvey and the late Malcolm X.

373 HOLDREDGE, Helen O'Donnell. *Mammy Pleasant.* New York, Putnam, 1953. 311 p.

374 HOLT, Rackham. *George Washington Carver; an American Biography.* Rev. ed. Garden City, N.Y., Doubleday, 1964. 306 p. $4.95. The life of the outstanding scientist from Tuskegee who revolutionized southern agriculture.

375 HOLT, Rackham. *Mary McLeod Bethune; a Biography.* Garden City, New York, Doubleday, 1964. 306 p. $4.95. Biography of a Negro educator who was a confidant and friend of Franklin D. and Eleanor Roosevelt and spokesman in the New Deal era.

376 HORNE, Lena and Richard Schickel. *Lena.* New York, Doubleday, 1965. 300 p. $4.95. The entertainer's life from her debut at the old Cotton Club in New York to her resounding triumphs of T.V.

377 HOYT, Edwin P. *Paul Robeson; the American Othello.* Cleveland, World Pub. Co., 1967. 228 p. $5.95. The Paul Robeson the author presents is the misunderstood defender of his people who became involved in, but not a member of, the Communist Party because it preached racial equality.

378 HUGHES, Langston. *The Big Sea; an Autobiography.* New York, Hill and Wang, 1963. 355 p. $4.50. Paperback (Knopf, 1940). $1.95. Autobiography of the Negro poet, novelist, and playwright. It recounts his life story up to the age of twenty-seven.

379  HUGHES, Langston. *I Wonder As I Wander; an Autobiographical Journey*. New York, Rinehart, 1956. 405 p. $6.00. Another installment of Hughes' autobiography begun in *The Big Sea*. This volume contains an account of his journeys through Russia, Spain, China, and Japan, as well as some incidents of his poetry readings in this country.

380  HUGHES, Louis. *Thirty Years a Slave. From Bondage to Freedom, The Institution of Slavery as Seen on the Plantation and in the Home of the Planter.* Autobiography of Louis Hughes. Milwaukee, South Side Printing Company, 1897. 210 p.

381  HUGHES, William Hardin and Frederick D. Patterson, eds. *Robert Russa Moton of Hampton and Tuskegee.* Chapel Hill, University of North Carolina Press, 1956. 238 p. Volume of tributes to the life of Dr. Robert Russa Moton.

382  HUIE, William Bradford. *Ruby McCollum; Woman in the Suwannee Jail.* Rev. ed. New York, New American Library, 1964. 190 p.

383  JACKSON, Mahalia with Evan McLeon Wylie. *Movin' On Up; the Mahalia Jackson Story.* New York, Hawthorn Books, 1966. 212 p. $5.95. This is an autobiography of the famous gospel singer and covers the details of life from her childhood in New Orleans to Chicago where she migrated and later gained international fame.

384  JEFFERSON, Isaac. *Memoirs of a Monticello Slave,* as dictated to Charles Campbell in the 1840's by Isaac, one of Thomas Jefferson's slaves. Edited by Rayford W. Logan. Charlottesville, Published by the University of Virginia Press for the Tracy W. McGregor Library, 1951. 45 p. Portrait.

385  JOHNSON, James Weldon. *Along This Way, the Autobiography of James Weldon Johnson.* New York, The Viking Press, 1933. 418 p. Portrait. Paperback (Penguin Books, 1941). The autobiography of a diplomat, reformer, poet, and Negro leader. His personal story reflects the struggles of his race.

386  JOHNSON, Thomas L. *Twenty-eight Years a Slave; or, The Story of My Life in Three Continents,* by Thomas L. Johnson. Bourne Mouth, England, W. Mate and Sons, Limited, 1909. 266 p.

387  JOHNSON, William. *William Johnson's Natchez; the Ante-Bellum Diary of a Free Negro.* Edited by William Ransom Hogan and Edwin

Adams Davis. Baton Rouge, Louisiana State University Press, 1951. 812 p. $10.00. See also Davis, Edwin Adams. *The Barber of Natchez.*

388  KECKLEY, Elizabeth. *Behind the Scenes, by Elizabeth Keckley, Or, Thirty Years a Slave, and Four Years in the White House.* New York, G.W. Carleton & Co., Publishers, 1868. 371 p.

389  KIRKEBY, W.T. *Ain't Misbehavin'; the Story of Fats Waller,* edited by Ed Kirkeby in collaboration with Duncan P. Schiedt and Sinclair Traill. New York, Dodd, Mead, 1966. 248 p. $5.00.

390  KITT, Eartha. *Thursday's Child.* 1st ed. New York, Duelln, Sloan and Pearce, 1956. 250 p.

391  KYTLE, Elizabeth. *Willie Mae.* New York, Alfred A. Knopf, 1958. 243 p. $3.50. This is the true story of a Negro servant from Georgia told in her own words.

392  LAWSON, Elizabeth with an introduction by William L. Patterson. *The Gentleman from Mississippi; Our First Negro Congressman, Hiram R. Revels.* New York, 1960. 63 p. Portraits.

393  LEE, Reba. *I Passed For White,* as told to Mary Hastings Bradley. 1st ed. New York, Longmans, Green, 1955. 274 p.

394  LEWIS, Claude. *Adam Clayton Powell.* Greenwich, Conn., Fawcett Publishing Co., 1963. 127 p. $0.40. An appraisal of the controversial clergyman and U.S. Congressman, who was, at the time of this book, chairman of House Committee on Education and Labor.

395  LITTLE, Malcolm with the assistance of Alex Haley. *The Autobiography of Malcolm X.* New York, Grove Press, 1965. 455 p. $2.50. Paperback. $0.95. The exciting story of the Negro leader which provides insights into the mind and character of the former Black Muslim leader.

396  LITTLE, Malcolm. *Malcolm X Speaks;* Selected Speeches and Statements edited with Prefatory Notes by George Breitman. New York, Merit Publishers, 1965. 242 p. Paperback (Grove Press). $0.95. The editor says in his foreword that the aim of this book is to present, in his own words, the major ideas Malcolm expounded and defended during his last year.

397  LITTLE, Malcolm. *The Speeches of Malcolm X at Harvard.* Edited with an Introductory Essay by Archie Epps. New York, William Morrow, 1968. 191 p. $4.95. Includes speeches given on three separate occasions from 1961 when he was deep in his Black Muslim period; in March 1964, when he had just resigned from the Black Muslims; and in December 1964, soon after he had returned from an extensive trip to Africa, two months before his assassination. A brief biographical sketch is included along with an analysis of his ideas, rebuttals by the Harvard faculty as well as the question-and-answer periods between Harvard students and Malcolm.

398  LOGUEN, Jermain Wesley. *The Rev. J.W. Loguen, as a Slave and as a Freeman.* A narrative of real life. Syracuse, N.Y., J.G.K. Truair & Co. Printers, 1859. 454 p. Written in the third person, but apparently the work of Loguen. Two letters at end of volume are dated 1860. Testimony of Rev. E.P. Rogers, including a poem "Loguen's position": p. 445-450.

399  LOVE, Nat. *The Life and Adventures of Nat Love.* Reprint of the 1907 ed.; with new Introduction by William L. Katz. New York, Arno Press, 1968. 162 p.

400  MAGOUN, F. Alexander. *Amos Fortune's Choice, The Story of a Negro Slave's Struggle for Self-Fulfillment.* Freeport, Maine, The Bond Wheelwright Co., 1964. 237 p.

MALCOLM X, See Little, Malcolm.

401  MALVIN, John. *North Into Freedom; the Autobiography of John Malvin, Free Negro, 1795-1880,* edited and with an Introduction by Allan Peskin. Cleveland, The Press of Western Reserve University, 1966. 87 p. $4.00. Contains the complete text of the original manuscript of a narrative with a few new bibliographical notes. The original title page includes the following subtitle — "A Narrative, Containing an Authentic Account of His Fifty Years' Struggle in the State of Ohio in Behalf of the American Slave, and the Equal Rights of All Men Before the Law Without Reference to Race or Color; Forty-Seven Years of Said Time Being Expended in the City of Cleveland."

402  MARSHALL, Herbert and Mildred Stock. *Ira Aldridge; the Negro Tragedian.* New York, Macmillan, 1959. 355 p. $7.00. Scholarly biography of the American-born Negro actor of the 19th century who won fame through his Shakespearean characterizations in

England and on the Continent, particularly in Czarist Russia.

403  MATHEWS, Marcia M. *Richard Allen.* Baltimore, Helicon Press, 1963. 151 p. $3.95.

404  MELBOURN, Julius. *Life and Opinions of Julius Melbourn;* With Sketches of the Lives and Characters of Thomas Jefferson, John Quincy Adams, John Randolph, and Several Other Eminent American Statesmen. Edited by a late member of Congress. Syracuse, Hall & Dickson; etc., 1847. 239 p.

405  MILLER, Floyd. *Ahdoola! A Biography of Matthew Henson.* New York, E.P. Dutton, 1963. 224 p. $4.50. Biography of the Negro American who is recognized as the man who was responsible for getting Peary to the Pole.

406  MILLER, William Robert. *Martin Luther King, Jr.: His Life, Martyrdom, and Meaning to the World.* New York, Weybright, 1968. $6.95.

407  MITCHELL, Joseph. *The Missionary Pioneer; or, A Brief Memoir of the Life, Labours, and Death of John Stewart, (Man of Colour), Founder, Under God, of the Mission Among the Wyandotts, at Upper Sandusky, Ohio.* Joseph Mitchell, New York, 1827. 96 p.

408  MORROW, Everett Frederic. *Black Man in the White House; a Diary of the Eisenhower Years by the Administrative Officer for Special Projects, White House, 1955-1961.* New York, Coward-McCann, 1963. 308 p. $5.95. Diary of the first Negro to serve on a Presidential staff in an executive capacity.

409  MORTON, Lena Beatrice. *My First Sixty Years: Passion and Wisdom.* New York, Philosophical Library, 1965. 177 p. $6.00. The autobiography of a veteran educator with particular attention to the struggle between Negroes and Caucasians.

410  MOTON, Robert Russa. *Finding a Way Out; an Autobiography.* Garden City, New York, Doubleday, Page & Company, 1920. 295 p.

411  MULZAC, Hugh. *A Star to Steer By, an Autobiography.* New York, International Publishers, 1963. 251 p. $5.00. Paperback $0.85. Autobiography of the first Negro in United States history to win his master's license and command his own ship.

412 MURRAY, Pauli. *Proud Shoes; the Story of an American Family.* New York, Harper and Row, 1956. 276 p. $3.50. Out of print. In a biography of her grandfather Fitzgerald, the author presents a small part of the pattern of Negro culture in the U.S., for her grandfather was of Irish African descent, one of the few Negro soldiers in the Union Army and a man who took it upon himself to come south after the Civil War to start schools for his newly freed people in Durham, North Carolina. It is more than a family chronicle. It is that, surely, but it is something more. It is a personal memoir, it is history, it is biography.

413 NEWMAN, Shirlee P. *Marian Anderson: Lady from Philadelphia.* Philadelphia, Westminster Press, 1966. 175 p. $3.75.

414 NORTHRUP, Solomon. *Twelve Years a Slave; Narrative of Solomon Northrup, a Citizen of New York, Kidnapped in Washington City in 1841, and Rescued in 1853 From a Cotton Plantation Near the Red River, in Louisiana.* Auburn, Derby and Miller; Buffalo, Derby, Orton and Mulligan; London, Sampson Low, Son and Co., 1853. 336 p. Illustrations. Reprint, Louisiana State University Press, 1968. $7.50.

415 OTTLEY, Roi. *The Lonely Warrior, the Life and Times of Robert S. Abbott.* Chicago, Ill., Henry Regnery Co., 1955. 381 p. Portraits.

416 PARKS, Gordon. *A Choice of Weapons.* New York, Harper and Row, 1966. 274 p. $5.95. Paperback $0.75. A quietly but bluntly told personal history of a gifted Negro in his formative years. A success story revealing an unvarnished glimpse of the ghetto, and personal recognition as a composer and photographer-historian for *Life* magazine.

417 PARKS, Gordon. *Gordon Parks; a Poet and His Camera.* Preface by Stephen Spencer. Introduction by Philip B. Kunhardt. New York, Viking Press, 1968. 92 p. $8.95.

418 PARKS, Lillian R. and Frances S. Leighton. *My Thirty Years Backstairs at the White House.* New York, Fleet Pub. Corp., 1961. 346 p. $4.95. Anecdotes and reminiscences of a maid and seamstress who followed her mother as number one White House maid. The book presents a backstage view of White House affairs covering a period of more than half a century.

419 PAULI, Hertha Ernestine. *Her Name was Sojourner Truth.* 1st ed.

New York, Appleton-Century-Crofts, 1962. 250 p.

420 PENNINGTON, James W.C. *The Fugitive Blacksmith; or, Events in the History of James W.C. Pennington formerly a Slave in the State of Maryland....* 2d ed. London, C. Galfin, 1849. 87 p.

421 PICKARD, Mrs. Kate E.R. *The Kidnapped and the Ransomed. Being the Personal Recollections of Peter Still and His Wife "Vina," After Forty Years of Slavery.* With an Introduction by Rev. Samuel J. May; and an Appendix, by William H. Furness, D.C. Syracuse, W.T. Hamilton; New York, etc., Miller, Orton and Mulligan, 1856. 409 p.

422 PONT, M.M. *Life and Times of Henry M. Turner; the Antecedent and Preliminary History of the Life and Times of Bishop H. M. Turner, His Boyhood, Education and Public Career and His Relation to His Associates, Colleagues and Contemporaries.* Atlanta, A. B. Caldwell Pub. Co., 1917. 173 p.

423 PRINCE, Mrs. Nancy (Gardener). *A Narrative of the Life and Travels of Mrs. Prince.* Boston, Nancy Gardener Prince, 1850. 87 p.

424 PROCTOR, Henry Hugh. *Between Black and White; Autobiographical Sketches.* Boston, Chicago, The Pilgrim Press, c1925. 189 p.

425 PURCELL, Leslie Harper. *Miracle in Mississippi: Laurence C. Jones of Piney Woods.* New York, Comet Press Books, 1956. 252 p.

426 REDDICK, Lawrence Dunbar. *Crusader Without Violence; a Biography of Martin Luther King, Jr.* 1st ed. New York, Harper, 1959. 243 p. Out of print.

427 REISNER, Robert George. *Bird: the Legend of Charlie Parker.* New York, Citadel Press, 1962. 256 p.

428 ROBESON, Eslanda Goode. *Paul Robeson, Negro.* New York, London, Harper and Brothers, 1930. 178 p. $3.50. Out of print.

429 ROBESON, Paul. *Here I Stand.* New York, Othello Associates, 1958. 128 p.

430 ROBINSON, Bradley and Matthew Henson. *Dark Companion: the Story of Matthew Henson.* New York, Fawcett Publications, 1967. 238 p. $0.75. The extraordinary biography of the Negro explorer

who with Peary discovered the North Pole, and who was immortalized by the Eskimos but completely neglected by a color-conscious American public.

431 ROBINSON, James Herman. *Road Without Turning. An Autobiography.* New York, Farrar, Straus and Co., 1950. 312 p. $3.50. Out of print. The autobiography of a Negro minister, who at the time the book was written was pastor of the Church of the Master (Presbyterian) in New York City. He is also founder of "Operation Crossroads Africa," after which President Kennedy patterned the Peace Corps.

432 ROBINSON, Sugar Ray. *Sugar Ray.* New York, Viking Press, 1968. "The former world boxing champion talks about his boxing career and his private life and thoughts."

433 RODMAN, Selden. *Horace Pippin, a Negro Painter in America.* New York, Quadrangle Press, 1947. 88 p.

434 ROPER, Moses. *A Narrative of the Adventures and Escape of Moses Roper, From American Slavery;* with a Preface by the Rev. R. Price. 4th ed. London, Harvey and Darton, 1840. 120 p.

435 ROWLAND, Mabel, ed. *Bert Williams, Son of Laughter;* a Symposium of Tribute to the Man and to His Work, by his Friends and Associates. With a Preface by David Belasco; New York City, The English Crafters c1923. 218 p.

436 RUDWICK, Elliott M. *W.E.B. DuBois; a Study in Minority Group Leadership.* Philadelphia, University of Pennsylvania Press, 1960. 382 p. $6.00.

437 SAVAGE, Horace C. *Life and Times of Bishop Isaac Lane.* Nashville, National Publication Co., 1958. 240 p.

438 SCHUYLER, George S. *Black and Conservative; the Autobiography of George S. Schuyler.* New Rochelle, N.Y., Arlington House, 1966. 362 p. $5.95.

439 SCHUYLER, Philippa Duke. *Adventures in Black and White.* Foreword by Deems Taylor. New York, R. Speller, 1960. 302 p. $4.95.

440 SHEPPERD, Gladys Byram. *Mary Church Terrell; Respectable*

*Person.* Baltimore, Human Relations Press, 1959. 125 p.

441   SINGLETON, George A. *The Autobiography of George A. Singleton.* Boston, Forum Publishing Co., 1964. 272 p. $5.00.

442   SMITH, Amanda (Berry), with an Introduction by Bishop Thoburn. *An Autobiography; the Story of the Lord's Dealings With Mrs. Amanda Smith, the Colored Evangelist; Containing an Account of Her Life Work of Faith, and Her Travels in America, England, Ireland, Scotland, India and Africa, as an Independent Missionary.* Chicago, Meyer & Brother, 1893. 506 p.

443   SMITH, David. *Biography of Rev. David Smith, of the A.M.E. Church, Being a Complete History Embracing Over Sixty Years Labor in the Advancement of the Redeemer's Kingdom on Earth. Including "The History of the Origin and Development of Wilberforce University."* Xenia, Ohio, Printed at the Xenia Gazette Office, 1881. 135 p.

444   SMITH, Homer. *Black Man in Red Russia.* With an Introduction by Harrison W. Salisbury. Chicago, Johnson Publishing Co., 1964. 217 p. $4.95. A black journalist's memoir of fourteen years (1932-46) spent in the USSR as consultant at the Moscow Post Office and as foreign correspondent.

445   SPELLMAN, Cecil Lloyd. *Rough Steps on My Stairway; the Life History of a Negro Educator.* 1st ed. New York, Exposition Press, 1953. 273 p.

446   SPENCER, Samuel R. *Booker T. Washington and the Negro's Place in American Life.* Boston, Little, Brown, 1955. Paperback $1.95. A brief biography of Booker T. Washington which is at the same time an attempt to show his influence for good on the American Negro.

447   STERLING, Dorothy. *Captain of the Planter; the Story of Robert Smalls.* New York, Doubleday & Co., Inc., 1958. 264 p. Illustrations. $2.95. Biography of the first Negro commissioned officer in the Union Navy. Born a South Carolina slave, Smalls helped to rebuild his state and nation during Reconstruction.

448   STEWARD, Austin. *Twenty-two Years a Slave and Forty Years a Freeman. Embracing a Correspondence of Several Years, While President of Wilberforce Colony.* London, Canada, West, Rochester, Alling, 1857. 360 p.

449 STEWARD, Theophilus Gould. *Memoirs of Mrs. Rebecca Steward. Containing a Full Sketch of Her Life, With Various Selections From Her Writings and Letters.* Philadelphia, Pa., Publication Department of the A.M.E. Church, 1877. 131 p.

450 STILL, James. *Early Recollections and Life of Dr. James Still.* Philadelphia, Printed for James Still by J.B. Lippincott & Co., 1877. 274 p.

451 TARRY, Ellen. *The Third Door; the Autobiography of an American Negro Woman.* New York, David McKay Co., Inc., 1955. $3.50. Out of print. The autobiography of a Negro Catholic writer, describing her experiences in New York and in Alabama. It is an honest, illuminating, and sometimes disheartening account of the American Negro woman's bumpy road in the United States.

452 TERRELL, Mary Church. *A Colored Woman in a White World,* by Mary Church Terrell. Washington, D.C., Ransdell Inc., 1940. 436 p.

453 THOMAS, Jesse O. *My Story in Black and White; the Autobiography of Jessie O. Thomas.* Foreword by Whitney M. Young, Jr. New York, Exposition Press, 1967. 300 p. $6.00.

454 THOMPSON, Era Bell. *American Daughter.* Chicago, The University of Chicago Press, 1946. 300 p.

455 THOMPSON, John. *The Life of John Thompson, a Fugitive Slave; Containing His History of 25 Years in Bondage, and His Providential Escape. Written by Himself.* Worcester, John Thompson, 1856. 143 p.

456 TURNER, Robert Emanuel. *Memories of a Retired Pullman Porter.* 1st ed. New York, Exposition Press, 1954. 191 p.

457 VAN DEUSEN, John George. *"Brown Bomber;" the Story of Joe Louis.* Philadelphia, Dorrance and Co., 1940. 163 p.

458 WALKER, David. *One Continual Cry, David Walker's Appeal to the Colored Citizens of the World (1829-1830).* New York, Humanities Press, 1964. 155 p. $4.00. An analysis by Herbert Aptheker together with the full text of the third edition of Walker's appeal.

459 WALKER, Thomas Calhoun. *The Honey-Pod Tree; the Life Story of Thomas Calhoun Walker.* New York, J. Day Co., 1958. 320 p.

460  WARD, Samuel Ringgold. *Autobiography of a Fugitive Negro: His Anti-Slavery Labours in the United States, Canada & England.* London, J. Snow, 1855. 412 p.

461  WASHINGTON, Booker T. *Up From Slavery; an Autobiography.* Garden City, N.Y., Doubleday, 1933. 243 p. $4.95. Paperback (Dell) $0.45. Classic autobiography of the Negro educator, first published in 1901.

462  WATERS, Ethel, with Charles Samuels. *His Eye is on the Sparrow; an Autobiography.* 1st ed. Garden City. N.Y., Doubleday, 1951. 278 p.

463  WEBB, Constance. *Richard Wright; a Biography.* New York, G.P. Putnam's Sons, 1968. 443 p. $8.95. This biography of the author of *Black Boy* and *Native Son* is a combination of personal reminiscence and literary analysis based on his diaries, letters, speeches, unpublished novels, and other materials. The author traces Wright's growth as a writer and man from his Mississippi boyhood to his days in Chicago and New York and his years as an expatriate in Paris. She also records his travels, his political beliefs and activities, and the influences that shaped his writing. She discusses and analyzes his major work.

464  WEINBERG, Kenneth G. *Black Victory: Carl Stokes and the Winning of Cleveland.* Chicago, Ill., Quadrangle, 1968. 256 p. $5.95.

465  WILLIAMS, James. *Narrative of James Williams. An American Slave; Who was for Several Years a Driver on a Cotton Plantation in Alabama.* New York, The American Anti-Slavery Society, 1838. 108 p. Written by J.G. Whittier from the verbal narrative of Williams, cf. G.R. Carpenter, John Greenleaf Whittier, 1903. 165 p.

466  WILLIAMSON, Henry. *Hustler.* Edited by H. Lincoln Keiser. With a Commentary by Paul Bohannon. Garden City, New York, Doubleday, 1966. 222 p. $4.50. Paperback (Avon). $0.60. The autobiography of a professional criminal recently parolled from the Illinois State Penitentiary dictated to and edited by a case worker in St. Leonard's House and Episcopal Home for parolees and ex-convicts.

467  WRIGHT, Richard. *Black Boy: a Record of Childhood and Youth.* New York, Harper, 1945. 228 p. Paperback (New American Library, 1962). $0.75. Autobiography of the early years of a famous Negro writer which tells of his life in transition from Mississippi to Chicago.

468 YATES, Elizabeth. *Howard Thurman: a Portrait of a Practical Dreamer.* New York, John Day, 1964. 249 p. $4.95. This biography recounts the life of a Negro boy who rose from humble beginnings in Florida to the post of Dean of the Chapel at Boston University.

## CULTURAL MILIEU
### ART

469 THE BOWDOIN COLLEGE MUSEUM OF ART. *The Portrayal of the Negro in American Painting.* Brunswick, Maine, Bowdoin College, 1964. 134 p. 80 plates. Notes on the exhibition by Sidney Kaplan.

470 CALIFORNIA ART COMMISSION. *The Negro in American Art:* An Exhibition Co-sponsored by the California Arts Commission. Los Angeles, UCLA Art Galleries, Dickson Art Center, 1967. 63 p. Includes essay: "One hundred and fifty years of Afro-American Art," by James A. Porter, pp. 5-12.

471 *CELEBRATING NEGRO HISTORY AND BROTHERHOOD;* a Folio of Prints by Chicago Artists. Chicago, Seven Arts Workshop, 1956. 6 plates.

472 DOVER, Cedric. *American Negro Art.* 2d ed. New York, New York Graphic Society, 1965. 186 p. $12.00.

473 *THE EVOLUTION OF AFRO-AMERICAN ARTISTS: 1800-1950,* at Great Hall, The City College. New York, 1967. 70 p. $1.50. Catalogue of an exhibition sponsored by the University of New York in Cooperation with the Harlem Cultural Council and the New York Urban League. Included are the paintings and sculpture of 48 contemporary artists and work from such earlier artists as Joshua Johnson, Robert Duncanson, and Edmonia Lewis.

474 GOLDEN STATE MUTUAL LIFE INSURANCE COMPANY. *Golden State's Mutual Negro Art Collection.* Los Angeles, 1967. Includes 35 plates with commentary and four pages of biographical notes.

475 HARMON FOUNDATION. New York City. *Negro Artists.* An illustrated review of their achievements. New York, The Harmon Foundation, 1935. 59 p.

476 JONES, Lois Mailou. *Peintures, 1937-1951.* Tourcoing, France, Presses Georges Frere, 1952. Portfolio of 112 plates. Biographical essay of painter by James A. Porter.

477 LOCKE, Alain LeRoy. *Negro Art: Past and Present.* Washington, D.C., Associates in Negro Folk Education, 1936. 122 p. Out of print.

478 LOCKE, Alain LeRoy. *The Negro in Art: A Pictorial Record of the Negro Artist and the Negro Theme in Art.* Washington, D.C., Associates in Negro Folk Education, 1940. 224 p. Out of print. See also no. 68.

479 MURRAY, Freeman Henry Morris. *Emancipation and the Freed in American Sculpture; A Study in Interpretation.* Washington, D.C., Freeman Henry Morris Murray, Black Folk in Art Series, 1916. 239 p. Out of print.

480 *THE NEGRO ARTIST COMES OF AGE.* A National Survey of Contemporary American Artists. Albany, New York, Albany Institute of History and Art, 1945. $1.00. 77 p.

481 PORTER, James A. *Modern Negro Art.* New York, Arno Press and the New York Times, 1969. 272 p.

482 PORTER, James A. *Robert S. Duncanson, Mid-western Romantic-Realist.* In *Art in America.* Vol. 39, No. 3, Oct. 1951, pp. 99-154. Plates.

483 PORTER, James A. *Ten Afro-American Artists of the Nineteenth Century.* An Exhibition Commemorating the Centennial of Howard University, Feb. 3-March 30, 1967. Washington, D.C., The Gallery of Art, Howard University, 1967. 33 p. $1.50.

484 RODMAN, Selden. *Horace Pippin; A Negro Painter in America.* New York, The Quadrangle Press, 1947. 48 plates, 88 p.

485 ROELOF-LANNER, T.V., ed. *Prints by American Negro Artists.* Los Angeles, Cultural Exchange Center, 1965. 11 p., 51 illustrations.

486 ROELOF-LANNER, T.V., ed. *Prints by American Negro Artists.* 2d ed. Los Angeles, California, Cultural Exchange Center of Los Angeles, 1967. 49 p., 60 illustrations. Introductory essay — "One Hundred-Fifty Years of Afro-American Art," by James A. Porter, pp. 9-19.

487 THOMPSON, Robert F. *African and Afro-American Art; the Transatlantic Tradition.* New York, McGraw-Hill, 1968. $4.50.

488  UNITED STATES COMMITTEE FOR THE FIRST WORLD FESTI-
VAL OF NEGRO ARTS. *Dix Artistes Nègres des États-Unis; Premier
Festival Mondial des Arts Nègres, Dakar, Sénégal, 1966. Ten Negro
Artists From the United States; First World Festival of Negro Arts,
Dakar, Senegal, 1966. An Exhibition Produced and Sponsored by
the United States Committee for the First World Festival of Negro
Arts, Inc., and the National Collection of Fine Arts, Smithsonian
Institution.* (Text Translation Prepared by Denise and Michel
Berthier. New York, Distributed by October House, 1966). 1 vol.
Illustrations.

489  UNITED STATES WORKS PROGRESS ADMINISTRATION. *Sub-
ject Index to Literature on Negro Art* Selected from the *Union
Catalog of Printed Materials on the Negro in the Chicago Libraries.*
Chicago, Chicago Public Library Omnibus Project, 1941. 49 p.

490  WHITE, Charles. *Images of Dignity: The Drawings of Charles White.*
Foreword by Harry Belafonte, Introduction by James A. Porter,
Commentary by Benjamin Horowitz. Los Angeles, Heritage Gallery,
1967. 121 p. See also no. 107.

## DANCE

491  BUCKLE, Richard, ed. *Katherine Dunham, Her Dancers, Singers,
Musicians.* London, Ballet Pub., 1949. 79 p. Illustrations.

492  CLUZEL, Magdeleine. *Glimpses of the Theatre and Dance.* Introductory letter by Michel de Ghelderode. New York, Kamin Pub., 1953.
112 p. Out of print.

493  COLE, Carriebel B., comp. and composer. *Dances Worth While.*
Washington, D.C., Murray Brothers, 1918. 18 p. Out of print.

494  DUNHAM, Katherine. *Katherine Dunham's Journey to Accompong.*
Drawings by Ted Cook. New York, Holt, 1946. 162 p. Out of print.
Famous American Negro dancer's travels.

495  DUNHAM, Katherine. *A Touch of Innocence.* 1st ed. New York,
Harcourt, Brace, 1959. 312 p. $4.95. Out of print. Dance auto-
biography.

496  HORST, Louis and Carroll Russell. *Modern Dance Forms in Relation
to the Other Modern Arts.* San Francisco, Impulse Publications,
1961. 149 p. Article on jazz and the dance, pp. 111-20.

497  HUNGERFORD, Mary Jane. *Creative Tap Dancing*. New York, Prentice-Hall, 1939. 213 p. Chapter I discusses the Negro minstrel, pp. 3-18.

498  LLOYD, Margaret. *The Borzoi Book of Modern Dance*. 1st ed. New York, Knopf, 1949. 356 p.

499  MAGRIEL, Paul David, ed. *Chronicles of the American Dance*. New York, Henry Holt and Co., 1948. 268 p. Illustrations. Juba, early American Negro dancer, pp. 38-63.

500  MARTIN, John Joseph. *Book of the Dance*. New York, Tudor Publishing Co., 1963. 192 p. Photographs. Contains an article on the history of the Negro in dance followed by biographies of famous Negro dancers.

501  MARTIN, John Joseph. *The Dance, the Story of the Dance Told in Pictures and Text*. New York, Tudor Publishing Co., 1947. 160 p.

502  SELDES, Gilbert Vivian. *The 7 Lively Arts*. New York, Sagamore, 1957. 306 p.

503  SORELL, Walter. *The Dance Has Many Faces*. Cleveland, World Pub. Co., 1951. 288 p.

504  SPAETH, Sigmund. *Music and Dance in New York State*. New York, Bureau of Musical Research, 1951. 435 p.

505  WOODY, Regina Llewellyn. *Student Dancer*. Boston, Houghton Mifflin Co., 1951. 276 p. Illustrations. Out of print.

506  WOOTEN, Betty Jane, ed. *Focus Dance III*. Washington, American Association for Health, Physical Education, Recreation, 1965. 64 p. Illustrations. African influences on American dance, pp. 35-40. The Negro spirtual: source material for dance, pp. 44-50.

## LITERATURE

### History and Criticism

507  *THE ARTS AND THE BLACK REVOLUTION. Special Issue of the Arts in Society*. Vol. 5, No. 11, Summer-Fall 1968. University Extension. The University of Wisconsin, Madison, Wisconsin. 359 p.

$11.50. Forty-three leading literary and art critics, black and white, contribute to this first of several issues to be devoted to the arts and to black revolution.

508   BONE, Robert A. *The Negro Novel in America.* Rev. ed. New Haven, Yale University Press, 1965. 289 p. $6.50. Paperback $1.95. 509

509   BRAWLEY, Benjamin Griffith. *Early Negro American Writers; Selections with Biographical and Critical Introductions.* Chapel Hill, The University of North Carolina Press, 1935. 305 p.

510   BRAWLEY, Benjamin Griffith. *The Negro Genius; a New Appraisal of the Achievement of the American Negro in Literature and the Fine Arts.* New York, Dodd, Mead & Co., 1937. 366 p.

511   BRAWLEY, Benjamin Griffith. *The Negro in Literature and Art in the United States.* New York, Duffield & Company, 1918. 176 p. Portraits.

512   BRONZ, Stephen H. *Roots of Negro Racial Consciousness; the 1920's; Three Harlem Renaissance Authors.* New York, Libra Publishers, Inc., 1964. 101 p. $1.95.

513   BROWN, Sterling Allen. *The Negro in American Fiction.* Port Washington, N.Y., Kennikat Press, 1967 (c1937). 209 p. $7.50.

514   BROWN, Sterling Allen. *Negro Poetry and Drama.* Washington, D.C., The Associates in Negro Folk Education, 1937. 142 p.

515   BUTCHER, Margaret. *The Negro in American Culture,* based on materials left by Alain Locke. New York, Knopf, 1956. 294 p. $5.95.

516   CHARTERS, Samuel Barclay. *The Poetry of the Blues.* With Photos by Ann Charters. New York, Oak Publications, 1963. 111 p.

517   CONFERENCE OF NEGRO WRITERS. 1st, New York, 1959. *The American Negro Writer and His Roots; Selected Papers.* New York, American Society of African Culture, 1960. 70 p.

518   DREER, Herman. *American Literature by Negro Authors.* New York, Macmillan Company, 1950. 334 p.

519   DYKES, Eva Beatrice. *The Negro in English Romantic Thought: or, A Study of Sympathy for the Oppressed.* Washington, D.C., The Associated Publishers, Inc., 1942. 197 p.

520   FORD, Nick Aaron. *The Contemporary Negro Novel, A Study in Race Relations.* Boston, Meador Publishing Company, 1936. 108 p.

521   GLOSTER, Hugh Morris. *Negro Voices in American Fiction.* New York, Russell and Russell, 1965. 295 p. $7.50. First published in 1948 by The University of North Carolina Press.

522   GREEN, Elizabeth Lay. *The Negro in Contemporary American Literature; an Outline for Individual and Group Study.* Chapel Hill, The University of North Carolina Press, 1928. 98 p.

523   GROSS, Seymour L. and John E. Hardy, eds. *Images of the Negro in American Literature.* Chicago, University of Chicago Press, 1966. 321 p. Paperback $2.95.

524   HOWARD UNIVERSITY, Washington, D.C. Graduate School. Division of the Social Sciences. *The New Negro Thirty Years Afterward;* Papers Contributed to the Sixteenth Annual Spring Conference April 20, 21 and 22, 1955. Edited by Rayford W. Logan, Chairman, Eugene C. Holmes and G. Franklin Edwards. Washington, Howard University Press, 1955 [i.e. 1956] 96 p.

525   HUGHES, Carl Milton. *The Negro Novelist; a Discussion of the Writings of American Negro Novelists, 1940-1950.* New York, The Citadel Press, 1953. 288 p. Reprint-Books for Libraries, 1968. $9.50.

526   JOHNSON, James Weldon. *Black Manhattan.* New York, Alfred A. Knopf, 1930. 284 p.

527   KERLIN, Robert Thomas. *Negro Poets and Their Poems.* Washington, D.C., The Associated Publishers, Inc. c1923. 285 p. Illustrations.

528   LITTLEJOHN, David. *Black on White; a Critical Survey of Writing by American Negroes.* New York, Grossman, 1966. 180 p. $4.50.

529   LOCKE, Alain LeRoy, ed. *The New Negro; an Interpretation.* Book decoration and portraits by Winold Reiss. New York, A. and C. Boni, 1925. 446 p. Illustrations. Reprinted by Arno Press, 1968. $9.00, and Johnson Reprint Corp., 1968. $9.00

530 LOGGINS, Vernon. *The Negro Author, His Development in America to 1900.* Port Washington, N.Y., Kennikat Press, 1964 (c1931). 480 p. $12.50.

531 MAYS, Benjamin Elijah. *The Negro's God as Reflected in His Literature.* Lithographs by James L. Wells. Boston, Chapman & Grimes, Inc., c1938. 269 p.

532 MOON, Bucklin, ed. *Primer for White Folks.* Garden City, N.Y., Doubleday, 1945. 491 p. A worthwhile collection of prose writings by and about the Negro contributed by both white and Negro writers.

533 NELSON, John Herbert. *The Negro Character in American Literature.* College Park, Maryland, McGrath Pub. Co., 1968, 1926. $10.00.

534 REDDING, Jay Saunders. *To Make a Poet Black.* Chapel Hill, The University of North Carolina Press, 1939. 142 p.

535 TURNER, Lorenzo Dow. *Anti-Slavery Sentiment in American Literature Prior to 1865.* Port Washington, N.Y., Kennikat Press, 1966. 188 p. First published in 1929 by the Association for the Study of Negro Life and History.

536 WAGNER, Jean. *Les Poètes Nègres des États-Unis: Le Sentiment, Racial et Religieux dans La Poèsie de P.L. Dunbar à L. Hughes (1890-1940).* Paris, Librairie Istra, 1963. 637 p.

### Anthologies — Poetry, Fiction, Essay

537 ADLER, Elmer. *Breaking Into Print: Being a Compilation of Papers Wherein Each of a Select Group of Authors Tells of the Difficulties of Authorship & How Such Trials Are Met, Together With Biographical Notes and Comment by an Editor of the Colophon, Elmer Adler.* New York, Simon and Schuster, 1937. 196 p.

538 ADOFF, Arnold, ed. *I Am the Darker Brother; an Anthology of Modern Poems by Negro Americans.* Drawings by Benny Andrews. Foreword by Charlemae Rollins. New York, Macmillan Co., 1968. 128 p. $4.95.

539 THE AMERICAN MERCURY. *The American Mercury Reader, a Selection of Distinguished Articles, Stories, and Poems Published in*

*the American Mercury During the Past 20 Years.* Garden City, N.Y., Blue Ribbon Books, 1944. 378 p.

540  BALTIMORE AFRO-AMERICAN. *Best Short Stories by Afro-American Writers, 1925-1950,* Selected and Edited by Nick Aaron Ford and H.L. Faggett. Boston, Meador Pub. Co., 1950. 307 p.

541  BONTEMPS, Arna Wendell. *American Negro Poetry.* New York, Hill and Wang, 1963. 197 p. $4.95. Paperback $1.45.

542  BONTEMPS, Arna Wendell, comp. *Golden Slippers, an Anthology of Negro Poetry for Young Readers.* With drawings by Henrietta Bruce Sharon. New York and London, Harper & Brothers, 1941. 220 p.

543  BREMAN, Paul, ed. *Sixes and Sevens; an Anthology of New Poetry.* London, P. Breman, 1962. 96 p. Six poets were asked to introduce their selections with a statement about the question, "whether being a Negro 'colors' one's writings?" The seven selections which follow are shorter, not necessarily as a reflection of comparative merit.

544  BROWN, Sterling Allen, Arthur P. Davis and Ulysses Lee, eds. *The Negro Caravan; Writings by American Negroes.* New York, Dryden Press, 1941. 1082 p. Out of print.

545  CALVERTON, Victor Francis, ed., with Introduction. *Anthology of American Negro Literature,* New York, The Modern Library, c1929. 535 p.

546  CLARKE, John Henrik, ed. *American Negro Short Stories.* New York, Hill and Wang, 1966. 355 p. $5.95. Paperback $1.45.

547  CONFERENCE OF NEGRO WRITERS. 1st, New York, 1959. *The American Negro Writer and His Roots; Selected Papers.* New York, American Society of African Culture, 1960. 70 p.

548  CROMWELL, Otelia, Lorenzo Dow Turner, and Eva B. Dykes, eds. *Readings From Negro Authors, for Schools and Colleges, With a Bibliography of Negro Literature.* New York, Harcourt, Brace and Co., c1931. 388 p.

549  CULLEN, Countee. *Caroling Dusk; an Anthology of Verse by Negro Poets.* Decorations by Aaron Douglas. New York, London, Harper & Bros. 1927. 237 p.

550 DUNBAR, Alice Moore, ed. *Masterpieces of Negro Eloquence: The Best Speeches Delivered by the Negro from the Days of Slavery to the Present Time.* New York, The Bookery Publishing Company, 1914. 512 p.

551 EMANUEL, James Andrew and Theodore L. Gross. *Dark Symphony; Negro Literature in America.* New York, Macmillan Co., 1968. $8.95. Paperback $4.98.

552 FEDERAL WRITERS' PROJECT. *American Stuff; an Anthology of Prose and Verse by Members of the Federal Writers' Project.* With Sixteen Prints by the Federal Art Project. New York, Viking Press, 1937. 301 p. Contains: "The Ethics of Jim Crow" by Richard Wright; "All are Gay" by Sterling Brown; "Autumnal" by Robert E. Hayden.

553 HAYDEN, Robert Earl, ed., with Introduction. *Kaleidoscope; Poems by American Negro Poets.* New York, Harcourt, Brace and World, 1967. 231 p. $3.95.

554 HICKS, Granville and others, eds. *Proletarian Literature in the United States; an Anthology.* With a Critical Introduction by Joseph Freeman. New York, International Publishers, 1935. 384 p. Contains writings by Langston Hughes and Richard Wright.

555 HILL, Herbert, ed., with Introduction. *Anger, and Beyond? the Negro Writer in the United States.* New York, Harper & Row, 1966. 227 p. $5.95.

556 HILL, Herbert. *Soon, One Morning; New Writing by American Negroes, 1940-1962.* Selected and edited with an Introduction and Biographical Notes, New York, Alfred A. Knopf, 1963. 617 p. $6.95.

557 HUGHES, Langston, comp. *Best Short Stories by Negro Writers? an Anthology,* From 1899 to the Present. Boston, Little, Brown, 1967. 508 p. $7.95.

558 HUGHES, Langston. *The Langston Hughes Reader.* New York, George Braziller, 1958. 501 p. $5.95.

559 HUGHES, Langston, ed. *Negro Poets, U.S.A.,* Foreword by Gwendolyn Brooks. Bloomington & London, Indiana University Press, 1966 (c1964). 127 p. $4.95.

560   HUGHES, Langston and Arna Bontemps, eds. *The Poetry of the Negro, 1746-1949.* Garden City, N.Y., Doubleday, 1949. 429 p. $6.50.

561   JOHNSON, Charles Spurgeon, ed. *Ebony and Topaz; a Collectanea.* Published by *Opportunity: Journal of Negro Life.* New York, National Urban League, 1927. 164 p.

562   JOHNSON, James Weldon, ed., with Essay. *The Book of American Negro Poetry.* New York, Harcourt, Brace and Co., c1931. 300 p.

563   JONES, LeRoi and Larry Neal, eds. *Black Fire; an Anthology of Afro-American Writing.* New York, William Morrow & Co., Inc., 1968. 670 p. $8.95. "In essays, poems, short stories and plays over seventy black writers, among whom are included Stokely Carmichael, Harold Cruse, A.B. Spellman, Sun-Ra, Ed Bullins, and the editors themselves, search for a definition of the black sensibility — the sensibility of a colonialized people waking up to the realities of the contemporary world."

564   JONES, LeRoi, ed. *The Moderns; an Anthology of New Writing in America.* New York, Corinth Books, Inc., 1963. 351 p. "This first anthology of the new writers in America provides a comprehensive view of their literary importance to the 1960's."

565   KERLIN, Robert Thomas. *Negro Poets and Their Poems.* Washington, D.C., The Associated Publishers, Inc., c1923. 285 p. Illustrations.

566   LANUSSE, Armand. *Creole Voices: Poems in French by Free Men of Color,* first published in 1845, edited by Edward Maceo Coleman, with a Foreword by H. Carrington Lancaster. Washington, D.C., The Associated Publishers, Inc., 1945. 130 p.

567   LOCKE, Alain LeRoy, ed. *The New Negro; an Interpretation.* Book decoration and portraits by Winold Reiss. New York, A. and C. Boni, 1925. 446 p. Illustrations. To be reprinted.

568   MOON, Bucklin, ed. *Primer for White Folks.* Garden City, New York, Doubleday, Doran and Co., Inc., 1945. 491 p. Presents a general picture of the Negro and his relationships with whites. Includes essays by both white and Negro persons.

569   MURPHY, Beatrice M., ed. *An Anthology of Contemporary Negro Voices.* Illustrations by Clifton Thompson Hill. New York, Henry

Harrison, Poetry Publishers, 1928. 173 p. Illustrations.

570 MURPHY, Beatrice M. *Ebony Rhythm, an Anthology of Contemporary Negro Verse.* New York, Exposition Press, 1948. 162 p.

571 POOL, Rosey E., ed., with Introduction. *Beyond the Blues; New Poems by American Negroes.* Kent, England, The Hand and Flower Press, 1962. 188 p.

572 ROLLINS, Charlemae Hill. *Christmas Gif'; an Anthology of Christmas Poems, Songs and Stories, Written by and About Negroes.* Chicago, Follett Pub. Co., 1963. 119 p. $4.95.

573 THE SCRIBES. *Sing, Laugh, Weep; a Book of Poems* by The Scribes. With Illustrations by Theopoius Williams, St. Louis, Press Publishing Co., 1944. 126 p. Poetry by Lorenzo D. Blanton, Frederick W. Bond, Laura Howard, Alice E. McGee, Arthur W. Reason, and Ezra W. Turner.

574 TALLEY, Thomas W. *Negro Folk Rhymes: Wise and Otherwise.* With a Study by Thomas W. Talley of Fisk University. New York, The Macmillan Company, 1922. 347 p.

575 WALROND, Eric and Rosey E. Pool, eds. *Black and Unknown Bards; a Collection of Negro Poetry.* Kent, England, The Hand and Flower Press, 1958. 43 p.

576 WATKINS, Sylvestre C. *Anthology of American Negro Literature.* Introduction by John T. Frederick. New York, The Modern Library, 1944. 481 p.

577 WILLIAMS, John Alfred, ed. *Beyond the Angry Black.* 2d ed. New York, Cooper Square Publishers, 1966. 198 p. A reissue with new material of *The Angry Black* published in 1962.

**Drama**                                              **History and Criticism**

578 *BLACK THEATRE.* Special Issue of *The Drama Review,* Vol. 12, No. 4, Summer, 1968. New York University, 32 Washington Place, New York, New York. 10003. 180 p. $2.00. Includes plays, directory of black theatre groups, bibliography of black plays, books and articles related to black theatre published from 1-1960 to 2-1968.

579 BOND, Frederick Weldon. *The Negro and the Drama; the Direct and Indirect Contribution Which the American Negro has Made to*

*Drama and the Legitimate Stage, With the Underlying Conditions Responsible.* Washington, D.C., The Associated Publishers, Inc.1940. 213 p. Contains a bibliography.

580  HUGHES, Langston and Milton Meltzer. *Black Magic; a Pictorial History of the Negro in American Entertainment.* Englewood Cliffs, N.J., Prentice-Hall, 1967. 367 p. $12.95.

581  ISAACS, Edith J.R. *The Negro in the American Theatre.* New York, Theatre Arts, 1947. 143 p. Out of print.

582  MARSHALL, Herbert, and Mildred Stock. *Ira Aldridge, the Negro Tragedian.* New York, The Macmillan Co., 1958. 355 p. $7.00.

583  MITCHELL, Lofton. *Black Drama; the Story of the American Negro in the Theatre.* New York, Hawthorn Books, 1967. 248 p. $5.95.

584  NATIONAL SERVICE BUREAU. *A List of Negro Plays.* New York, National Service Bureau, 1938. 53 p.

585  PATTERSON, Lindsay, comp. *Anthology of the American Negro in the Theatre; a Critical Approach.* 1st ed. New York, Publishers Co., (International Library of Negro Life and History). 1967. 306 p.

586  RABKIN, Gerald. *Drama and Commitment: Politics in the American Theatre of the Thirties.* Bloomington, Indiana University Press, 1964. $6.00.

**Anthologies**

587  COUCH, William, ed. *New Black Playwrights; an Anthology.* Baton Rouge, Louisiana State University Press, 1968. $7.50.

588  EDMONDS, Randolph. *The Land of Cotton, and. Other Plays.* Washington, D.C., The Associated Publishers, Inc., 1942. 267 p.

589  EDMONDS, Randolph. *Six Plays for a Negro Theatre.* Foreword by Frederick H. Koch. Boston, Walter H. Baker Company, c1934. 155 p. One of the plays is entitled "Nat Turner."

590  HUGHES, Langston. *Five Plays.* Edited with an Introduction by Webster Smalley. Bloomington, Indiana University Press, 1963. 258 p. $5.95. Contents: "Mulatto;" "Soul Gone Home;" "Little Ham;" "Simply Heavenly;" "Tambourines to Glory."

591  JONES, LeRoi. *Baptism and the Toilet.* New York, The Grove Press, 1967 (c1963), 1966. 62 p. $1.00. *(Evergreen* Playscript, No. 10).

592  JONES, LeRoi. *The Dutchman and the Slave.* Two Plays. New York, William Morrow and Co., 1964. 88 p. $3.75.

593  LOCKE, Alain LeRoy, and Montgomery Gregory, eds. *Plays of Negro Life; a Source-Book of Native American Drama.* Decorations and illustrations by Aaron Douglas. New York, Harper and Brothers, 1927. 430 p. Bibliography of Negro drama, pp. 424-30.

594  RICHARDSON, Willis, and May Miller. *Negro History in Thirteen Plays.* Washington, D.C., The Associated Publishers, Inc. 1935. 333 p.

595  RICHARDSON, Willis, comp. *Plays and Pageants From the Life of the Negro.* Washington, D.C., The Associated Publishers, Inc., c1930. 373 p.

596  TORRENCE, Frederic Ridgely. *Granny Maumee, the Rider of Dreams. Simon the Cyrenian: Plays for a Negro Theater.* New York, The Macmillan Company, 1917. 111 p.

### Individual Plays

597  BALDWIN, James. *Amen Corner.* New York, Dial Press, 1967. 128 p. $3.95.

598  BALDWIN, James. *Blues for Mister Charlie.* New York, Dial Press, 1964. 121 p. Considered a classic — a play which combines all the author's talents as novelist and essayist.

599  BRANCH, William Blackwell. *Fifty Steps Toward Freedom. A Dramatic Presentation in Observance of the Fiftieth Anniversary of the National Association for the Advancement of Colored People.* New York, N.A.A.C.P., 1959. 26 p.

600  BULLINS, Ed. *How Do You Do.* Illuminations Press, Mill Valley, California, 1968. $1.50.

601  CALDWELL, Ben. *Militant Preacher.* Newark, Jihad Productions, 1967.

602 CONNELLY, Marcus Cook. *The Green Pastures, a Fable,* Suggested by Roark Bradford's Southern Sketches, "Ol' Man Adam an' His Chillun." New York, Farrar & Rinehart, Inc., 1930. 141 p.

603 COTTER, Joseph Seamon. *Caleb, the Degenerate, a Play in Four Acts; a Study of the Types, Customs, and Needs of the American Negro.* Louisville, Ky., The Bradley & Gilbert Company, 1903. 57 p.

604 DAVIS, Ossie. *Purlie Victorious, a Comedy in Three Acts.* New York, S. French, c1961. 90 p. Out of print.

605 DUBERMAN, Martin. *In White America; a Documentary Play.* Boston, Houghton Mifflin, 1964. 112 p. $3.95. Paperback $1.75. The race question as revealed in drama.

606 D'USSEAU, Arnaud and James Gow. *Deep Are the Roots.* New York, C. Scribner's Sons, 1946. 205 p.

607 EDMONDS, Randolph. *Earth and Stars; a Problem Play Concerning Negro and White Leadership in the South,* Including Desegregation, Freedom Riders, Sit-ins, the Failure of Intelligent White Majority Control, and Other Controversies Confronting Today's Crisis-Ridden South. Tallahassee, Fla., Florida A. and M. University, 1961. 146 leaves.

608 EDMONDS, Randolph. *Shades and Shadows.* Boston, Meador Publishing Co., 1930. 171 p.

609 ERROL, John. *Moon on a Rainbow Shawl.* New York, Grove Press, 1967.

610 GRIMKE, Angelina W. *Rachel: A Play in Three Acts.* Boston, The Cornhill Company, 1920. 96 p.

611 HANSBERRY, Lorraine. *A Raisin in the Sun; a Drama in Three Acts.* New York, Random House, 1959. 142 p. $2.95. Paperback (Signet Book, 1961).

612 HEYWARD, Dorothy and DuBose. *Mamba's Daughters, a Play.* Dramatized from the novel *Mamba's Daughters,* by DuBose Heyward. New York, Farrar & Rinehart, 1939. 182 p.

613 HILL, Leslie Pinckney. *Toussaint L'Ouverture, a Dramatic History.* Boston, The Christopher Publishing House, 1928. 137 p.

614 IMAN, Yusef. *Praise the Lord, But Pass the Ammunition.* Newark, Jihad Productions, 1967.

615 JONES, LeRoi. *Arm Yourself or Harm Yourself.* Newark, Jihad Productions, 1967.

616 MITCHELL, Loften. *Land Beyond the River.* Cody, Wyoming, Pioneer Drama Service, 1963.

617 PETERS, Paul, and George Sklar. *Stevedore, a Play in Three Acts.* New York, Covici, Friede, c1934. 123 p.

618 SACKLER, Howard. *The Great White Hope. A Play.* New York, Dial Press, 1968. 264 p. $4.95. Jack Johnson became the first Negro heavyweight champion of the world in 1908; this is an epic drama based on his life.

619 SPENCE, Eulalie. *Fool's Errand: Play in One Act.* New York, Samuel French, 1927.

620 WRIGHT, Richard, and Paul Green. *Native Son* (The Biography of a Young American). A play in ten scenes. From the novel by Richard Wright. New York and London, Harper & Brothers, 1941. 148 p.

### Poetry by Negro Authors

621 BELL, James Madison. *The Poetical Works of James Madison Bell.* Lansing, Mich., Wynkoop, Hallenbeck, Crawford Co., 1901. 208 p.

622 BRAITHWAITE, William Stanley Beaumont. *The House of Falling Leaves, With Other Poems.* Boston, J.W. Luce and Company, 1908. 112 p.

623 BRAITHWAITE, William Stanley Beaumont. *Lyrics of Life and Love.* Boston, H.B. Turner & Company, 1904. 80 p.

624 BRAITHWAITE, William Stanley Beaumont. *Selected Poems.* New York, Coward-McCann, Inc., 1948. 96 p.

625 BROOKS, Gwendolyn. *Annie Allen. Poems.* 1st ed. New York, Harper, 1949. 60 p. Out of print.

626 BROOKS, Gwendolyn. *The Bean Eaters; Poems.* 1st ed. New York, Harper, 1960. 71 p.

627 BROOKS, Gwendolyn. *Bronzeville Boys and Girls.* Pictures by Ronni Solbert. New York, Harper, 1956. 40 p.

628 BROOKS, Gwendolyn. *Selected Poems.* New York, Harper and Row, 1963. 127 p. $3.95. Paperback $1.65.

629 BROOKS, Gwendolyn. *A Street in Bronzeville.* New York and London, Harper & Brothers, 1945. 57 p.

630 BROWN, Sterling. *Southern Road; Poems.* New York, Harcourt, Brace and Co., 1932. 135 p.

631 CAMPBELL, James Edwin. *Echoes from the Cabin and Elsewhere.* Chicago, Donohue and Henneberry, 1895. 86 p.

632 CANNON, David Wadsworth. *Black Labor Chant, and Other Poems.* Illustrations by John Borican. New York, The National Council on Religion in Higher Education, c1939. 56 p.

633 COTTER, Joseph Seamon. *A White Song and a Black One.* Louisville, Ky., Bradley and Gilbert Co., 1909. 64 p.

634 CULLEN, Countee. *The Ballad of the Brown Girl, an Old Ballad Retold.* With illustrations and decorations by Charles Cullen. New York and London, Harper & Brothers, 1927. 11 p.

635 CULLEN, Countee. *The Black Christ & Other Poems.* With decoration by Charles Cullen. New York and London, Harper & Brothers, 1929. 110 p.

636 CULLEN, Countee. *Color.* New York and London, Harper & Brothers, 1925. 108 p.

637 CULLEN, Countee. *Copper Sun.* With decorations by Charles Cullen. New York and London, Harper & Brothers, 1927. 89 p.

638 CULLEN, Countee. *On These I Stand; an Anthology of the Best Poems of Countee Cullen.* New York, Harper & Brothers, 1947. 197 p. $4.95.

639 CUTHBERT, Marion Vera. *April Grasses.* New York, The Woman's Press, c1936. 30 p.

640 CUTHBERT, Marion Vera. *Songs of Creation.* New York, Woman's Press, 1949. 46 p.

641 DANNER, Margaret. *To Flower: Poems,* n.p., Hemphill House, 1963. 30 p.

642 DAVIS, Frank Marshall. *Black Man's Verse.* Chicago, Ill., The Black Cat Press, 1935. 83 p.

643 DAVIS, Frank Marshall. *47th Street; Poems.* Prairie City, Ill., Decker Press, 1948. 105 p.

644 DAVIS, Frank Marshall. *I Am the American Negro.* Chicago, Ill., Black Cat Press, 1937. 69 p.

645 DAVIS, Frank Marshall. *Through Sepia Eyes.* Chicago, Black Cat Press, 1938. 10 p.

646 DODSON, Owen. *Powerful Long Ladder.* New York, Farrar, Straus and Company, Inc., 1946. 103 p.

647 DUNBAR, Paul Laurence. *Candle-Lightin' Time.* Illustrated with photographs by the Hampton Institute Camera Club and decorations by Margaret Armstrong. New York, Dodd, Mead, & Co., 1901. 127 p.

648 DUNBAR, Paul Laurence. *Complete Poems.* New York, Dodd, Mead, & Co., 1940. 289 p. $4.50.

649 DUNBAR, Paul Laurence. *Howdy, Honey, Howdy.* Illustrated with photographs by Leigh Richmond Miner and decorations by Will Jenkins. New York, Dodd, Mead & Co., 1905. 125 p.

650 DUNBAR, Paul Laurence. *Joggin' Erlong.* Illustrated with photographs by Leigh Richmond Miner and decorations by John Rae. New York, Dodd, Mead, & Co., 1906. 119 p.

651 DUNBAR, Paul Laurence. *Li'l' Gal.* Illustrated with photographs by Leigh Richmond Miner, decorations by Margaret Armstrong. New York, Dodd, Mead, & Co., 1904. 123 p.

652 DUNBAR, Paul Laurence. *Little Brown Baby; Poems for Young People.* Selections, with biographical sketch by Bertha Rodgers. Illustrated by Erick Berry [pseud.] New York, Dodd, Mead, & Co., 1940. 106 p.

653  DUNBAR, Paul Laurence. *Lyrics of Love and Laughter.* New York, Dodd, Mead, & Co., 1903. 180 p.

654  DUNBAR, Paul Laurence. *Lyrics of Lowly Life.* With an Introduction by W.D. Howells. New York, Dodd, Mead, & Co., 1896. 208 p.

655  DUNBAR, Paul Laurence. *Lyrics of Sunshine and Shadow.* New York, Dodd, Mead, & Co., 1905. 109 p.

656  DUNBAR, Paul Laurence. *Lyrics of the Hearthside.* New York, Dodd, Mead, & Co., 1899. 227 p.

657  DUNBAR, Paul Laurence. *Poems of Cabin and Field.* Illustrated with photographs by the Hampton Institute Camera Club and decorations by Alice Morse. New York, Dodd, Mead, & Co., 1899. 125 p.

658  DUNBAR, Paul Laurence. *When Malindy Sings (Poems).* Illustrated with photographs by the Hampton Institute Camera Club and decorations by Margaret Armstrong. New York, Dodd, Mead, & Co., 1903. 144p.

659  HARPER, Frances Ellen Watkins. *Atlanta Offering: Poems.* Philadelphia, 1895. 70 p.

660  HARPER, Frances Ellen Watkins. *Idylls of the Bible.* Philadelphia, 1901. 64 p.

661  HARPER, Frances Ellen Watkins. *Moses: a Story of the Nile.* 2d ed. Philadelphia, Merrihew and Son, 1869. 47 p.

662  HARPER, Frances Ellen Watkins. *Poems on Miscellaneous Subjects.* 20th ed. Philadelphia, Merrihew and Son, 1874. 56 p.

663  HARPER, Frances Ellen Watkins. *Sketches of Southern Life.* Philadelphia, Merrihew and Son, 1888. 58 p.

664  HARPER, Frances Ellen Watkins. *The Sparrow's Fall and Other Poems.* n.p., n.d. 22 p. Portrait.

665  HAYDEN, Robert Earl. *A Ballad of Remembrance.* 1st ed. London, P. Breman, 1962. 72 p.

666 HAYDEN, Robert Earl. *Heart-shape in the Dust; Poems by Robert Hayden.* Detroit, Mich., The Falcon Press, c1940. 63 p.

667 HAYDEN, Robert Earl, ed. *Kaleidoscope; Poems by American Negro Poets.* New York, Harcourt, Brace & World, 1967. 231 p.

668 HAYDEN, Robert Earl. *Selected Poems.* New York, October House, 1966. 79 p. $4.50. Paperback $1.95.

669 HILL, Leslie Pinckney. *The Wings of Oppression.* Boston, The Stratford Co., 1921. 124 p.

670 HORNE, Frank. *Haverstraw.* London, P. Breman, 1963. 40 p.

671 HUGHES, Langston. *Ask Your Mama; 12 Moods for Jazz.* New York, Alfred A. Knopf, 1961. 92 p. $3.95.

672 HUGHES, Langston. *Dear Lovely Death.* Amenia, N.Y., Priv. Print. at the Troutbeck Press, 1931. 18 p.

673 HUGHES, Langston. *The Dream Keeper and Other Poems.* With illustrations by Helen Sewell. New York, Alfred A. Knopf, 1932. 77 p.

674 HUGHES, Langston. *Fields of Wonder.* New York, Alfred A. Knopf, 1947. 114 p.

675 HUGHES, Langston. *Fine Clothes to the Jew.* New York, Alfred A. Knopf, 1927. 89 p.

676 HUGHES, Langston. *Freedom's Plow.* New York, Musette Publishers, 1943. 14 p.

677 HUGHES, Langston. *The Negro Mother and Other Dramatic Recitations.* With decorations by Prentiss Taylor. New York, The Golden Stair Press, 1931. 20 p.

678 HUGHES, Langston. *A New Song.* Introduction by Michael Gold; Frontispiece by Joe Jones. New York, International Workers Order, c1938. 31 p.

679 HUGHES, Langston. *One-Way Ticket Poems.* Illustrations by Jacob Lawrence. 1st ed. New York, Alfred A. Knopf, 1949, c1948. 136 p.

680  HUGHES, Langston. *The Panther & the Lash. Poems of Our Times.* New York, Alfred A. Knopf, 1967. 101 p.

681  HUGHES, Langston. *Scottsboro Limited; Four Poems and a Play in Verse.* With illustrations by Prentiss Taylor. New York, The Golden Stair Press, 1932. 20 p.

682  HUGHES, Langston. *Shakespeare in Harlem.* With drawings by E. McKnight Kauffer. New York, Alfred A. Knopf, 1942. 124 p.

683  HUGHES, Langston. *The Weary Blues.* With an Introduction by Carl Van Vechten. New York, Alfred A. Knopf, 1926. 109 p.

684  JOHNSON, Georgia Douglas. *An Autumn Love Cycle.* New York, H. Vinal, Ltd., 1928. 70 p.

685  JOHNSON, Georgia Douglas. *Bronze: a Book of Verse.* With an Introduction by W.E.B. DuBois. Boston, B.J. Brimmer Company, 1922. 101 p.

686  JOHNSON, Georgia Douglas. *The Heart of a Woman, and Other Poems.* With an Introduction by William Stanley Braithwaite. Boston, The Cornhill Company, 1918. 62 p.

687  JOHNSON, Georgia Douglas. *Share My World; a Book of Poems.* Washington, D.C., Halfway House, 1962. 32 p.

688  JOHNSON, James Weldon. *Fifty Years & Other Poems.* With an Introduction by Brander Matthews. Boston, The Cornhill Company, c1917. 92 p.

689  JOHNSON, James Weldon. *God's Trombones; Seven Negro Sermons in Verse.* Drawings by Aaron Douglas, lettering by C.B. Falls. New York, The Viking Press, 1927. 56 p.

690  JOHNSON, James Weldon. *Saint Peter Relates an Incident, Selected Poems.* New York, Viking Press, 1935. 105 p.

691  JOHNSTON, Percy Edward. *"Concerto for Girl and Convertible" Opus No. 5 and Other Poems.* Washington, D.C., Murray, 1960. 24 p.

692  JOHNSTON, Percy Edward. *Sean Pendragon Requiem.* Poetical Texture by Percy Edward Johnston. Artistical Texture by William A. White. 1st ed. New York, Dasein-Jupiter Hammon, 1964. 27 p.

693  JOHNSTON, Percy Edward. *Six Cylinder Olympus.* Chicago, Jupiter Hammon Press, 1964. 36 p.

694  JONES, LeRoi. *The Dead Lecturer: Poems.* New York, Grove Press, 1964. 79 p.

695  MADGETT, Naomi Long. *Star by Star; Poems.* Detroit, Harlo Press, 1965. 64 p. $3.00.

696  MARGETSON, George Reginald. *England In The West Indies; a Neglected and Degenerated Empire.* Cambridge, Mass., George Reginald Margetson, 1906. 35 p.

697  MARGETSON, George Reginald. *Ethiopia's Flight; the Negro Question or, the White Man's Fear.* Cambridge, Mass., George Reginald Margetson, 1907. 12 p.

698  MARGETSON, George Reginald. *The Fledgling Bard and the Poetry Society.* Boston, R.G. Badger, etc., c1916. 111 p.

699  McCLELLAN, George Marion. *The Path of Dreams.* Louisville, Ky., J.P. Morton & Company, Inc., c1916. 76 p.

700  MILLER, May. *Into the Clearing.* Washington, The Charioteer Press, 1959. 24 p.

701  MILLER, May. *Poems.* Thetford, Vt., Cricket Press, 1962. 12 p.

702  ODEN, Gloria. *The Naked Frame, a Love Poem and Sonnets.* 1st ed. New York, Exposition Press, 1952. Unpaged.

703  PAYNE, Daniel Alexander. *The Pleasures, and Other Miscellaneous Poems.* Baltimore, Sherwood & Co., 1850. 43 p.

704  ROGERS, James Overton. *Blues and Ballads of a Black Yankee; a Journey with Sad Sam.* New York, Exposition Press, 1965. 63 p. $3.00.

705  SMITH, Lucy. *No Middle Ground.* Philadelphia, Council of the Arts, Science and Professions, 1952. 30 p.

706  TOLSON, Melvin Beaunorus. *Harlem Gallery:* Book I, *the Curator.* With an Introduction by Karl Shapiro. New York, Twayne Publishers, Inc., 1965. $4.00.

# PORTER BIBLIOGRAPHY

707 TOLSON, Melvin Beaunorus. *Rendezvous With America.* New York, Dodd, Mead, & Co., 1944. 121 p.

708 WALKER, Margaret. *For My People.* With a Foreword by Stephen Benet. New Haven, Yale University Press, 1968. 58 p. $5.00. Paperback $1.65. First published in 1942— this book won the Yale Series of Younger Poets award.

709 WHEATLEY, Phillis. *Poems of Phillis Wheatley.* Edited by Julian D. Mason. Chapel Hill, University of North Carolina Press, 1966. 113 p. $6.50.

710 WHEATLEY, Phillis. *Poems on Various Subjects, Religious and Moral.* By Phillis Wheatley, Negro Servant to Mr. John Wheatley, of Boston, in New-England. Albany: Reprinted, From the London Edition, by Barber & Southwick, for Thomas Spencer, Book-Seller, Market-street, 1793. 89 p.

711 WHITMAN, Albery Allson. *An Idyl of the South; an Epic Poem in Two Parts.* New York, Metaphysical Pub. Co., 1901. 126 p.

712 WHITMAN, Albery Allson. *Not a Man, and Yet a Man.* Springfield, Ohio, Republic Printing Co., 1877. 254 p.

713 WHITMAN, Albery Allson. *Twasinta's Seminoles; or, Rape of Florida.* Rev. ed. St. Louis, Nixon-Jones Printing Co., 1885. 97 p.

714 YEISER, Idabelle. *Lyric and Legend. Poems.* Boston, Christopher Pub. House, 1947. 77 p.

### Fiction by Negro Authors

715 ASHBY, William Mobile. *Redder Blood; a Novel.* by William M. Ashby, New York, The Cosmopolitan Press, 1915. 188 p.

716 ATTAWAY, William. *Blood on the Forge, a Novel.* Garden City, N.Y., Doubleday, Doran & Co., Inc., 1941. 279 p.

717 BALDWIN, James. *Another Country.* New York, Dial Press, 1962. 436 p. $5.95. Paperback (New York, Dell Pub. Co., 1962) $0.75.

718 BALDWIN, James. *Giovanni's Room; a Novel.* New York, Dial Press, 1956. 248 p. Paperback (Dell).

719  BALDWIN, James. *Go Tell It on the Mountain.* New York, Alfred A. Knopf, 1953. 303 p. $3.50.

720  BALDWIN, James. *Going to Meet the Man.* New York, Dial Press, 1965. 249 p. $4.95. Paperback (New York, Dell Pub. Co., 1965). $0.75.

721  BENNETT, George H. *A Wilderness of Vines.* London, Cape, 1967. 345 p.

722  BOLES, Robert. *Curling.* Boston, Houghton Mifflin Co., 1968. 259 p. $4.50.

723  BONTEMPS, Arna Wendell. *Black Thunder.* Boston, Beacon Press, 1968. 298 p. $4.95. Paperback $1.95. Reprint of a classic. First published in 1936. Contains new introduction by author.

724  BONTEMPS, Arna Wendell. *Chariot in the Sky; a Story of the Jubilee Singers.* Illustrated by Cyrus Leroy Baldridge. 1st ed. Philadelphia, Winston, c1956. 234 p.

725  BONTEMPS, Arna Wendell. *Drums at Dusk; a Novel.* New York, The Macmillan Co., 1939. 226 p.

726  BONTEMPS, Arna Wendell. *God Sends Sunday.* New York, Harcourt, Brace and Company, 1931. 199 p.

727  BONTEMPS, Arna Wendell. *Lonesome Boy.* Boston, Houghton Mifflin Co., 1955. 28 p.

728  BONTEMPS, Arna Wendell. *Sad-Faced Boy.* Illustrated by Virginia Lee Burton. Boston, Houghton Mifflin Co., 1937. 118 p.

729  BROOKS, Gwendolyn. *Maude Martha, a Novel.* 1st ed. New York, Harper, 1953. 180 p.

730  BROWN, Frank London. *Trumbull Park, a Novel.* Chicago, Regnery, 1959. 432 p. $3.95.

731  BROWN, Lloyd L. *Iron City, a Novel.* New York, Masses & Mainstream, 1951. 255 p. $3.00.

732  BROWN, William Wells. *Clotel.* New York, Arno Press, 1969. 245 p. Reprint of 1853 edition. First novel by an American Negro.

733 CHASTAIN, Thomas. *Judgment Day*. Garden City, N.Y., Doubleday, 1962. 213 p.

734 CHESNUTT, Charles Waddell. *The Colonel's Dream*. New York, Doubleday, Page & Company, 1905. 294 p.

735 CHESNUTT, Charles Waddell. *The Conjure Woman*. Cambridge, Riverside Press, 1899. 229 p.

736 CHESNUTT, Charles Waddell. *The House Behind the Cedars*. Boston and New York, Houghton Mifflin Co., 1900. 294 p.

737 CHESNUTT, Charles Waddell. *The Marrow of Tradition*. Boston and New York, Houghton Mifflin Co., 1901. 329 p.

738 CHESNUTT, Charles Waddell. *The Wife of His Youth and Other Stories of the Color Line*. With illustrations by Clyde O. DeLand. Boston and New York, Houghton Mifflin Co., 1899. 323 p. Reprint: The Gregg Press, 1967. (American Fiction Series, no. 4).

739 COTTER, Joseph S. *Negro Tales*. New York, Cosmopolitan Press, 1912. 148 p.

740 CRUMP, Paul. *Burn, Killer, Burn!* Chicago, Johnson Publishing Co., 1962. 391 p. $4.95.

741 CULLEN, Countee. *My Lives and How I Lost Them,* by Christopher Cat in Collaboration With Countee Cullen, With Drawings by Robert Reid Macguire. New York and London, Harper & Brothers, c1942. 160 p.

742 CULLEN, Countee. *One Way to Heaven*. New York and London, Harper & Brothers, 1932. 280 p.

743 DALY, Victor. *Not Only War, a Story of Two Great Conflicts*. Boston, The Christopher Publishing House, 1932. 106 p.

744 DAVIS, Christopher. *First Family*. New York, Coward-McCann, 1961. 253 p.

745 DEMBY, William. *Beetlecreek*. Afterword by Herbert Hill. New York, Avon Books, 1967. 190 p. $0.75.

746 DEMBY, William. *The Catacombs*. New York, Pantheon Books, 1965. 244 p. $4.95.

747 DODSON, Owen. *Boy at the Window, a Novel.* New York, Farrar, Straus and Young, Inc., 1951. 212 p. $2.75. Reprint-title: *When Trees are Green.* N.Y., Popular, 1951. $0.60.

748 DuBOIS, William Edward Burghardt. *Dark Princess, a Romance.* New York, Harcourt, Brace and Company, c1928. 311 p.

749 DuBOIS, William Edward Burghardt. *Mansart Builds a School.* New York, Mainstream Publishers, 1959. 367 p. His *The Black Flame,* a Trilogy, Book II.

750 DuBOIS, William Edward Burghardt. *The Ordeal of Mansart.* New York, Mainstream Publishers, 1957. 316 p. His *The Black Flame,* a Trilogy, Book I.

751 DuBOIS, William Edward Burghardt. *The Quest of the Silver Fleece; a Novel.* Chicago, A.C. McClurg & Co., 1911. 434 p.

752 DuBOIS, William Edward Burghardt. *Worlds of Color.* New York, Mainstream Publishers, 1961. 349 p. His *The Black Flame,* a Trilogy, Book III.

753 DUNBAR, Paul Laurence. *The Fanatics.* New York, Dodd, Mead & Company, 1901. 312 p.

754 DUNBAR, Paul Laurence. *Folks From Dixie.* With illustrations by E.W. Kemble. New York, Dodd, Mead, & Co., 1898. 263 p.

755 DUNBAR, Paul Laurence. *The Love of Landry.* New York, Dodd, Mead, & Co., c1900. 200 p.

756 DUNBAR, Paul Laurence. *The Sport of the Gods.* New York, Dodd, Mead, & Co., 1902. 255 p.

757 DUNBAR, Paul Laurence. *The Strength of Gideon, and Other Stories.* With illustrations by E.W. Kemble. New York, Dodd, Mead, & Co., 1900. 362 p.

758 DUNBAR, Paul Laurence. *The Uncalled: a Novel.* New York, Dodd, Mead, & Co., 1898. 255 p.

759 ELLISON, Ralph. *Invisible Man.* New York, Random House, 1952. 439 p. $5.95. Paperback (New York, New American Library, 1960). $0.95.

760 FAUSET, Jessie. *The Chinaberry Tree; a Novel of American Life.* New York, Frederick A. Stokes Company, 1931. 341 p.

761 FAUSET, Jessie. *Comedy, American Style.* New York, Frederick A. Stokes Company, 1933. 327 p.

762 FAUSET, Jessie. *There is Confusion.* New York, Boni and Liveright, 1924. 297 p.

763 FISHER, Rudolph. *The Conjure-man Dies, a Mystery Tale of Dark Harlem.* New York, Covici, Friede, 1932. 316 p.

764 FISHER, Rudolph. *The Walls of Jericho.* New York & London, Alfred A. Knopf, 1928. 307 p.

765 GRAHAM, Lorenz B. *South Town.* Chicago, Follett Pub. Co., 1958. 189 p.

766 GRAHAM, Shirley. *The Story of Phillis Wheatley.* Illustrated by Robert Burns. New York, J. Messner, c1949. 176 p.

767 GRAHAM, Shirley. *The Story of Pocahontas.* Illustrated by Mario Cooper, Enid La Monte Meadowcroft, Supervising Editor. New York, Grosset & Dunlap, 1953. 180 p.

768 GRANT, John Wesley. *Out of the Darkness; or, Diabolism and Destiny.* Nashville, Tenn., National Baptist Publishing Board, 1909. 316 p.

769 GRIGGS, Sutton Elbert. *The Hindered Hand: or, The Reign of the Repressionist.* Nashville, Tenn., The Orion Publishing Company, 1905. 303 p.

770 GRIGGS, Sutton Elbert. *Overshadowed, a Novel.* Nashville, Tenn., The Orion Publishing Co., 1901. 219 p.

771 GRIGGS, Sutton Elbert. *Pointing the Way.* Nashville, Tenn., The Orion Publishing Company, 1908. 233 p.

772 GRIGGS, Sutton Elbert. *Unfettered, a Novel.* Nashville, The Orion Publishing Co., 1902. 276 p.

773 HARPER, Frances Ellen Watkins. *Iola Leroy: or, Shadows Uplifted.* Philadelphia, Pa., Garrigues Brothers, 1892. 282 p.

774  HENDERSON, George Wylie. *Jule.* New York, Creative Age Press, Inc., 1946. 234 p.

775  HENDERSON, George Wylie. *Ollie Miss, a Novel.* New York, Frederick A. Stokes Company, 1935. 276 p.

776  HILL, John H. *Princess Malah.* Washington, D.C., The Associated Publishers, Inc., c1933. 330 p.

777  HIMES, Chester B. *All Shot Up.* New York, Avon Book Division, 1960. 160 p.

778  HIMES, Chester B. *The Big Gold Dream.* New York, Avon Book Division, 1960. 160 p.

779  HIMES, Chester B. *Cast the First Stone, a Novel.* New York, Coward-McCann, 1952. 346 p.

780  HIMES, Chester B. *Cotton Comes to Harlem.* New York, G. P. Putnam, 1965. 223 p. $4.50.

781  HIMES, Chester B. *The Heat's On.* New York, 1966. 220 p.

782  HIMES, Chester B. *If He Hollers Let Him Go.* Garden City, New York, Doubleday & Garden, Inc., 1945. 249 p. $2.50.

783  HIMES, Chester B. *Lonely Crusade.* 1st ed. New York, Alfred A. Knopf, 1947. 398 p.

784  HIMES, Chester B. *Pinktoes, a Novel.* Paris, Olympia Press, 1961. 207 p.

785  HIMES, Chester B. *The Primitive.* New York, New American Library, 1955. 151 p.

786  HIMES, Chester B. *The Real Cook Killers.* New York, Avon Publications, Inc., 1959. 160 p.

787  HIMES, Chester B. *Run Man Run.* New York, G.P. Putnam, 1966. 192 p. $4.95.

788  HIMES, Chester B. *The Third Generation.* Cleveland, World Pub. Co., 1954. 350 p.

789 HUGHES, Langston. *Best of Simple*. New York, Hill and Wang, 1961. 245 p. $3.95. Paperback $1.65.

790 HUGHES, Langston. *Not Without Laughter*. New York, London, Alfred A. Knopf, 1930. 324 p. $2.50.

791 HUGHES, Langston. *Something in Common and Other Stories*. New York, Hill and Wang, 1963. 236 p. $3.95. Paperback $1.75.

792 HUGHES, Langston. *Tambourines to Glory, a Novel*. New York, J. Day Co., 1958. 188 p.

793 HUGHES, Langston. *The Ways of White Folks*. New York, Alfred A. Knopf, 1934. 248 p.

794 HUNTER, Kristin. *God Bless the Child*. New York, Scribner, 1964. 307 p. $4.95.

795 HUNTER, Kristin. *The Landlord*. New York, Scribner, 1966. 338 p. $5.95.

796 HURSTON, Zora Neale. *Seraph on the Suwanee, a Novel*. New York, C. Scribner's Sons, 1948. 311 p.

797 HURSTON, Zora Neale. *Their Eyes Were Watching God; a Novel*. Philadelphia, London, J.B. Lippincott Company, 1937. 286 p.

798 JOHNSON, James Weldon. *The Autobiography of an Ex-Coloured Man*. New York, Alfred A. Knopf, 1927. 211 p. $3.95.

799 JONES, LeRoi. *The System of Dante's Hell (a Novel)*. New York, Grove Press, 1965. 154 p.

800 KELLEY, William Melvin. *Dancers on the Shore*. Garden City, New York, Doubleday, 1964. 201 p.

801 KELLEY, William Melvin. *Dem*. 1st ed. Garden City, N.Y., Doubleday, 1967. 210 p.

802 KELLEY, William Melvin. *A Drop of Patience*. Garden City, New York, Doubleday, 1965. 237 p. $4.50.

803 KILLENS, John Oliver. *And Then We Heard the Thunder*. New York, Alfred A. Knopf, 1962. 485 p. $5.95.

804 KILLENS, John Oliver. *'Sippi.* New York, Trident Press, 1967. 434 p. $5.95.

805 KILLENS, John Oliver. *Youngblood.* New York, Dial Press, 1954. 566 p.

806 LARSEN, Nella. *Passing.* New York & London, Alfred A. Knopf, 1929. 215 p.

807 LARSEN, Nella. *Quicksand.* New York & London, Alfred A. Knopf, 1928. 301 p.

808 LEE, George Washington. *Beale Street Sundown.* New York, House of Field, Inc., 1942. 176 p.

809 LEE, George Washington. *River George.* New York, The Macaulay Company, 1937. 275 p.

810 MARSHALL, Paule. *Brown Girl, Brownstones.* New York, Random House, 1959. 310 p. $3.95.

811 MAYFIELD, Julian. *The Grand Parade.* New York, Vanguard Press, 1960. 448 p. $4.95.

812 MAYFIELD, Julian. *The Hit.* New York, Vanguard Press, 1957. 212 p. $3.50

813 MAYFIELD, Julian. *The Long Night.* New York, Vanguard Press, 1958. 156 p.

814 MICHEAUX, Oscar. *The Homesteader.* Sioux City, Iowa, Western Book Supply Co., 1917. 533 p.

815 MICHEAUX, Oscar. *The Story of Dorothy Stanfield, Based on a Great Insurance Swindle, and a Woman!* A Novel, by Oscar Micheaux. New York, Book Supply Company, 1946. 416 p.

816 MILLER, Warren. *The Cool World.* New York, Fawcett Publications, 1968. 160 p. Paperback $0.60. The story of a Harlem Negro boy's relentless quest for identity and his final rejection of violence as a means of escape from the ghetto.

817 MOTLEY, Willard. *Knock on Any Door.* New York, New American Library, 1947. 504 p. Paperback $0.75.

818 MOTLEY, Willard. *Let No Man Write My Epitaph.* New York, Random House, 1958. 467 p. $4.95.

819 MOTLEY, Willard. *Let Noon Be Fair, a Novel.* New York, Putnam, c1965. 416 p.

820 MOTLEY, Willard. *We Fished All Night.* New York, Appleton-Century-Crofts, 1951. 560 p.

821 OTTLEY, Roi. *White Marble Lady.* New York, Farrar, Straus and Giroux, 1965. 287 p. $4.95.

822 PARKS, Gordon. *The Learning Tree.* New York, Harper and Row, 1963. 303 p. $4.95. Paperback, (Fawcett Publications, Inc.) $0.75. Powerful novel about a young Negro boy growing up in Kansas in the 1920's.

823 PAYNTER, John E. *Fugitives of the Pearl.* Washington, D.C., The Associated Publishers, Inc., 1930. 209 p.

824 PETRY, Ann Lane. *Country Place.* Boston, Houghton Mifflin Co., 1947. 266 p.

825 PETRY, Ann Lane. *The Narrows.* Boston, Houghton Mifflin, 1953. 428 p. $3.95.

826 PETRY, Ann Lane. *The Street.* Boston, Houghton Mifflin, 1946. 435 p.

827 PICKENS, William. *The Vengeance of the Gods, and Three Other Stories of Real American Color Line Life.* Introduction by Bishop John Hurst. Philadelphia, Pa., The A.M.E. Book Concern, c1922. 125 p.

828 POLITE, Carlene Hatcher. *The Flagellants.* New York, Farrar, Straus & Giroux, 1967. 214 p.

829 REDDING, Jay Saunders. *No Day of Triumph.* With an Introduction by Richard Wright. New York and London, Harper & Brothers, 1942. 342 p.

830 REDDING, Jay Saunders. *Stranger and Alone, a Novel.* 1st ed. New York, Harcourt, Brace, 1950. 308 p.

831 ROGERS, Joel Augustus. *She Walks in Beauty.* Los Angeles, Western Publishers, 1963. 316 p.

832 ROGERS, Joel Augustus. *From Superman to Man.* Chicago, M.A. Donohue & Co., Printers, 1917. 128 p.

833 ROLLINS, Bryant. *Danger Song.* 1st ed. Garden City, N.Y., Doubleday, 1967. 280 p.

834 SAVOY, Willard W. *Alien Land.* 1st ed. New York, E.P. Dutton, 1949. 320 p.

835 SCHUYLER, George S. *Black No More, Being an Account of the Strange and Wonderful Workings of Science in the Land of the Free, A.D. 1933-1940.* New York, The Macaulay Company, 1931. 250 p. Out of print.

836 SMITH, William Gardner. *Anger at Innocence.* New York, Farrar, Straus and Company, 1950. 300 p. $3.00.

837 SMITH, William Gardner. *Last of the Conquerors.* New York, Farrar, Straus, 1948. 191 p.

838 SMITH, William Gardner. *The Stone Face, a Novel.* New York, Farrar, Straus, 1963. 213 p.

839 THOMAS, Piri. *Down These Mean Streets.* New York, Alfred A. Knopf, 1967. 333 p. $5.95.

840 THOMAS, Will. *God is for White Folks.* New York, Creative Age Press, c1947. 305 p.

841 THOMAS, Will. *The Seeking.* New York, A.A. Wyn, 1953. 290 p. $3.50.

842 THURMAN, Wallace. *The Blacker the Berry; a Novel of Negro Life.* New York, The Macaulay Company, 1929. 262 p.

843 THURMAN, Wallace. *Infants of the Spring.* New York, The Macaulay Company, 1932. 284 p. $2.00.

844 THURMAN, Wallace and A.L. Furman, *The Interne.* New York, The Macaulay Company, c1932. 252 p.

845 TOOMER, Jean. *Crane.* With a Foreword by Waldo Frank. New York, Boni and Liveright, 1923. 239 p. Reprint: University Place Press, 1967. $6.00.

846 TURPIN, Waters Edward. *O Canaan! A Novel.* New York, Doubleday, Doran & Company, Inc., 1939. 311 p.

847 TURPIN, Waters Edward. *The Rootless.* New York, Vantage Press, 1957. 340 p.

848 TURPIN, Waters Edward. *These Low Grounds.* New York, Harper & Brothers Publishers, 1937. 341 p. $2.50.

849 WALKER, Margaret. *Jubilee.* New York, Houghton Mifflin, and Co. 1966. 497 p. $5.95.

850 WALROND, Eric. *Tropic Death.* New York, Boni & Liveright, 1926. 283 p.

851 WARD, Thomas P. *The Right to Live.* New York, Pageant Press, 1953. 239 p. $3.00.

852 WEBB, Frank J. *The Garies and Their Friends.* With an Introductory Preface by Mrs. Harriet B. Stowe. London, G. Rutledge & Co., 1857. 392 p. Reprint by Arno Press, 1969.

853 WEST, Dorothy. *The Living Is Easy.* Boston, Houghton Mifflin, and Co., 1948. 347 p. $3.50.

854 WEST, John B. *Bullets are My Business.* New York, The New American Library, 1960. 128 p.

855 WEST, John B. *Cobra Venom.* New York, The New American Library, 1960. 126 p.

856 WEST, John B. *A Taste for Blood.* New York, The New American Library, 1960. 144 p.

857 WHITE, Walter. *Fire in the Flint.* New York, Alfred A. Knopf, 1924. 300 p.

858 WHITE, Walter. *Flight.* New York, Alfred A. Knopf, 1926. 300 p.

859 WILLIAMS, Chancellor. *Have You Been to the River?* New York, Exposition Press, 1952. 350 p. $3.00.

860 WILLIAMS, Chancellor. *The Raven.* Philadelphia, Dorrance and Company, 1943. 562 p.

861 WILLIAMS, John Alfred. *The Angry Ones.* New York, Ace Books, Inc., 1960. 192 p.

862 WILLIAMS, John Alfred. *The Man Who Cried I Am; a Novel.* Boston, Little, Brown, 1967. 403 p. $6.95.

863 WILLIAMS, John Alfred. *Night Song.* New York, Farrar, Straus and Cudahy, 1961. 219 p. $3.50.

864 WILLIAMS, John Alfred. *Sissie.* New York, Farrar, Straus and Cudahy, 1963. 277 p. $4.50.

865 WOOBY, Philip. *Nude to the Meaning of Tomorrow; a Novel of a Lonely Search.* New York, Exposition Press, 1959. 285 p. $4.50.

866 WRIGHT, Charles. *The Messenger.* New York, Farrar, Straus and Cudahy, 1963. 217 p. $3.95.

867 WRIGHT, Charles. *The Wig, a Mirror Image.* New York, Farrar, Straus and Girous, 1966. 179 p.

868 WRIGHT, Richard. *Bright Morning Star.* New York, International Publishers, 1938. 48 p.

869 WRIGHT, Richard. *Eight Men.* Cleveland, World Pub. Co., 1961. 250 p.

870 WRIGHT, Richard. *Lawd Today.* New York, Walker, 1963. 189 p.

871 WRIGHT, Richard. *The Long Dream, a Novel.* 1st ed. Garden City, N.Y., Doubleday, 1958. 384 p.

872 WRIGHT, Richard. *Native Son.* New York, New American Library, 1962. 413 p. Paperback $0.75.

873 WRIGHT, Richard. *The Outsider.* New York, Harper & Brothers, 1953. 405 p. $3.95.

874 WRIGHT, Richard. *Uncle Tom's Children.* New York, Harper & Brothers, 1940. 317 p. Paperback $0.60.

875   YERBY, Frank. *Bride of Liberty*. 1st ed. Garden City, N.Y., Doubleday, 1954. 219 p.

876   YERBY, Frank. *Captain Rebel*. New York, Dial Press, 1956. 343 p.

877   YERBY, Frank. *The Devil's Laughter*. New York, Dial Press, 1953. 376 p.

878   YERBY, Frank. *Fairoaks, a Novel*. New York, Dial Press, 1957. 405 p.

879   YERBY, Frank. *Floodtide*. New York, Dial Press, 1950. 342 p.

880   YERBY, Frank. *Foxes of Harrow*. New York, Dial Press, 1946. 534 p. $4.95. Paperback (New York, Dell Pub. Co., 1966). $0.75.

881   YERBY, Frank. *The Garfield Honor*. New York, Dial Press, 1961. 347 p.

882   YERBY, Frank. *Gillian*. New York, Dial Press, 1960. 346 p.

883   YERBY, Frank. *Goat Song: a Novel of Ancient Greece*. New York, Dial Press, 1967. 469 p.

884   YERBY, Frank. *The Golden Hawk*. New York, Dial Press, 1948. 312 p.

885   YERBY, Frank. *Griffin's Way*. New York, Dial Press, 1962. 345 p. $4.95.

886   YERBY, Frank. *Jarrett's Jade, a Novel*. New York, Dial Press, 1959. 342 p.

887   YERBY, Frank. *Judas My Brother. The Story of the Thirteenth Disciple*. An Historical Novel. New York, Dial Press, 1968. 540 p. This is Yerby's twenty-first book and the result of thirty years of intensive research.

888   YERBY, Frank. *An Odor of Sanctity*. New York, Dial Press, 1968. 563 p. $6.95.

889   YERBY, Frank. *Pride's Castle*. New York, Dial Press, 1949. 382 p.

890 YERBY, Frank. *The Saracen Blade, a Novel.* New York, Dial Press, 1952. 406 p.

891 YERBY, Frank. *The Serpent and the Staff.* New York, Dial Press, 1958. 377 p.

892 YERBY, Frank. *The Treasure of Pleasant Valley.* New York, Dial Press, 1955.

893 YERBY, Frank. *The Vixens, A Novel.* New York, Dial Press, 1947. 347 p.

894 YERBY, Frank. *A Woman Called Fancy.* New York, Dial Press, 1951. 309 p.

### Essays by Negro Writers

895 BALDWIN, James. *Nobody Knows My Name; More Notes of a Native Son.* New York, Dial Press, 1961. 241 p. Paperback (Dell).

896 BALDWIN, James. *Notes of a Native Son.* Boston, Beacon, 1955. 175 p. Paperback (Bantam).

897 BENNETT, Lerone. *The Negro Mood, and Other Essays.* Chicago, Johnson Pub. Co., 1964. New York, Ballantine Books, 1965. 104 p. $3.95. Paperback $0.60.

898 CRUMMELL, Alexander. *Africa and America: Addresses and Discourses.* Springfield, Mass., Willey & Co., 1891. 466 p.

899 CRUMMELL, Alexander. *The Relations and Duties of Free Colored Men in America to Africa.* A letter to Charles B. Dunbar. . .by the Rev. Alex. Crummell. . .Hartford, Press of Case, Lockwood and Company, 1861. 54 p.

900 DUBOIS, William Edward Burghardt. *Darkwater; Voices from Within the Veil.* New York, Harcourt, Brace and Howe, 1920. 276 p.

901 DUBOIS, William Edward Burghardt. *Dusk of Dawn; An Essay toward an Autobiography of a Race Concept.* New York, Schocke Books, 1968. 334 p. $6.50. Paperback $2.45.

902 DUBOIS, William Edward Burghardt. *The Souls of Black Folk.* Introduction by Saunders Redding. Greenwich, Conn., Fawcett Publications, Inc., c1953. 1968. 192 p. Paperback $0.60.

903  ELLISON, Ralph. *Shadow and Act.* New York, Random House, 1964. 317 p. $5.95. Paperback $0.95.

904  EMBRY, James Crawford. *Thoughts for Today, Upon the Past, Present & Future of the Colored Americans.* In six chapters. Fort Scott, Kansas, Pioneer Book and Job Publishing House, 1878. 66 p.

905  GRIMKE, Francis James. *Christianity and Race Prejudice: Two Discourses Delivered in the Fifteenth Street Presbyterian Church, Washington, D.C., May 29th, and June 5th, 1910.* Washington, D.C., Press of W.E. Cobb, 1910. 29 p.

906  GRIMKE, Francis James. *Equality of Rights for All Citizens, Black and White, Alike, A Discourse Delivered in the Fifteenth Street Presbyterian Church, Washington, D.C., Sunday, March 7th, 1909.* Washington, D.C., 1909. 19 p.

907  JOHNSON, James Weldon. *Negro Americans. What Now?* New York, The Viking Press, 1934. 103 p.

908  JONES, LeRoi. *Home: Social Essays.* New York, William Morrow and Company, 1966. 252 p. $1.75.

909  KILLENS, John Oliver. *Black Man's Burden.* New York, Trident, 1965. 176 p. $3.95.

910  MITCHELL, Glenford E. and William H. Peace, III, eds. *The Angry Black South.* New York, Corinth Books, 1962. 159 p. $1.45.

911  PLATO, Ann. *Essays: Including Biographies and Miscellaneous Pieces in Prose and Poetry.* With an Introduction by the Rev. James W.C. Pennington. Hartford, 1841. 122 p. Out of print.

912  THURMAN, Howard. *The Luminous Darkness: A Personal Interpretation of the Anatomy of Segregation and the Ground of Hope.* New York, Harper and Row, 1965. 113 p. $3.00.

## JOURNALISM

913  BROOKS, Maxwell. *The Negro Press Re-Examined: Political Content of Leading Negro Newspapers.* Boston, Christopher Publishing House, 1959. 125 p. Dr. Brooks examines five Negro newspapers: *Afro-American, Amsterdam News, Courier, Defender, Journal* and *Guide.* He finds that these newspapers reflect the

traditional American values rather than revolutionary doctrines. These are journals of reform, says Dr. Brooks, rather than organs of protest. Bibliography, pp. 123-25.

914  BROWN, Warren. *Checklist of Negro Newspapers in the United States (1827-1946).* Jefferson City, Missouri, School of Journalism, Lincoln University, 1946. 37 p. Out of print. 467 newspapers are listed alphabetically by name. The checklist locates all known copies. Entry includes names of editors, dates of founding, and expiration.

915  CLARK, Thomas D. *The Southern Country Editor.* Indianapolis, Bobbs-Merrill, 1948. 365 p. Out of print. A rather light-hearted look at the rural weekly in the South from the Civil War to the forties. Some 1,800 weeklies were examined. No Negro papers were included, but there are revealing chapters on the white reporting of lynchings, racial attitudes, and so forth. Bibliography, pp. 339-46.

916  DETWEILER, Frederick German. *The Negro Press in the United States.* Chicago, Illinois, The University of Chicago Press, 1922. 274 p. Reprint: McGrath Publishing Company, College Park, Md., 20740. 1968. $12.50. Statistics and history as well as an examination of the format and theme content of the Negro Press. Bibliography, pp. 270-72.

917  *DIRECTORY OF U.S. NEGRO NEWSPAPERS, MAGAZINES AND PERIODICALS, 1966.* New York, U.S. Negro World, 1966. 40 leaves. $7.50. In addition to the directory section, this spiral bound volume contains an essay: "The Negro Press; Past, Present and Future" by Thelma T. Gorham. Areas of suggested study are given. Unpublished materials are included in the Bibliography, pp. 22-25. Order from: U.S. Negro World, Box 595, Manhattanville, New York, N.Y., 10027.

918  FISHER, Paul and Ralph Lowenstein, eds. *Race and News Media.* New York, Praeger, 1967. 158 p. $4.95. Papers from the eighth annual conference of the Freedom of Information Center of the University of Missouri. The conference was entitled "The Racial Crisis and the News Media." Twenty contributors cover the topics: "Reporting the Racial Crisis in the North and South," "The Changing Content of Racial News," "The Role of the Negro Press in the Civil Rights Struggle."

919  GORE, George William, Jr. *Negro Journalism; an Essay on the*

*History and Present Conditions of the Negro Press.* Greencastle, Indiana, Journalism Press, 1922. 35 p. Out of print.

920   GRAHAM, Hugh Davis. *Crisis in Print, Desegregation and the Press in Tennessee.* Nashville, Tenn., Vanderbilt University Press, 1967. 338 p. $7.50.

921   HILL, Roy L. *Who's Who in the American Negro Press.* Dallas Royal Publishing Co., 1960. 80 p. $3.95. Out of print. Biographical sketches were compiled from a questionnaire. The respondents included their views on the strengths and weaknesses of the American Negro press. Methods for improvement are given. These statements are tabulated. Respondents are classified by political affiliation, religious affiliation, educational background, etc.

922   KERLIN, Robert T. *The Voice of the Negro.* New York, E.P. Dutton Co., 1920. 188 p. Out of print. A compilation of Negro newspapers for a four month period. Reaction to the Washington Riot, World War I and the Versailles Treaty are central themes.

923   LOGAN, Rayford W. *Attitude of the Southern White Press Towards the Negro.* Washington, D.C., Foundation Publishers, 1940. 115 p.

924   LYLE, Jack. *The Black American and the Press,* by Jack Lyle and others. Los Angeles, Ward Ritchie Press, 1968. 86 p. $3.95. Paperback $1.50. Papers and related comments presented at a symposium during the UCLA Foreign Journalism Awards Program, 1967. Gunnar Mydral, Charles Evers, residents of Watts, and others discuss "The Racial Crisis," "Coverage in the Domestic Press," "International Reporting," "Negro Reaction to Press Coverage." Crisis reporting and its effect is the common theme.

925   OAK, Vishnu V. *The Negro Newspaper.* Yellow Springs, Ohio, Antioch Press, 1948. 170 p. Out of print.

926   OTTLEY, Roi. *The Lonely Warrior, The Life and Times of Robert S. Abbott.* Chicago, Ill., Henry Regnery Co., 1955. 381 p. Portraits. Out of print. Abbott was the founder of the Chicago *Defender* Bibliography, pp. 369-70.

927   PENN, Irvine Garland. *The Afro-American Press and its Editors.* With Contributions by Hon. Frederick Douglass, Hon. John R. Lynch. Springfield, Massachusetts, Wiley & Company, 1891. 565 p. Illustrations. Out of print.

928 SCHUYLER, George S. *Black and Conservative.* New Rochelle, N.Y., Arlington House Publishers, 1966. 362 p. $5.95. Author began journalism career as assistant editor of Harlem's *Messenger* . Schuyler is a columnist for the *Pittsburgh Courier* and a contributor to the North American Newspaper Alliance, a syndicate serving the dailies.

929 SCHUYLER, George S. *Fifty Years of Progress in Negro Journalism.* Pittsburgh, Pennsylvania, Pittsburgh Courier Publishing Company, 1950. 7 p. Illustrations. Out of print.

930 SIMPSON, George Eaton. *The Negro in the Philadelphia Press.* Philadelphia, University of Pennsylvania, 1936. 158 p. Illustrations. Out of print. Written as a sociology dissertation. Both white and Negro newspapers are examined, and the coverage classified and tabulated. Anti-social news coverage (crime and criminals) is the largest category.

931 WEDLOCK, Lunabelle. *The Reaction of Negro Publications and Organizations to German Anti-Semitism.* Washington, D.C., Howard University, 1942. 208 p. *(Howard University Studies in the Social Sciences,* Vol. 3, No. 2). Out of print.

## MUSIC

932 ALLEN, William Francis. *Charles P. Ware and Lucy McKim Garrison. Slave Songs of the United States.* New York, A Simpson and Co., 1967. 115 p.

933 BRADFORD, Perry. *Born With the Blues; Perry Bradford's Own Story.* The True Story of the Pioneering Blues Singers and Musicians in the Early Days of Jazz. New York, Oak Publications, c1965. 175 p. Illustrations.

934 BRYANT, Lawrence Chesterfield. *A Study of Music Programs in Private Negro Colleges.* Orangeburg, S.C., South Carolina State College, 1962. 14 leaves.

935 CARAWAN, Guy. *Ain't You Got a Right to the Tree of Life? The People of Johns Island, South Carolina, Their Faces, Their Words, and Their Songs.* Recorded by Guy and Candy Carawan. Photographed by Robert Yellin. Music transcribed by Ethel Raim, With a preface by Alan Lomax. New York, Simon and Schuster, 1967, c1966. 190 p. Illustrations.

936 CHAMBERS, H.A. *The Treasury of Negro Spirituals.* Foreword by Marian Anderson. New York, Emerson Books, 1963. 125 p. $5.50.

937  CHARTERS, Samuel Barclay. *The Bluesmen: the Story and the Music of the Men Who Made the Blues.* New York, Oak Publications, 1967. Illustrations.

938  CHARTERS, Samuel Barclay and Leon Kunstadt. *Jazz; a History of the New York Scene.* Garden City, New York, Doubleday and Co., 1962. 382 p. $5.95.

939  CHARTERS, Samuel Barclay. *The Poetry of the Blues.* With photos by Ann Charters. New York, Oak Publications, 1963. 111 p. Illustrations.

940  CLARK, Edgar Rogie, comp. *Negro Art Songs.* Album by contemporary composers for voice and piano. New York, Edward B. Marks, 1946. 72 p. $1.50. Includes compositions by eleven Negro composers with brief biographies.

941  COURLANDER, Harold. *Negro Folk Music, U.S.A.* New York, Columbia University Press, 1963. 324 p. $10.00.

942  DENNISON, Tim. *The American Negro and His Amazing Music.* 1st ed. New York, Vantage Press, 1963. 76 p.

943  DETT, Robert Nathaniel, ed. *Religious Folk-Songs of the Negro as Sung at Hampton Institute.* Hampton, Va., Hampton Institute Press, 1927. 236 p. Out of print.

944  DIXON, Robert M.W. and John Godrich, comps. *Blues & Gospel Records, 1902-1942.* (n.p.) 1963. 765 p.

945  FAHEY, John Aloysius. *A Textual and Musicological Analysis of the Repertoire of Charley Patton.* Los Angeles, 1966. 176 leaves.

946  FENNER, Thomas Putnam, arranger. *Religious Folk Songs of the Negro as Sung on the Plantations.* New ed. Arranged by the musical director of the Hampton Normal and Agricultural Institute from the original edition. Hampton, Va., The Institute Press, 1909. 175 p. Out of print.

947  FISHER, Miles Mark. *Negro Slave Songs in the United States.* New York, Russell & Russell, 1968 (c1953). 223 p. $8.50.

948  FRIML, Rudolf. *Don't Take Away My Jesus.* (Negro Spiritual) For voice and piano. Words by Katharine Bainbridge. New York, G. Schirmer, 1950. 7 p.

949  HANDY, William Christopher. *Blues; an Anthology Tracing the Development of the Most Spontaneous and Appealing Branch of Negro Folk Music from the Folk Blues to Modern Jazz.* New York, A. & C. Boni, 1926. 180 p.

950  HANDY, William Christopher. *Father of the Blues; an Autobiography of W.C. Handy.* Edited by Arna W. Bontemps. New York, Macmillan, 1941. 317 p.

951  HANDY, William Christopher. *A Treasury of the Blues;* Complete Words and Music of 67 Great Songs from Memphis Blues to the Present Day. With an Historical and Critical Text by Abbe Niles. With Pictures by Miguel Covarrubias. New York, C. Boni, distributed by Simon and Schuster, 1949. 258 p. Illustrations. Bibliography.

952  HARE, Maud Cuney. *Negro Musicians and Their Music.* Washington, D.C., The Associated Publishers Inc., 1936. 439 p. Out of print.

953  HARRIS, Joel Chandler. *Uncle Remus; His Songs and Sayings.* With a foreword by Marc Connolly and woodcuts by Seong Moy. New York, for the members of the Limited Editions Club, 1957. 158 p. Illustrations.

954  HUGHES, Langston. *Famous Negro Music Makers;* Illustrated with photos. New York, Dodd, Mead, 1955. 179 p. Illustrations. (Famous Biographies for Young People).

955  JACKSON, Clyde Owen. *The Songs of Our Years; a Study of Negro Folk Music.* New York, Exposition Press, 1968. 54 p. $4.00.

956  JOHNSON, James Weldon. *The Book of American Negro Spirituals.* New York, Viking Press, 1940. 2 vols. $6.95.

957  JONES, LeRoi. *Black Music.* New York, W. Morrow, 1967. 221 p. $5.00.

958  JONES, LeRoi. *Blues People; Negro Music in White America.* New York, W. Morrow, 1963. 244 p. $5.00. Paperback $1.65.

959  KEEPNEWS, Orrin and Bill Grauer. *A Pictorial History of Jazz.* New York, Crown Pub., 1955. 282 p.

960  KEIL, Charles. *Urban Blues.* Chicago, University of Chicago Press, 1966. 231 p. $4.95.

961   KREHBIEL, Henry Edward. *Afro-American Folksongs; a Study in Racial and National Music.* New York, Frederick Ungar Pub. Co., 1962. 176 p. $4.75.

962   LOCKE, Alain LeRoy. *The Negro and His Music.* Port Washington, N.Y., Kennikat Press, 1967 (c1936). 142 p. $6.25.

963   LUCAS, John. *Basic Jazz on Long Play.* The Great Soloists: Ragtime, Folksong, Blues, Jazz, Swing, and the Great Bands; New Orleans, Swing, Dixieland. Northfield, Minn., Carleton Jazz Club, Carleton College, 1954. 103 p. (Carleton College, Northfield, Minn. Carleton Jazz Club. Bulletin no. 1).

964   LUCAS, John. *The Great Revival on Long Play.* Northfield, Minn., Carleton Jazz Club, Carleton College, 1957. 56 p. (Carleton College, Northfield, Minn. Carleton Jazz Club. Bulletin no. 2).

965   MAHONEY, Jack. *Modern Minstrels.* New York, Central Music Pub. Co., c1945. 39 p.

966   MARSH, J.B.T. *The Story of the Jubilee Singers? with their Songs.* Revised edition. Boston, Houghton, Osgood and Co., 1880. viii, 243 p. illus. music scores. Out of print.

967   NATHAN, Hans. *Dan Emmett and the Rise of Early Negro Minstrelsy.* 1st ed. Norman, University of Oklahoma Press, 1962. 496 p. Illustrations. $10.00

968   ODUM, Howard Washington and Guy B. Johnson. *The Negro and His Songs; a Study of Typical Negro Songs in the South.* Hatboro, Pa., Folklore Associates, 1964 (c1925). 306 p.

969   OLIVER, Paul. *The Meaning of the Blues.* With a Foreword by Richard Wright. New York, Collier, 1963. 383 p. Paperback $0.95.

970   PATTERSON, Lindsay, comp. *The Negro in Music and Art.* 1st ed. New York, Publishers Co., 1967. 304 p. (International Library of Negro Life and History).

971   RAMSEY, Frederic. *Been Here and Gone.* New Brunswick, N.J., Rutgers University Press, 1960. 177 p. Illustrations.

972   RAMSEY, Frederic, Jr. and Charles Edward Smith, eds. *Jazzmen.* New York, Harcourt, Brace, 1959 (c1939). 360 p. Illustrations.

973  REVETT, Marion S. *A Minstrel Town.* 1st ed. New York, Pageant Press, c1955. 335 p. Illustrations.

974  SCARBOROUGH, Dorothy, assisted by Ola Lee Gulledge. *On the Trail of Negro Folksongs.* Foreword by Roger D. Abrahams. Hatboro, Pa., Folklore Associates, 1963. 295 p.

975  SCHLEIN, Irving. *Slave Songs of the United States.* New York, Oak Publications, 1965. 175 p. $5.95.

976  SPELLMAN, A.B. *Four Lives in the Bebop Business.* New York, Pantheon Books, 1966. 241 p.

977  TROTTER, James M. *Music and Some Highly Musical People.* Boston, Lee & Shepard. New York, C.T. Dillingham, 1878. 505 p. Out of print.

978  WHITNEY, Maurice C. *River Jordan, Fantasy on Negro Spirituals.* New York, G. Schirmer, 1950. Score (26 p.). (University of Michigan Band Series, pt. 1, no. 10).

979  WILLIAMS, Martin. *Jazz Masters of New Orleans.* New York, Macmillan Co., 1967. 287 p. $5.95.

## FOLKLORE AND FOLKTALES

980  ABRAHAMS, Roger D. *Deep Down in the Jungle. Negro Narrative Folklore from the Streets of Philadelphia.* Hatboro, Pa., Folklore Associates, 1964. 287 p.

981  ADAMS, Edward C.L. *Congaree Sketches; Scenes from Negro Life in the Swamps of the Congaree and Tales by Tad and Scip of Heaven and Hell with Other Miscellany.* Chapel Hill, University of North Carolina Press, 1927. 116 p. Folklore of the South Carolina Negro.

982  ADAMS, Edward C.L. *Nigger to Nigger.* New York, Charles Scribner's Sons, 1928. 270 p.

983  ADAMS, Edward C.L. *Potee's Gal, a Drama of Negro Life Near the Big Congaree Swamp.* Columbus, S.C., The State Company, 1929. 49 p.

984  BALLOWE, Hewitt Leonard. *The Laud Sayin' the Same.* Negro Folk Tales of the Creole Country. Baton Rouge, La., Louisiana State

University Press, 1947. 254 p. $2.75. Twenty-four tales of Louisiana sugar plantation workers.

985 BENNETT, John. *The Doctor to the Dead; Grotesque Legends and Folk Tales of Old Charleston.* New York, Toronto, Rinehart and Company, 1946. 260 p. $2.50.

986 BLACKBURN, M.J. *Folklore from Mammy Days.* Boston, Walter H. Baker Co., 1924. 105 p. $1.25.

987 BOTKIN, Benjamin Albert. *A Treasury of Mississippi River Folklore; Stories, Ballads, Traditions, and Folkways of the Mid-American River Country.* Foreword by Carl Carmer. New York, Crown Publishers, 1955. 620 p.

988 BRADFORD, Roark. *Ol' Man Adam an' His Chillun'.* New York, Harper and Bros., 1928. 264 p. $2.50.

989 BRADFORD, Roark. *This Side of Jordan.* New York, Harper and Bros., 1929. 255 p. $2.50.

990 BREWER, John Mason. *Aunt Dicy Tales; Snuff-Dipping Tales of the Texas Negro.* Austin, Texas, New York, 1956. 80 p.

991 BREWER, John Mason. *Dog Ghosts, and Other Texas Negro Folk Tales.* Austin, University of Texas Press, 1958. 124 p. $3.95.

992 BREWER, John Mason. *Humorous Folk Tales of the South Carolina Negro.* Orangeburg, Claflin College, South Carolina Negro Folklore Guild, 1945. 64 p.

993 BREWER, John Mason. *The Word on the Brazos; Negro Preacher Tales from the Brazos Bottoms of Texas.* Austin, University of Texas Press, 1953. 109 p. $3.50.

994 BREWER, John Mason. *Worser Days and Better Times; the Folklore of the North Carolina Negro.* Chicago, Quadrangle Books, 1965. 192 p. $5.00.

995 CHRISTENSEN, Mrs. Abigail M.H. *Afro-American Folk Lore; Told Round Cabin Fires on the Sea Islands of South Carolina.* Boston, J.G. Cupples Co., 1892. 116 p.

996 COCKE, Sarah Johnson. *Bypaths in Dixie; Folk Tales of the South.*

With an Introduction by Harry Stillwell Edwards. New York, E.P. Dutton and Co., c1911. 316 p.

997 COHN, David L. *God Shakes Creation*. New York, Harper & Bros., 1935. 299 p. $3.50.

998 COURLANDER, Harold. *Terrapin's Pot of Sense*. New York, Holt, 1957. 125 p. $3.00.

999 CRUM, Mason. *Gullah: Negro Life in the Carolina Sea Islands*. Durham, N.C., Duke University Press, 1940. 351 p. $3.50.

1000 DOBIE, James Frank. *Follow De Drinkin' Gou'd*. Austin, Texas, Texas Folklore Society, 1928. 201 p. $2.75.

1001 DOBIE, James Frank. *Tone the Bell Easy*. Austin, Texas, Texas Folklore Society, 1932. 199 p.

1002 DORSON, Richard Mercer, collector, with Introduction and Notes. *American Negro Folktales*. New York, Fawcett Publications, 1967. $0.75. paper. A comprehensive collection which includes not only the well-known stories of talking animals but also the cycle concerning Old Marster and his clever slave John, and ranges from supernatural accounts, of specters and bogies, through comical and satirical anecdotes, to the more realistic reports of racial injustice. With bibliography and indices of motifs and tale types.

1003 DORSON, Richard Mercer. *Negro Folktales in Michigan*. Cambridge, Harvard University Press, 1956. 245 p. $3.00.

1004 DORSON, Richard Mercer. *Negro Tales from Pine Bluff, Arkansas and Calvin, Michigan*. Bloomington, Indiana University Press, 1958. 292 p. $3.00.

1005 DUNCAN, Eula Griffin. *Big Road Walker,* based on stories told by Alice Cannon. New York, Frederick A. Stokes Company, 1940. 121 p. $1.75.

1006 GOLDSBOROUGH, Edmund K. *Ole Man an' Ole Miss*. Washington, D.C., National Publishing Co., 1900. 219 p.

1007 GONZALES, Ambrose Elliott. *The Black Border; Gullah Stories of the Carolina Coast*. Columbia, S.C., The State Co., 1922. 384 p. $3.00.

1008 GONZALES, Ambrose Elliott. *Laguere, a Gascon of the Black Border.* Columbia, S.C., The State Co., 1924. 318 p. $2.00.

1009 GONZALES, Ambrose Elliott. *With Aesop Along the Black Border.* Columbia, S.C., The State Co., 1924. 298 p. $2.00.

1010 HARRIS, Joel Chandler. *Uncle Remus; His Songs and His Sayings. The Folklore of the Old Plantation.* With illustrations by Frederick S. Church and James H. Moser. New York, D. Appleton and Co., 1881. 231 p.

1011 HATCHCOCK, Louise. *True Stories of Little Dixie.* San Antonio, Naylor Co., 1962. 281 p. $4.95.

1012 HEYWARD, Jane Screven. *Brown Jackets.* Columbia, S.C., The State Co., 1923. 64 p. $1.00.

1013 HOBSON, Anne. *In Old Alabama; Being the Chronicles of Miss Mouse, the Little Black Merchant.* New York, Doubleday, Page and Co., 1903. 237 p.

1014 HUGHES, Langston, and Anna Bontemps, eds. *The Book of Negro Folklore.* New York, Dodd, Mead, 1958. 624. $6.50.

1015 HURSTON, Zora Neale. *Mules and Men.* With an Introduction by Frank Boas. 10 Illustrations by Miguel Covarrubias. Philadelphia. London, J.B. Lippincott Company, 1935. 342 p.

1016 JACKSON, Bruce. *The Negro and His Folklore in Nineteenth-Century Periodicals.* Austin, University of Texas Press, 1967. 274 p. $8.50. Thirty-five selections from periodicals.

1017 JOHNSON, Guy B. *Folk Culture in St. Helena Island, South Carolina.* Chapel Hill, University of North Carolina Press, 1930. 183 p. $3.00.

1018 JOHNSON, Guy B. *John Henry; Tracking Down a Negro Legend.* Chapel Hill, University of North Carolina, 1929. 155 p. $2.00.

1019 JONES, Charles Colcock. *Negro Myths from the Georgia Coast Told in the Vernacular.* Boston, Houghton Mifflin Co., 1888. 192 p. $2.00. Reprinted by The State Co., 1925.

1020 LOVE, Rose Leary, ed. *A Collection of Folklore for Children in Elementary School and at Home.* New York, Vantage Press, 1964. 83 p.

1021 MIKELL, I. Jenkins. *Rumbling of the Chariot Wheels.* Columbia, S.C., The State Co., 1923. 273 p. $1.75. Lore of the Gullah.

1022 ODUM, Howard W. *Cold Blue Moon, Black Ulysses Afar Off.* Indianapolis, Bobbs-Merrill Company, 1931. 98 p. $2.50.

1023 OTT, Eleanore. *Plantation Cookery of Old Louisiana.* New Orleans, Harmanson, 1938. 96 p. $0.50.

1024 OWEN, Mary Alicia. *Ole Rabbit's Plantation Stories, as Told Among the Negroes of the Southwest.* Philadelphia, George W. Jacobs, 1898. 310 p.

1025 OWEN, Mary Alicia. *Voodoo Tales, as Told Among the Negroes of the Southwest,* Collected from Original Sources by Mary Alicia Owen. New York, G.P. Putnam's Sons, 1893. 310 p.

1026 PARSONS, Elsie Clews. *Folk-lore of the Sea Islands, South Carolina.* Cambridge, Mass., The American Folklore Society, 1923. 219 p. $3.50.

1027 PETERKIN, Julia Mood. *Roll Jordan Roll.* New York, R.O. Ballou, 1933. 341 p. $25.00.

1028 PIPES, James. *Ziba.* Norman, Oklahoma, University of Oklahoma Press, 1943. 188 p. $2.50.

1029 PUCKETT, Newbell Niles. *Folk Beliefs of the Southern Negro.* Chapel Hill, University of North Carolina Press, London, Milford, 1926. 644 p. $5.00. Out of print.

1030 RICE, James Henry. *Glories of the Carolina Coast.* Columbus, S.C., R.L. Bryan Company, 1936. 211 p. $2.50.

1031 ROBB, Bernard. *Welcum Hinges.* New York, E.P. Dutton & Co., 1942. 215 p. $2.50.

1032 SALE, John B. *The Tree Named John.* With twenty-two silhouettes by Joseph Cranston Jones. Chapel Hill, University of North Carolina Press, 1929. 151 p. $2.00.

1033 SMYTHE, Augustine T. and Herbert R. Sass. *The Carolina Low Country.* New York, Macmillan, 1931. 186 p. $5.00.

1034 STERLING, Philip. *Laughing on the Outside: The Intelligent White Reader's Guide to Negro Tales and Humor.* Collected and edited by Philip Sterling. Introduction essay by Saunders Redding,, Cartoons by Ollie Harrington. New York, Grosset & Dunlap, Inc., 1965. 254 p. $3.95.

1035 STONEY, Samuel Gaillard. *Black Genesis: a Chronicle.* New York, Macmillan Co., 1930. 192 p. $3.50. "Tales of the Gullah Negroes of the Carolina Low Country (told in the Gullah dialect)."

1036 TALLEY, Thomas Washington. *Negro Folk Rhymes, Wise and Otherwise.* New York, Macmillan Co., 1922. 347 p. $2.25.

1037 TURNER, L.M. *'Bout Cullud Folkses.* New York, Henry Harrison, 1938. 64 p. $1.50.

1038 WHALEY, Marcellus S. *The Old Types Pass— Gullah Sketches of the South Carolina Sea Islands.* Boston, Christopher Publishing House, 1925. $2.50.

1039 WHITING, Helen Adele. *Negro Folk Tales for Pupils in the Primary Grades.* Washington, D.C., The Associated Press Inc., 1938. 28 p. $1.00.

1040 WILLIAMS, John G. *De Ole Plantation.* Charleston, S.C., Walter, Evans and Cogswell Co., 1896. 67 p.

1041 WRITERS' PROGRAM. Georgia. *Drums and Shadows; Survival Studies Among the Georgia Coastal Negroes,* by the Savannah Unit, Georgia Writers' Project, Work Projects Administration; Foreword by Guy B. Johnson, Photographs by Muriel and Malcolm Bell, Jr. Athens, University of Georgia Press, 1940. 274 p. $3.00.

1042 WRITERS' PROGRAM. Tennessee. *God Bless the Devil! Liars' Bench Tales.* Chapel Hill, University of North Carolina Press, 1940. 254 p.

## ECONOMIC CONDITIONS

### THEORY

1043 ALLEN, James Stewart. *The Negro Question in the United States.* New York, International Publishers, 1936. 224 p.

1044 BECKER, Gary S. *The Economics of Discrimination*. Chicago, University of Chicago Press, 1957. 137 p. $5.00.

1045 BELL, William Kenan. *Fifteen Million Negroes and Fifteen Billion Dollars*. New York, W.K. Bell Publications, 1956. 147 p.

1046 BLAIR, Lewis Harvie. *A Southern Prophecy: the Prosperity of the South Dependent Upon the Elevation of the Negro (1889)*. Edited with an Introduction by C. Vann Woodward. Boston, Little, Brown, 1964. 201 p.

1047 CALIFORNIA. State Fair Employment Practice Commission. *Negro Californians: Population, Employment, Income, Education*. San Francisco, Division of Fair Employment Practices, 1963. 34 p.

1048 CLARK, Kenneth B. *Dark Ghetto: Dilemmas of Social Power*. New York, Harper and Row, 1965. 251 p. $5.95. Paperback, $1.75.

1049 CLARKE, John Henrik. *Harlem, A Community in Transition*. New York, Citadel Press, 1964. 223 p. Paperback $1.95.

1050 DE MOND, Albert Lawrence. *Certain Aspects of the Economic Development of the American Negro, 1865-1900*. Washington, D.C., The Catholic University of America Press, 1945. 187 p.

1051 DRAKE, St. Clair and Horace R. Cayton. *Black Metropolis; A Study of Negro Life in a Northern City*. Introduction by Richard Wright. Introduction to Torchbook ed. by Everett C. Hughes. Rev. and enl. ed. New York, Harper and Row, 1962. 2 vols. Paperback $2.75 each.

1052 Du BOIS, William Edward Burghardt, ed. *Economic Co-operation Among Negro Americans*. Report of a Social Study Made by Atlanta University, under the Patronage of the Carnegie Institution of Washington, D.C., together with the Proceedings of the 12th Conference for the Study of the Negro Problems, held at Atlanta University, on Tuesday, May 28th, 1907. Atlanta, Georgia. The Atlanta University Press, 1907. 184 p.

1053 DUTCHER, Dean. *The Negro in Modern Industrial Society; an Analysis of Changes in the Occupations of Negro Workers, 1910-1920*. Lancaster, Pa., 1930. 137 p. Out of print.

1054 EDWARDS, G. Franklin. *The Negro Professional Class*. Glencoe, Illinois, Free Press, 1959. 224 p. Out of print.

1055 EDWARDS, Paul K. *The Southern Urban Negro as a Consumer.* New York, Prentice-Hall, 1932. 323 p. Out of print.

1056 FIEN, Rashi. *An Economic and Social Profile of the Negro American.* Washington, D.C., Brookings Institution, 1966. pp. 815-46. (Brookings Institution Reprints, 110).

1057 FELDMAN, Herman. *Racial Factors in American Industry.* New York, Harper & Bros., 1931. 318 p. Out of print.

1058 FOLEY, Eugene P. *The Achieving Ghetto.* Washington, D.C., National Press, Inc., 1968. $4.95. Paperback $2.45.

1059 FRAZIER, E. Franklin. *Black Bourgeoisie: the Rise of a New Middle Class in the United States.* New York, Collier Books, 1966. 222 p. Paperback $0.95.

1060 FRAZIER, E. Franklin. *The Negro Family in the United States.* Rev. and abridged ed. Chicago, University of Chicago Press, 1966. 372 p. $6.00. Paperback $2.45.

1061 GINZBERG, Eli. *The Negro Potential.* New York, Columbia University Press, 1956. 144 p. Paperback $1.45.

1062 HAYNES, George Edmund. *The Negro at Work in New York City: a Study in Economic Progress.* New York, Columbia University, Longmans, Green & Company, Agents, 1912. 158 p.

1063 HAYWOOD, Harry. *Negro Liberation.* New York, International Publishers, 1948. 245 p. Out of print.

1064 HENDERSON, Vivian W. *The Economic Status of Negroes; in the Nation and in the South.* Atlanta, Southern Regional Council, 1963. 23 p. $0.25.

1065 HENTOFF, Nat. *The New Equality.* New York, Viking Press, 1964. 243 p. $4.50.

1066 HILL, Timothy Arnold. *The Negro and Economic Reconstruction.* Washington, D.C., The Associates in Negro Folk Education, 1937. 78 p. Out of print.

1067 JACOBS, Paul. *Prelude to Riot; a View of Urban America from the Bottom.* New York, Random House, 1968 (c1967). 298 p. $5.95. Vantage Books, Paperback $1.95.

1068 JOHNSON, Charles Spurgeon. *The Economic Status of Negroes;* Summary and Analysis of the Materials Presented at the Conference on the Economic Status of the Negro, held in Washington, D.C., May 11-13, 1933. under the Sponsorship of the Julius Rosenwald Fund. Report prepared for the Committee on Findings by Charles S. Johnson. Nashville, Fisk University Press, 1933. 53 p.

1069 JOHNSON, Charles Spurgeon. *Growing Up in the Black Belt; Negro Youth in the Rural South.* New York, Shocken Books, 1967 (c1941). 358 p. $6.95. Paperback $2.45.

1070 KAHN, Tom. *The Economics of Equality.* New York, League for Industrial Democracy, distributed by the Industrial Union Dept. American Federation of Labor, Congress of Industrial Organizations, 1964. 70 p. (An L.I.D. Pamphlet).

1071 LARSSON, Cloyte M. *Marriage Across the Color Line.* Chicago, Johnson Publishing Company, 1965. 204 p. $4.95.

1072 LUMER, Hyman. *Poverty; Its Roots and Its Future.* New York, International Publishers, 1965. 127 p.

1073 MACK, Raymond W. *Race, Class and Power.* New York, American Book Company, 1964. 399 p. Paperback $4.25.

1074 MYRDAL, Gunnar. *An American Dilemma.* New York, Harper & Brothers, 1944. 2 vols. (Vol. 1 - Chapters 13, 14, 16, 17, 18, 19, and Appendix 6).

1075 NATIONAL URBAN LEAGUE. *Economic and Social Status of the Negro in the United States.* New York, 1961. 32 p.

1076 NORTHRUP, Herbert. *Organized Labor and the Negro.* Foreword by Sumner H. Slichter. New York, Harper, 1944. Out of print.

1077 STERNER, Richard Mauritz Edward in collaboration with Lenore A. Epstein, Ellen Winston and others.. *The Negro's Share; a Study of Income, Consumption, Housing and Public Assistance.* New York, London, Harper & Brothers, 1943. 433 p.

1078 STUART, Merah Steven. *An Economic Detour; a History of Insurance in the Lives of American Negroes.* New York, W. Malliet and Company, 1940. 339 p.

1079 THOMPSON, Daniel. *The Negro Leadership Class.* Englewood Cliffs, New Jersey, Prentice-Hall, 1963. 178 p. Paperback $1.95.

1080 U.S. AREA REDEVELOPMENT ADMINISTRATION. *Negro-White Differences in Geographic Mobility.* Washington, D.C., for sale by Supt. of Documents U.S. Goverment Printing Office, 1964. 22 p.

1081 U.S. BUREAU OF THE CENSUS. *Social and Economic Conditions of Negroes in the United States.* Washington, D.C., U.S. Government Printing Office, 1967. 97 p. $0.55.

1082 U.S. BUREAU OF LABOR STATISTICS. *The Economic Situation of Negroes in the United States.* Rev. Washington, D.C., U.S. Department of Labor, for sale by the Superintendent of Documents, U.S. Government Printing Office, 1962. 32 p.

1083 U.S. BUREAU OF LABOR STATISTICS. *Employment and Economic Status of Negroes in the United States.* Staff Report to the Sub-committee on Labor and Labor-Management Relations of the Committee on Labor and Public Welfare, United States Senate, Eighty-second Congress, Second Session, by Helen H. Ringe with the Assistance of Sophia Cooper, division of Manpower and Employment Statistics. Washington, U.S. Government Printing Office, 1952. 20 p.

1084 U.S. BUREAU OF LABOR STATISTICS. *The Negroes in the United States, Their Economic and Social Situation.* Washington, D.C., U.S. Government Printing Office, 1966. 241 p. $1.25.

1085 U.S. BUREAU OF LABOR STATISTICS. *Notes on the Economic Situation of Negroes in the United States.* Washington, D.C., 1957.

1086 U.S. BUREAU OF LABOR STATISTICS. *Social and Economic Conditions of Negroes in the U.S.* October 1967. (BLS Report, No. 332). (Bureau of Census. Current Population Reports, Ser. p-23, No. 24). Washington, D.C., Supt. of Docs., 1967. $0.55.

1087 U.S. DEPARTMENT OF LABOR. Office of Policy Planning and Research. *The Negro Family, the Case for National Action.* Washington, D.C., U.S. Government Printing Office, 1965. 78 p. $0.45.

1088 U.S. DEPARTMENT OF THE INTERIOR. Office of the Adviser on Negro Affairs. *The Urban Negro Worker in the United States,*

*1925-1936.* Washington, D.C., U.S. Govt. Printing Office, 1938-1939. 2 vols.

1089 WASHINGTON, Booker T. and W. E. Burghardt DuBois. *The Negro in the South, His Economic Progress in Relation to His Moral and Religious Development;* Being the William Levi Bull Lectures for the year 1907. Philadelphia, G.W. Jacobs & Company, 1907. 222 p.

1090 WHITING, Helen Adele (Johnson). *Climbing the Economic Ladder.* Atlanta, Helen Adele Johnson Whiting, 1948. 100 p.

## BUSINESS

1091 ALEXANDER, Richard D. and others. *The Management of Racial Integration in Business.* McGraw-Hill, 1964. 147 p. $10.00.

1092 ASSOCIATION FOR THE STUDY OF NEGRO LIFE AND HISTORY. *The Negro as a Business Man,* by J.H. Harmon, Jr., Arnett G. Lindsay and Carter G. Woodson. Washington, D.C., The Association for the Study of Negro Life and History, 1929. 111 p.

1093 BRINK, William. *The Negro Revolution in America; What Negroes Want, Why and How They Are Fighting, Whom They Support, What Whites Think of Them and Their Demands.* New York, Simon and Schuster, 1964 (c1963). 249 p. $4.50. Paperback $1.45.

1094 CARTER, Wilmoth Annette. *The Urban Negro in the South.* New York, Vantage Press, 1962. 272 p. Bibliography. Out of print.

1095 CHAMBER OF COMMERCE OF THE UNITED STATES. *The Disadvantaged Poor; Education and Employment.* Washington, D.C., Chamber of Commerce of the United States, 1966. pp. 101-8, 419-433.

1096 DREXEL INSTITUTE OF TECHNOLOGY. *The Census of Negro-Owned Businesses, Philadelphia, 1964.* Philadelphia, 1965. 227 p.

1097 DuBOIS, William Edward Burghardt. *The Negro in Business; a Report of a Social Study made under the Direction of Atlanta University: Together with the Proceedings of the Fourth Conference for the Study of the Negro Problems, Atlanta University, May 30-31, 1899.* Atlanta, Ga., Atlanta University Press, 1899. 77 p. To be reprinted by Arno Press, Inc.

1098 FLEMING, Walter Lynwood. *The Freedman's Savings Bank; A*

*Chapter in the Economic History of the Negro Race.* Chapel Hill, N.C., University of North Carolina Press, 1927. 170 p.

1099 GINZBERG, Eli, ed. *Business Leadership in the Negro Crisis.* New York, McGraw-Hill Book Co., 1968. $5.95.

1100 GINZBERG, Eli. *The Negro Challenge to the Business Community.* New York, McGraw-Hill Book Co., 1964. 111 p. $4.95. Paperback $1.65.

1101 GUTTMAN, Egon. *The Barber Shop.* Washington, D.C., Howard University, Small Business Guidance and Development Center 1967. 53 p.

1102 GUTTMAN, Egon. *The Valet Service Establishment: Dry Cleaning, Shoe Repairing and Hat Blocking.* Washington, D.C., Howard University, Small Business Guidance and Development Center, 1967. 44 p.

1103 HARRIS, Abram Lincoln. *The Negro as Capitalist; a Study of Banking and Business among American Negroes.* Philadelphia, American Academy of Political and Social Science, 1936. 205 p.

1104 HOWARD UNIVERSITY. Small Business Guidance and Development Center. *A Directory of Negro-Owned and Operated Businesses in Washington, D.C.* Washington, D.C., Howard University, 1965. 80 p.

1105 HOWARD UNIVERSITY. *Small Business Guidance and Development Center. Essays By Students on Small Businessmen.* Washington, D.C., Howard University, 1967. 21 p.

1106 HOWARD UNIVERSITY. Studies in the Social Sciences. *The Post-War Outlook for Negroes in Small Business, the Engineering Professions, and the Technical Vocations.* Ninth Annual Conference. April 1946. 194 p.

1107 JOHNSON, Joseph T. *The Potential Negro Market.* New York, Pageant Press, 1952. 185 p. Out of print.

1108 KINZER, Robert H. and Edward Sagarin. *The Negro in American Business; the Conflict Between Separatism and Integration.* New York, Greenberg, 1950. 220 p. Out of print.

1109 MITCHELL, James R. *The Collapse of the National Benefit Life Insurance Company.* Washington, D.C., The Graduate School for the

Divisions of the Social Sciences, Howard University, 1939. 150 p. (Howard Studies in the Social Sciences, Vol. 2, No. 1). Out of print.

1110 NATIONAL CONFERENCE ON SMALL BUSINESS. *Problems and Opportunities Confronting Negroes in the Field of Business.* H. Naylor Fitzhugh, ed. Washington, D.C., U.S. Government Printing Office, 1962. 103 p. Paperback $0.35.

1111 OAK, Vishnu V. *The Negro's Adventure in General Business.* Yellow Springs, Ohio, Antioch Press, 1949. 223 p. $4.75.

1112 PETTIGREW, Thomas F. *A Profile of the Negro American.* Princeton, N.J., D. Van Nostrand, 1964. 250 p.

1113 PIERCE, Joseph A. *Negro Business and Business Education.* New York, Harper & Bros., 1947. 338 p. Out of print.

1114 SCHUSTER, Louis H. *Business Enterprises of Negroes in Tennessee.* Washington, D.C., Small Business Administration, 1961. 93 p.

1115 STUART, Merah Steven. *An Economic Detour.* New York, Wendell Malliet & Company, 1940. 339 p. Out of print. Inquiry into the origin and growth of Negro life insurance companies.

1116 TENNESSEE AGRICULTURAL AND INDUSTRIAL STATE UNIVERSITY, NASHVILLE. *Business Enterprises of Negroes in Tennessee.* Nashville, 1961. 93 p. (Small Business Management Research Study).

1117 TRENT, William J. *Development of Negro Life Insurance Enterprises.* Salisbury, N.C., Salisbury College, 1932. 62 p. Out of print.

1118 U.S. DEPARTMENT OF COMMERCE. *A Guide to Negro Marketing Information.* Washington, D.C., U.S. Government Printing Office, 1966. 50 p.

1119 U.S. DEPARTMENT OF COMMERCE. *Negro Chambers of Commerce: 1936.* Washington, D.C., Bureau of Foreign and Domestic Commerce, 1936. 21 p. Structure and function of above; states plus their names and locations.

1120 U.S. DEPARTMENT OF COMMERCE. *The Negro in Business, 1935: a Bibliography.* Washington, D.C., July 1935. 9 p.

1121 U.S. DEPARTMENT OF LABOR. Bureau of Labor Statistics, and U.S. Department of Commerce. Bureau of the Census. *The Negroes in the United States, Their Economic and Social Condition.* Washington, D.C., U.S. Government Printing Office, 1965. 241 p.

1122 U.S. DEPARTMENT OF LABOR. Bureau of Labor Statistics, and U.S. Department of Commerce. Bureau of the Census. *Social and Economic Conditions of Negroes in the United States.* Washington, D.C., U.S. Government Printing Office, 1967. 97 p.

1123 WORK, Monroe N. *The Negro in Business and the Professions.* In: *Annals of the American Academy of Political and Social Sciences,* Vol. CXL, Nov. 1928. pp. 138-44.

## EMPLOYMENT

1124 ALEXANDER, Richard D. and others. *The Management of Racial Integration in Business: Special Report to the Management.* Prepared under the Supervision of Georges F. Doriot. New York, McGraw-Hill, 1964. 147 p.

1125 *AT WORK IN INDUSTRY TODAY.* Schenectady, New York, General Electric Co. Employee Relations Publications Bldg. 2, 1965. 30 p. Gratis.

1126 CAYTON, Horace R. and George S. Mitchell. *Black Workers and the New Unions.* Chapel Hill, University of North Carolina Press, 1939. 473 p.

1127 COMMONS, John Rogers, ed. *Trade Unionism and Labor Problems.* New York, A.M. Kelley, 1967 (c1905). 628 p.

1128 FERMAN, Louis A. and others. *Negroes and Jobs; A Book of Readings;* Foreword by A. Philip Randolph. Ann Arbor, University of Michigan Press, 1968. 440 p. $7.95. Paperback $5.25.

1129 FRANKLIN, Charles Lionel. *The Negro Labor Unionist of New York: Problems and Conditions Among Negroes in the Labor Unions in Manhattan with Special Reference to the N.R.A. and Post-N.R.A. Situations.* New York, Columbia University Press, 1936. 417 p.

1130 GARFINKEL, Herbert. *When Negroes March; the March on Washington Movement in the Organizational Politics for FEPC.* Glencoe, Ill., Free Press, 1959. 224 p. Out of print.

110

1131 GINZBERG, Eli. *The Negro Potential.* New York, Columbia University Press, 1956. 144 p. Paperback $1.45.

1132 GOURLAY, Jack G. *The Negro Salaried Worker.* New York, American Management Association, 1965. 103 p. $4.50.

1133 GREENE, Lorenzo Johnston and Carter G. Woodson. *The Negro Wage Earner.* Washington, D.C., The Association for the Study of Negro Life and History, Inc., 1930. 388 p.

1134 HIESTAND, Dale L. *Economic Growth and Employment Opportunities for Minorities.* Foreword by John F. Henning. Introduction by Eli Ginzberg. New York, Columbia University Press, 1964. 127 p.

1135 HILL, Herbert. *The Racial Practices of Organized Labor in the Age of Gompers and After.* New York, National Association for the Advancement of Colored People, 1965. 23 p.

1136 HYMER, Bennett. *Negro Labor Market in Chicago, 1966; Conditions in Employment and Manpower Training.* Chicago, 1966. 16 p. Gratis.

1137 JACOBSON, Julius. *The Negro and the American Labor Movement.* New York, Doubleday Anchor Original, 1968. 430 p. $1.75 Paperback.

1138 KRISLOV, Samuel. *The Negro in Federal Employment; the Quest for Equal Opportunity.* Minneapolis, University of Minnesota, 1967. 157 p. $5.00.

1139 LEE, Irvin H. *Negro Medal of Honor Men.* New York, Dodd, Mead, 1967. 139 p. $4.00.

1140 LEE, Ulysses. *The Employment of Negro Troops; United States Army in World War II.* Washington, D.C., U.S. Government Printing Office, 1966. 740 p. $7.75.

1141 LEWIS, Edward Erwin. *The Mobility of the Negro; a Study in the American Labor Supply.* New York, Columbia University Press, 1931. 144 p.

1142 MARSHALL, F. Ray and Vernon Briggs. *The Negro and Apprenticeship.* Baltimore, Johns Hopkins Press, 1967. 283 p. $8.00.

1143 MARSHALL, F. Ray. *The Negro and Organized Labor.* New York, John W. Wiley, 1965. 327 p. $6.95.

1144 MARSHALL, F. Ray. *The Negro Worker.* New York, Random House, 1967. 180 p. $2.45 Paperback.

1145 NATIONAL ASSOCIATION FOR THE ADVANCEMENT OF COLORED PEOPLE. *The Negro Wage-Earner and Apprenticeship Training Programs; a Critical Analysis with Recommendations.* New York, National Association for the Advancement of Colored People, 1960. 60 p.

1146 NATIONAL CONFERENCE ON EQUAL EMPLOYMENT OPPORTUNITY, Washington, D.C. *A Time for Action; Proceedings.* Washington, D.C., U.S. Government Printing Office, 1963. 70 p. Portraits.

1147 NICHOLS, Lee. *Breakthrough on the Color Front.* New York, Random House, 1954. 235 p. Out of print.

1148 NORGREN, Paul Herbert. *Employing the Negro in American Industry; a Study of Management Practices.* New York, Industrial Relations Counselors, 1959. 171 p. Out of print.

1149 NORGREN, Paul Herbert, and Samuel E. Hill, with the Assistance of F. Ray Marshall. *Toward Fair Employment.* New York, Columbia University Press, 1964. 296 p.

1150 NORTHRUP, Herbert R. and Richard L. Rowan, editors. *The Negro and Employment Opportunity; Problems and Practices.* Ann Arbor, Bureau of Industrial Relations, Graduate School of Business Administration, University of Michigan, 1965. 411 p. $8.50.

1151 NORTHRUP, Herbert R. *Negro in the Automobile Industry.* Philadelphia, University of Pennsylvania., Wharton School of Finance and Commerce, 1968. 75 p. $2.50.

1152 PAYNTER, John Henry. *Horse and Buggy Days with Uncle Sam.* New York, Margent Press, 1943. 190 p.

1153 REITZES, Dietrich C. *Negroes and Medicine.* Cambridge, Mass., Harvard University Press, 1958. 400 p. $7.00.

1154 ROSS, Arthur M. and Herbert Hill, eds. *Employment, Race and*

*Poverty.* New York, Harcourt, Brace and World, 1967. 598 p. $7.50. Paperback $3.95.

1155 SMITH, Stanley Hugh. *Freedom to Work.* New York, Vantage Press, 1955. 217 p.

1156 SOVERN, Michael I. *Legal Restraints on Racial Discrimination in Employment.* New York, Twentieth Century Fund, 1966. 270 p. $6.00.

1157 SPERO, Sterling and Abram L. Harris. *The Black Worker; the Negro and the Labor Movement.* With a new preface by Herbert G. Gutman. New York, Atheneum, 1968. 509 p. $3.75. (Studies in American Negro Life, August Meier, General Editor). Paperback.

1158 STAUPERS, Mabel Keaton. *No Time for Prejudices; a Study of the Integration of Negroes in Nursing in the United States.* New York, Macmillan, 1961. 206 p. $4.95.

1159 U.S. PRESIDENT'S COMMITTEE ON EQUAL OPPORTUNITY IN THE ARMED FORCES. *Equality of Treatment and Opportunity for Negro Military Personnel Stationed Within the United States; Initial Report,* Washington, D.C., 1963. 93 p.

1160 WACHTEL, Dawn. *The Negro and Discrimination in Employment.* Ann Arbor, Institute of Labor and Industrial Relations, University of Michigan, 1965. 96 p. $2.00.

1161 WASHINGTON, Booker T. *The Negro in Business.* Boston, Chicago, Hertel, Jenkins & Co., c1907. 379 p.

1162 WESLEY, Charles Harris. *Negro Labor in the United States, 1850-1925; a Study in American Economic History.* New York, Russell & Russell, 1967 (c1927). 343 p. $9.00

## EDUCATION

1163 ASHMORE, Harry S. *The Negro and the Schools.* Rev. ed. Chapel Hill, University of North Carolina Press, 1954. 228 p. Paperback $1.50.

1164 BERMAN, Daniel M. *It is Ordered: the Supreme Court Rules on School Segregation.* New York, Norton, 1966. 161 p.

1165 BERNSTEIN, Abraham. *The Education of Urban Populations.* New York, Random House, 1966. 398 p. $3.95.

1166 BLOSSOM, Virgil T. *It Has Happened Here*. New York, Harper and Bros., 1959. 209 p. $2.95.

1167 BOND, Horace Mann. *The Education of the Negro in the American Social Order*. New York, Octagon Books, 1966 (c1934). 531 p. $12.50.

1168 BOND, Horace Mann. *Negro Education in Alabama; a Study in Cotton and Steel*. Washington, D.C., The Associated Publishers, Inc., 1939. 358 p.

1169 BRICKMAN, William W. and Stanley Lehrer, eds. *The Countdown on Segregated Education*. New York, Society for the Advancement of Education, 1960. 175 p. $3.50.

1170 BROWN, Hugh Victor. *A History of the Education of Negroes in North Carolina*. Raleigh, Irving Swain Press, 1961. 167 p.

1171 BULLOCK, Henry Allen. *A History of Negro Education in the South; from 1619 to the Present*. Cambridge, Mass., Harvard University Press, 1967. 339 p. $7.95.

1172 CALDWELL, Dista H. *The Education of the Negro Child*. New York, Carleton Press, 1961. 51 p. $2.00.

1173 CHAMBER OF COMMERCE OF THE UNITED STATES OF AMERICA. Task Force on Economic Growth and Opportunity. *The Disadvantaged Poor: Education and Employment*. Washington, D.C., 1966. 447 p.

1174 CLIFT, Virgil A. *Negro Education in America; Its Adequacy, Problems and Needs*. Sixteenth yearbook of the John Dewey Society. New York, Harper and Bros., 1962. 315 p. $5.95.

1175 COLEMAN, James Samuel. *Equality of Educational Opportunity*. Washington, D.C., U.S. Department of Health, Education and Welfare, Office of Education; for sale by the Superintendent of Documents, U.S. Government Printing Office, 1966. 737 p. $4.25.

1176 COLES, Robert. *Children of Crisis: a Study of Courage and Fear*. Boston, Little, Brown and Co., 1967. 401 p. $8.50.

1177 CONFERENCE ON THE ROLE OF THE LIBRARY IN IMPROVING EDUCATION IN THE SOUTH, Atlanta University,

Atlanta, Ga. *The Role of the Library in Improving Education in the South.* Papers Presented at a Conference, April 8-10, 1965. Edited with an Introduction by Hallie Beachem Brooks. Atlanta, Ga., School of Library Service, Atlanta University, 1965. 112 p.

1178 CRAIN, Robert L., with the assistance of Mortan Inger, Gerald McSorter, and James J. Vanecko. *The Politics of School Desegregation: Comparative Case Studies of Community Structure and Policy-Making.* Chicago, Aldine Publishing Co., 1968. 390 p. $7.95. (NORC monographs in Social Research, No. 14).

1179 CRUSE, Harold. *The Crisis of the Negro Intellectual.* New York, Morrow, 1967. 594 p.

1180 DABNEY, Lillian Gertrude. *The History of Schools for Negroes in the District of Columbia, 1807-1947.* Washington, D.C., Catholic University of America Press, 1949. 287 p.

1181 DAMERELL, Reginald G. *Triumph in a White Suburb; the Dramatic Story of Teaneck, N.J., The First Town in the Nation to Vote for Integrated Schools.* New York, Morrow and Co., Inc., 1968. 351 p. $6.50.

1182 DANIEL, Walter Green. *The Reading Interests and Needs of Negro College Freshmen Regarding Social Science Materials.* New York, Teachers College, Columbia University, 1942. 129 p.

1183 DERBIGNY, Irving Antony. *General Education in the Negro College.* Stanford University Press, 1947. 255 p. $3.00.

1184 FUCHS, Estelle. *Pickets at the Gates.* New York, Free Press, 1966. 205 p.

1185 GALLAGHER, Buell Gordon. *American Caste and the Negro College.* Foreword by William H. Kilpatrick. Staten Island, N.Y., Gordian Press, 1966 (c1938). 463 p. $10.00.

1186 GATES, Robbins L. *The Making of Massive Resistance: Virginia's Politics of Public School Desegregation, 1954-1956.* Chapel Hill, University of North Carolina Press, 1964. 222 p. $6.50.

1187 GINZBERG, Eli. *The Middle-class Negro in the White Man's World.* New York, Columbia University Press, 1967. 182 p. $5.00.

1188 GORDON, Edmund W., and Doxey A. Wilkerson. *Compensatory Education for the Disadvantaged; Programs and Practices, Preschool Through College.* New York, College Entrance Examination Board, 1966. 299 p.

1189 GURIN, Patricia and Daniel Katz. *Motivation and Aspiration in the Negro College.* Ann Arbor, Mich., Institute for Social Research, University of Michigan, 1966. 346 p. $4.25.

1190 HENTOFF, Nat. *Our Children are Dying.* New York, Viking Press, 1966. 141 p. $4.50.

1191 HILDEBRANDT, Herbert William. *Issues of Our Time: A Summons to Speak.* New York, Macmillan, 1963. 375 p.

1192 HOLLEY, Joseph Winthrop. *Education and the Segregation Issue; a Program of Education for the Economic and Social Regeneration of the Southern Negro.* New York, William-Frederick Press, 1955. 62 p.

1193 HUMPHREY, Hubert H. *Integration vs. Segregation.* New York, Thomas Crowell, 1964. 314 p. $4.95.

1194 HUNDLEY, Mary Gibson. *The Dunbar Story, 1870-1955.* New York, Vantage Press, 1965. 179 p. $3.50. Story of a segregated Washington, D.C., high school.

1195 JOHNSON, Charles Spurgeon. *The Negro College Graduate.* Chapel Hill, University of North Carolina Press, 1938. 399 p. Out of print.

1196 KOBLITZ, M.W. *Negro in Schoolroom Literature; Resource Materials for the Teacher of Kindergarten through the Sixth Grade.* New York, Center for Urban Education, 33 42nd St., 1966. 66 p. $0.25.

1197 KOZOL, Jonathan. *Death at an Early Age, the Destruction of the Hearts and Minds of Negro Children in the Boston Public schools.* Boston, Houghton Mifflin, 1967. 240 p. $4.95. Paperback, (Bantam) $0.95.

1198 MALLERY, David. *Negro Students in Independent Schools.* Boston, National Association of Independent Schools, 1963. 93 p. $1.00.

1199 McGINNIS, Frederick A. *A History and an Interpretation of Wilberforce University.* Wilberforce, Ohio, 1941. 215 p.

1200 McGRATH, Earl James. *The Predominantly Negro Colleges and Universities in Transition.* New York, Bureau of Publications, Teachers College, Columbia University, 1965. 204 p. $4.75. Paperback $2.75.

1201 McMILLAN, Lewis K. *Negro Higher Education in the State of South Carolina.* Orangeburg, S.C., South Carolina State A. & M. College, 1952. 296 p.

1202 MEREDITH, James. *Three Years in Mississippi.* Bloomington, Indiana University Press, 1966. 328 p. $5.95.

1203 MUSE, Benjamin. *Ten Years of Prelude: the Story of Integration Since the Supreme Court's 1954 Decision.* New York, Viking Press, 1964. 308 p. $5.00.

1204 NOBLE, Jeanne L. *The Negro Woman's College Education.* New York, Columbia University, Teachers College, 1956. 163 p. $4.25.

1205 PASSOW, A. Harry. *Education in Depressed Areas.* New York, Bureau of Publications, Teachers College, Columbia University, 1963. 359 p. Paperback $2.50.

1206 PLANS FOR PROGRESS. *Directory of Negro Colleges and Universities, March 1967.* Compiled by Plans for Progress, Washington, D.C., U.S. Government Printing Office, 1967. 106 p.

1207 RANGE, Willard. *The Rise and Progress of Negro Colleges in Georgia, 1865-1949.* Athens, Ga., University of Georgia Press, 1951. 254 p. $3.75.

1208 SEXTON, Patricia Cayo. *Education and Income: Inequalities of Opportunity in Our Public Schools.* Foreword by Kenneth B. Clark. New York, The Viking Press, 1961. 298 p. $5.00. Paperback $1.65. "One of the most devastating documents of the degree to which social class factors have insidiously permeated the American educational system that I have read." Kenneth B. Clark.

1209 SMITH, Bob. *They Closed Their Schools.* Chapel Hill, University of North Carolina Press, 1965. 281 p. $5.95.

1210 SOUTHERN EDUCATION REPORTING SERVICE. *Southern Schools: Progress and Problems;* Prepared by staff members and associates of Southern Education Reporting Service. Edited by Patrick McCauley and Edward D. Ball. Data collection directed by Bennie Carmichael. Nashville, Tenn., Southern Education Reporting Service, 1959. 174 p. $4.75.

1211 SOUTHERN EDUCATION REPORTING SERVICE. *Statistical Summary of School Segregation – Desegregation in the Southern and Border States.* Nashville, Tenn., Southern Education Reporting Service, 1967. 44 p. $1.00.

1212 SOUTHERN EDUCATION REPORTING SERVICE. *With All Deliberate Speed; Segregation – Desegregation in Southern Schools.* Prepared by staff members and associates of Southern Education Reporting Service; Bert Collier and others. Edited by Don Shoemaker. 1st ed. New York, Harper, 1957. 239 p.

1213 STOFF, Sheldon. *The Two-Way Street; Guideposts to Peaceful School Desegregation.* Indianapolis, David – Stewart Pub. Co. 1967. 184 p.

1214 TRILLIN, Calvin. *An Education in Georgia; the Integration of Charlayne Hunter and Hamilton Holmes.* New York, Viking Press, 1964. 180 p. $3.95.

1215 U.S. COMMISSION ON CIVIL RIGHTS. *Civil Rights U.S.A.: Public Schools, Cities in the North and West.* Washington, D.C., U.S. Government Printing Office, 1962. 309 p. $2.00.

1216 U.S. COMMISSION ON CIVIL RIGHTS. *Civil Rights U.S.A.: Public Schools, Southern States.* Washington, D.C., U.S. Government Printing Office, 1962. 217 p. $0.75.

1217 U.S. COMMISSION ON CIVIL RIGHTS. *Racial Isolation in the Public Schools; A Report.* Washington, D.C. For sale by the Superintendent of Documents, U.S. Government Printing Office, 1967. 2 vols.

1218 U.S. COMMISSION ON CIVIL RIGHTS. *Southern School Desegregation 1966-67.* Washington, D.C., U.S. Commission on Civil Rights, 1967. 262 p.

1219 U.S. OFFICE FOR ECONOMIC OPPORTUNITY. Community Action Program. *Upward Bound; a Program to Help Youth from Low-Income Families Achieve a College Education. Policy*

*Guidelines and Appreciation Instructions.* Washington, D.C., Office of Economic Opportunity, 1965. 75 p.

1220 WALKER, Anne K. *Tuskegee and the Black Belt; a Portrait of a Race.* Richmond, Va., The Dietz Press, Inc., 1944. 180 p.

1221 WASHINGTON, Booker T., ed. *Tuskegee, Its People: Their Ideals and Achievements.* New York, D. Appleton and Company, 1905. 354 p.

1222 WIGGINS, Samuel Paul. *The Desegregation Era in Higher Education.* Berkeley, Calif., McCutchan Publishers, 1966. 106 p. $3.95.

1223 WOODSON, Carter Godwin. *The Education of the Negro Prior to 1861; a History of the Education of the Colored People of the United States from the Beginning of Slavery to the Civil War.* New York and London, G.P. Putnam's Sons, 1915. 454 p. Reprint Arno Press, Inc., 1968. $14.00.

## HISTORY

1224 ABBOTT, Martin, *The Freedmen's Bureau in South Carolina, 1865-1872.* Chapel Hill, University of North Carolina Press, 1967. 162 p. $5.00.

1225 ALLEN, James Egert. *The Negro in New York.* New York, Exposition Press, 1964. 94 p. $3.00.

1226 ALLEN, James S. *Reconstruction, the Battle for Democracy (1865-1876).* New York, The International Publishers, 1937. 256 p.

1227 AMES, William C. *The Negro Struggle for Equality in the Twentieth Century.* Boston, Heath, 1965. 182 p.

1228 ANDREWS, Sidney. *The South Since the War, as Shown by Fourteen Weeks of Travel and Observation in Georgia and the Carolinas.* Boston, Ticknor and Fields, 1866. 400 p.

1229 APTHEKER, Herbert. *American Negro Slave Revolts.* New York, International Publishers, 1963. 409 p. $5.00. Paperback $2.25.

1230 APTHEKER, Herbert. *Documentary History of the Negro People in the United States.* New York, Citadel Press, 1964. 2 vols. Paperback $2.25 each.

1231 APTHEKER, Herbert. *Essays in the History of the American Negro.* New York, International Publishers, 1964. 216 p. $3.50.

1232 APTHEKER, Herbert. *The Negro in the Civil War.* New York, International Publishers, 1938. Out of print, 48 p.

1233 APTHEKER, Herbert. *Soul of the Republic; the Negro Today.* New York, Marzani & Munsell, 1964. 122 p. Paperback $1.65.

1234 APTHEKER, Herbert. *To Be Free; Studies in American Negro History.* New York, International Publishers, 1948. 256 p.

1235 AUSTIN, Frank Eugene. *The History of Segregation.* Winter Park, Fla., Rollins Press, 1956. 260 p.

1236 AVINS, Alfred, ed. *The Reconstruction Amendments' Debates; the Legislative History and Contemporary Debates in Congress on the 13th, 14th, and 15th Amendments,* Richmond, Virginia Commission on Constitutional Government, 1967. 764 p. Includes subject and name index.

1237 BALLAGH, James C. *A History of Slavery in Virginia.* Baltimore, Johns Hopkins Press, 1902. 160 p. Out of print.

1238 BARDOLPH, Richard. *The Negro Vanguard.* New York, Rinehart, 1959. 388 p. Paperback $1.85.

1239 BARTLETT, Irving H. *From Slave to Citizen; the Story of the Negro in Rhode Island.* Providence, Urban League of Greater Providence, 1954. 76 p.

1240 BARTLETT, Irving H. *Wendell Phillips: Brahmin Radical.* Boston, Beacon Press, 1961. 438 p. Profile of a tireless abolitionist.

1241 BAUGHAM, Lawrence E. Alan. *Southern Rape Complex; Hundred Year Psychosis.* Atlanta, Pendulum Books, 1966. 222 p.

1242 BEAM, Lura. *He Called Them By Lightning; a Teacher's Odyssey in the Negro South, 1908-1919.* Indianapolis, Bobbs-Merrill Company, 1967. 230 p. $5.75.

1243 BEASLEY, Delilah L. *The Negro Trail Blazers of California.* Los Angeles, Delilah L. Beasley, 1919. 323 p. Reprinted by Rand E. Research Associates, San Francisco, 1968.

1244 BENNETT, Lerone. *Before the Mayflower: a History of the Negro in America, 1619-1966.* 3d ed. Chicago, Johnson Pub. Co., 1966, 449 p. Illustrated. $6.95. Paperback, Penguin. $2.45.

1245 BENNETT, Lerone. *Black Power, U.S.A., the Human Side of Reconstruction, 1867-1877.* Chicago, Johnson Pub. Co., 1967. 401 p. $6.95.

1246 BENNETT, Lerone. *Confrontation: Black and White.* Chicago, Johnson Pub. Co., 1965. 321 p. $5.95.

1247 BERGER, Morroe. *Equality By Statute.* New York, Doubleday and Co., Inc., 1952. 253 p. $5.95.

1248 BILLINGTON, Ray Allen, ed. *The Journal of Charlotte L. Forten.* New York, The Dryden Press, 1953. $5.00. Diary of a free Negro woman.

1249 BITTLE, William E. and Gilbert Geis. *The Longest Way Home; Chief Alfred C. Sam's Back-to-Africa Movement.* Detroit, Wayne State University Press, 1964. 229 p. $8.50.

1250 BONTEMPS, Arna Wendell and Jack Conroy. *Anyplace But Here.* New York, Hill and Wang, 1966. 372 p. Paperback (American Century) $1.95.

1251 BONTEMPS, Arna Wendell. *Story of the Negro.* 3d ed. rev. New York, Alfred A. Knopf, 1958. 243 p.

1252 BOTKIN, Benjamin Albert, ed. *Lay My Burden Down. A Folk History of Slavery,* Chicago, University of Chicago Press, 1945. Paperback $3.50.

1253 BOWERS, Claude Gernade. *The Tragic Era; the Revolution After Lincoln.* Cambridge, Houghton Mifflin Company, 1929. 567 p. Historians generally reject the racist hyperbole of Bowers.

1254 BOYKIN, James H. *The Negro in North Carolina Prior to 1861; an Historical Monograph.* New York, Pageant Press, 1958. 84 p. $3.00.

1255 BROCK, William Ranulf. *An American Crisis: Congress and Reconstruction, 1865-1867.* New York, St. Martin's Press, 1963. 312 p.

1256 BROOM, Leonard. *Transformation of the Negro American.* New York, Harper & Row, 1965. 207 p. $5.75.

1257 BROTZ, Howard. *Negro Social and Political Thought, 1850-1920; representative texts.* New York, Basic Books, 1966. 593 p. $12.50.

1258 BROWN, Ina Corinne. *The Story of the American Negro.* New York, Friendship Press, 1957. 212 p. $2.75.

1259 BUCKMASTER, Henrietta. *Freedom Bound: the Real Story of the Reconstruction, 1868-1875.* New York, Macmillan, 1965. 155 p.

1260 BUCKMASTER, Henrietta. *Let My People Go; the Story of the Underground Railroad and the Growth of the Abolition Movement.* New ed. Boston, Beacon Press, 1959 (c1941). 398 p. $4.00 Paperback $1.95.

1261 CAIN, Alfred E., ed. *The Winding Road to Freedom; a Documentary Survey of Negro Experiences in America.* Yonkers, Educational Heritage, 1965. 384 p. $10.00.

1262 CHAMBERS, Lucile Arcola. *America's Tenth Man; a Pictorial Review of One-Tenth of a Nation, Presenting the Negro Contribution to American Life Today.* New York, Twayne Publishers, 1957. 351 p. Out of print.

1263 CINCINNATI. Public Schools. *The Negro in American Life,* by Mable Morsbach. Cincinnati. Printed by Cincinnati Lithographing, 1966. 218 p.

1264 CLARK, Peter Wellington. *Delta Shadows, "a Pageant of Negro Progress in New Orleans."* New Orleans, Graphic Arts Studios, 1942. 200 p.

1265 CLEMONS, Lulamae. *The American Negro.* St. Louis, Webster Division, McGraw-Hill, 1965. 138 p.

1266 COLEMAN, J. Winston. *Slavery Times in Kentucky.* Chapel Hill, University of North Carolina Press, 1940. 351 p.

1267 CONRAD, Earl. *The Invention of the Negro.* New York, P.S. Eriksson, 1967. 244 p. $5.95.

1268 CORNISH, Dudley Taylor. *The Sable Arm; Negro Troops in the Union Army, 1861-1865.* New York, Norton, 1966. 337 p. Paperback $1.75.

1269 COULTER, Ellis Merton. *The Civil War and Readjustment in Kentucky.* Gloucester, Mass., P. Smith, 1966 (c1926). 468 p.

1270 CROMWELL, John Wesley. *The Negro in American History; Men and Women Eminent in the Evolution of the American of African Descent.* Washington, D.C., The American Negro Academy, 1914. 284 p. Reprinted by Bergman Publishers, 1968. $38.00.

1271 CROWE, Charles, ed. *The Age of Civil War and Reconstruction, 1830-1900: a Book of Readings.* Homewood, Illinois, The Dorsey Press, 1966. 489 p. Paperback $4.95.

1272 CURRENT, Richard Nelson, ed. *Reconstruction, 1865-1877.* Englewood Cliffs, N.J., Prentice-Hall, 1965. 183 p. Documents.

1273 DAVIE, Maurice Rea. *Negroes in American Society.* New York, Whittlesey House, 1949. 542 p. $6.95.

1274 DAVIS, David Brion. *The Problem of Slavery in Western Culture.* Ithaca, New York, Cornell University Press, 1966. 505 p. $10.00.

1275 *DAEDALUS, THE NEGRO AMERICAN.* American Academy of Arts and Sciences, 1965-1966. 2 vols., special issues, Fall 1965 and Winter 1966.

1276 DENNETT, John Richard. *The South as it is: 1865-1866.* New York, Viking Press, 1965. 370 p. $6.95. Eyewitness account of the South during the first years of Reconstruction.

1277 DETROIT. Public Schools. Dept. of Social Studies. *The Struggle for Freedom and Rights; Basic Facts About the Negro in American History.* Preliminary ed. Detroit, Board of Education of the City of Detroit, 1966 (c1963). 52 p.

1278 DILLON, Merton. *Benjamin Lundy and the Struggle for Negro Freedom.* Urbana, Illinois, University of Illinois Press, 1966. 285 p. $6.75.

1279 DONALD, Henderson H. *The Negro Freedman.* New York, Henry Schuman, 1932. 270 p. $4.00.

1280 DRIMMER, Melvin, ed., with commentary. *Black History: a Reappraisal.* 1st ed. Garden City, N.Y., Doubleday, 1968. 553 p. $6.95. "Essays which present the Negro's role in American history, each prefaced by an analysis of the historical events surrounding the period it covers."

1281 DUBERMAN, Martin. *The Anti-Slavery Vanguard; New Essays on the Abolitionists.* Princeton, N.J., Princeton University Press, 1965. 508 p. $10.00.

1282 DuBOIS, William Edward Burghardt. *Black Reconstruction in America, 1860-1880.* New York, Meridian Books, 1964 (c1962). 738 p. Paperback $3.45.

1283 DuBOIS, William Edward Burghardt. *The Souls of Black Folks: Essays and Sketches.* Greenwich, Conn., Fawcett, 1961. 192 p. Paperback $0.60. "A passionate unfolding of the Negro's bitter struggle for his human rights by the outstanding Negro scholar. No serious research in the Negro field can be done without reference to this book." Roy Wilkins.

1284 DUMOND, Dwight Lowell. *America's Shame and Redemption.* Marquette, Northern Michigan University Press, 1965. 171 p.

1285 DUMOND, Dwight Lowell. *Anti-slavery: the Crusade for Freedom in America.* Ann Arbor, University of Michigan Press, 1961. 422 p. Illustrations. $2.00.

1286 DURHAM, Philip and Everett L. Jones. *The Negro Cowboys.* New York, Dodd, Mead, 1965. 278 p. $5.00.

1287 EPPSE, Merl Raymond. *A Guide to the Study of the Negro in American History.* Nashville, National Publication Co., 1953. 186 p.

1288 EPPSE, Merl Raymond. *The Negro, Too, in American History.* Nashville, New York, National Educational Publishing Co., 1938. 544 p.

1289 EVANS, William McKee. *Ballots and Fence Rails; Reconstruction on the Lower Cape Fear.* Chapel Hill, University of North Carolina Press, 1967. 314 p. $7.50.

1290 FILLER, Louis. *The Crusade Against Slavery, 1830-1860.* New York, Harper and Brothers, 1960. 318 p. Paperback $5.00.

1291 FISHEL, Leslie H. and Benjamin Quarles. *The Negro American: a Documentary History.* Glenview, Ill., Scott, Foresman, 1967. 536 p. $3.95.

1292 FLEMING, Walter Lynwood, ed. *Documentary History of Reconstruction: Political, Military, Social, Religious, Educational and Industrial, 1865 to 1906.* New York, McGraw-Hill Book Company, 1966. 2 vols. Paperback $2.45 each. Must be used with care because Fleming edited out anything favorable to Negroes, carpetbaggers, and scalawags.

1293 FLEMING, William Henry. *Treaty-Making Power: Slavery and the Race Problem in the South.* Boston, The Stratford Company, 1920. 100 p.

1294 FOSTER, William Zebulon. *The Negro People in American History.* New York, International Publishers, 1954. 608 p. $6.00.

1295 FRANCIS, Charles E. *The Tuskegee Airmen: the Story of the Negro in the U.S. Air Force.* Boston, Bruce Humphries, 1955. 225 p.

1296 FRANKLIN, John Hope. *The Emancipation Proclamation.* Garden City, N.Y., Doubleday, 1963. 181 p. $3.50. Paperback $0.95.

1297 FRANKLIN, John Hope. *The Free Negro in North Carolina, 1790-1860.* Chapel Hill, University of North Carolina Press, 1943. 271 p. $4.00.

1298 FRANKLIN, John Hope. *From Slavery to Freedom; a History of American Negroes.* 3d ed. New York, Alfred A. Knopf, 1967. 686 p. $10.75.

1299 FRANKLIN, John Hope. *Reconstruction: After the Civil War.* Chicago, University of Chicago Press, 1961. 258 p. $5.00. Paperback $1.95.

1300 FRAZIER, E. Franklin. *The Negro in the United States.* Rev. ed. New York, Macmillan Co., 1957. 769 p. $8.95.

1301 GARA, Larry. *The Liberty Line: the Legend of the Underground Railroad.* Lexington, University of Kentucky Press, 1961. 201 p. $5.00.

1302 GENOVESE, Eugene D. *The Political Economy of Slavery; Studies in the Economy and Society of the Slave South.* New York, Pantheon Books, 1965. 304 p.

1303 GINZBERG, Eli and Alfred S. Eichner. *The Troublesome Presence; American Democracy and the Negro.* New York, Free Press of Glencoe, 1964. 339 p. $5.95.

1304 GOLSTON, Robert. *The Negro Revolution.* New York, Macmillan, 1968. 247 p. $4.95. Primarily a history of Negro protest. Ages 14 up.

1305 GREENE, Lorenzo Johnston. *The Negro in Colonial New England, 1620-1776.* New York, Columbia University Press, 1942. 404 p. Paperback.

1306 HALASZ, Nicholas. *The Rattling Chains: Slave Unrest and Revolt in the Antebellum South.* New York, David McKay Company, 1966. 274 p. $4.95.

1307 HANDLIN, Oscar. *The Newcomers: Negroes and Puerto Ricans in a Changing Metropolis.* Cambridge, Harvard University Press, 1959. 171 p. Paperback.

1308 HARLAN, Louis R. *The Negro in American History.* Washington, D.C., American Historical Association, 1965. 29 p. $5.00.

1309 HARRIS, Norman Dwight. *The History of Negro Servitude in Illinois, and of the Slavery Agitation in that State, 1719-1864.* Chicago, A.C. McClurg & Co., 1904. 276 p.

1310 HERSKOVITS, Melville Jean. *The Myth of the Negro Past.* Boston, Beacon Press, 1958. 368 p. $2.25.

1311 HESSELTINE, William Best. *The Tragic Conflict; the Civil War and Reconstruction.* New York, G. Braziller, 1962. 528 p. $7.50.

1312 HIGGINSON, Thomas Wentworth. *Army Life in a Black Regiment.* With a new Introduction by Howard N. Meyer. New York, Collier Books, 1962. 287 p. Paperback $0.95.

1313 HILL, Roy L. *Rhetoric of Racial Revolt.* Denver, Golden Bell Press, 1964. 378 p.

1314 HODGES, Carl, and Helen H. Levene. *Illinois Negro Historymakers.* Chicago, Illinois Emancipation Centennial Commission, 1964. 91 p.

1315 HOLLANDER, Barnett. *Slavery in America; its Legal History.* London, Bowes and Bowes, 1962. 212 p. $4.90.

1316 HUGHES, Langston, and Milton Meltzer. *A Pictorial History of the Negro in America.* Rev. ed. New York, Crown Publishers, 1963. 337 p. $5.95. New edition, augmented by C. Eric Lincoln.

1317 ISAACS, Harold R. *The New World of Negro Americans.* New York, John Day Co., 1963. 366 p. $7.50.

1318 JACKSON, Luther P. *Free Negro Labor and Property Holding in Virginia, 1830-1860.* New York, London, D. Appleton-Century Company, Inc., 1942. 270 p.

1319 JARRELL, Hampton M. *Wade Hampton and the Negro; the Road Not Taken.* Columbia, University of South Carolina Press, 1949. 209 p.

1320 JERNEGAN, Marcus Wilson. *Laboring and Dependent Classes in Colonial America, 1607-1783; Studies of the Economic, Educational, and Social Significance of Slaves, Servants, Apprentices, and Poor Folk.* Chicago, Ill., The University of Chicago Press, 1931. 256 p.

1321 JOHNSON, Charles Spurgeon. *Patterns of Negro Segregation.* New York, Harper, 1943. 332 p. Out of print.

1322 JOHNSON, Charles Spurgeon. *Shadow of the Plantation.* Chicago, University of Chicago Press, 1934. Out of print. Paperback (Phoenix). 214 p. $1.95.

1323 JOHNSON, F. Roy. *The Nat Turner Slave Insurrection.* Murfreesboro, N.C., Johnson Publishing Company, 1966. 248 p. $6.50.

1324 JOHNSON, Haynes. *Dusk at the Mountain: the Negro, the Nation and the Capital.* Garden City, N.Y., Doubleday, 1963. 273 p. $4.50.

1325 JOINER, William A. *A Half Century of Freedom of the Negro in Ohio.* Xenia, Ohio, Press of Smith Adv. Co., 1915. 134 p.

1326 KALVEN, Harry, Jr. *The Negro and the First Amendment.* Columbus, Ohio State University Press, 1965. 190 p.

1327 KATZ, William Loren, comp. *Eyewitness; the Negro in American History.* New York, Pitman Pub. Corp., 1967. 554 p. Illustrated. $9.75.

1328 KEMBLE, Frances Anne. *Journal of a Residence on a Georgian Plantation in 1838-1839.* New York, Knopf, 1961. 415 p.

1329 KENNEDY, Louise V. *The Negro Peasant Turns Cityward.* New York, Columbia University Press, 1930. 271 p.

1330 KLEIN, Herbert S. *Slavery in the Americas: a Comparative Study of Virginia and Cuba.* Chicago, University of Chicago Press, 1967. 270 p. $6.95.

1331 KOGER, Azzie Briscoe. *The Maryland Negro in Our Wars.* Baltimore, Clarke Press, 1942. 31 p.

1332 LARKIN, John R. *The Negro Population of North Carolina 1945-1955.* Raleigh, North Carolina State Board of Public Welfare, 1957. 78 p.

1333 LECKIE, William H. *The Buffalo Soldiers: a Narrative of the Negro Cavalry in the West.* Norman, Oklahoma, University of Oklahoma Press, 1967. 290 p. $5.95.

1334 LEE, Irvin H. *Negro Medal of Honor Men.* New York, Dodd, Mead, 1967. 139 p. $4.00.

1335 LITWACK, Leon F. *North of Slavery; the Negro in the Free States, 1790-1860.* Chicago, University of Chicago Press, 1961. 318 p. $6.00. Paperback (Phoenix). $2.45.

1336 LOFTON, John. *Insurrection in South Carolina: the Turbulent World of Denmark Vesey.* Yellow Springs, Ohio, The Antioch Press, 1964. 294 p. $6.00.

1337 LOGAN, Rayford W., and Irving S. Cohen, with the Editorial Assistance of Howard R. Anderson. *The American Negro; Old World Background and New World Experience.* Boston, Houghton Mifflin Co., 1967. 278 p. $2.80. Paperback $1.60.

1338 LOGAN, Rayford W. *The Betrayal of the Negro; from Rutherford B. Hayes to Woodrow Wilson.* New enl. ed. New York, Collier Books, 1965. 447 p. Paperback $1.50. Originally published as *The Negro in American Life and Thought: The Nadir, 1877-1901.*

1339 LYDA, John W. *The Negro in the History of Indiana.* Terre Haute, Indiana, 1953. 136 p.

1340 LYNCH, John Roy. *The Facts of Reconstruction.* New York, The Neal Publishing Company, 1913. 325 p.

1341 MAGDOL, Edward. *Owen Lovejoy: Abolitionist in Congress.* New Brunswick, N.J., Rutgers University Press, 1967. 493 p. $10.00.

1342 MAZYCK, Walter H. *George Washington and the Negro.* Washington, D.C., The Associated Publishers, Inc., 1932. 191 p. $2.15.

1343 McCARTHY, Agnes and Lawrence Reddick. *Worth Fighting for: a History of the Negro in the United States During the Civil War and Reconstruction.* Garden City, N.Y., Doubleday, 1965. 118 p. $2.95.

1344 McMANUS, Edgar J. *A History of Negro Slavery in New York.* Syracuse, N.Y., Syracuse University Press, 1966. 219 p.

1345 McPHERSON, James M. *The Negro's Civil War; How American Negroes Felt and Acted During the War for the Union.* New York, Pantheon Books, 1964. 358 p. $6.95.

1346 McPHERSON, James M. *The Struggle for Equality; Abolitionists and the Negro in the Civil War and Reconstruction.* Princeton, N.J., Princeton University Press, 1964. 474 p. Illustrated.

1347 MEIER, August and Elliott M. Rudwick. *From Plantation to Ghetto; an Interpretive History of the American Negroes.* New York, Hill & Wang, 1966. $5.95.

1348 MEIER, August. *Negro Thought in America, 1880-1915; Racial Ideologies in the Age of Booker T. Washington.* Ann Arbor, University of Michigan Press, 1963. 336 p. $7.50. Paperback $2.25.

1349 MELTZER, Milton, ed. *In Their Own Words: a History of the American Negro, 1619-1966.* New York, Thomas Crowell, 1964-67. 3 v. $4.95 each. Vol. 1, 1619-1865; Vol. 2, 1865-1916; Vol. 3, 1916-66.

1350 MELTZER, Milton and August Meier. *Time of Trial, Time of Hope; the Negro in America, 1919-1941.* Illustrated by Moneta Barnett. Garden City, N.Y., Doubleday, 1966. 120 p.

1351 MINN, Joseph Karl. *The Large Slaveholders of Louisiana – 1860.* New Orleans, Pelican Pub. Co., 1964. 432 p.

1352 MITCHELL, Glenford E. and William H. Peace, III. *The Angry Black South*. New York, Corinth Books, 1962. 159 p.

1353 MONTGOMERY, David. *Beyond Equality: Labor and the Radical Republicans, 1862-1872*. New York, Alfred A. Knopf, 1967. 508 p. $10.00.

1354 MORGAN, Albert Talmon. *Yazoo; On the Picket Line of Freedom in the South. A Personal Narrative*. Washington, D.C., Albert Talmon Morgan, 1884. 512 p.

1355 MORSBACH, Mabel. *The Negro in American Life*. New York, Harcourt, Brace and World, 1967. 273 p. Illustrations. $6.95.

1356 MUELDER, Hermann Richard. *Fighters for Freedom; the History of Anti-Slavery Activities of Men and Women Associated with Knox College*. New York, Columbia University Press, 1959. 428 p.

1357 MUSE, Benjamin. *Virginia's Massive Resistance*. Bloomington, Indiana University Press, 1961. 184 p. $3.95.

1358 NELL, William C. *The Colored Patriots of the American Revolution*. New York, Arno Press, Inc., 1968. $12.00. (Reprint of 1855 ed.).

1359 NEWBY, I.A. *Jim Crow's Defense: Anti-Negro Thought in America, 1900-1930*. Baton Rouge, Louisiana State University Press, 1965. 230 p. $6.50.

1360 NICHOLS, Charles Harold. *Many Thousand Gone; the Ex-slaves' Account of Their Bondage and Freedom*. Leiden, Netherlands, Brill, 1963. 229 p. $10.00.

1361 NOLEN, Claude H. *The Negro's Image in the South: the Anatomy of White Supremacy*. Lexington, University of Kentucky Press, 1967. 232 p. $6.50.

1362 NUNN, William Curtis. *Texas Under the Carpetbaggers*. Austin, University of Texas Press, 1962. 304 p.

1363 OLSEN, Otto H. *Carpetbagger's Crusade: the Life of Albion Winegar Tourgée*. Baltimore, Johns Hopkins Press, 1965. 395 p. $7.95.

1364 OSOFSKY, Gilbert. *The Burden of Race; a Documentary History of Negro-White Relations in America.* New York, Harper & Row, 1967. 654 p. Illustrations. $7.95. Paperback (Torchbooks) $3.75.

1365 OTTLEY, Roi. *Black Odyssey: the Story of the Negro in America.* New York, Charles Scribner, 1948. 340 p. Out of print.

1366 OTTLEY, Roi and William J. Weatherby, eds. *The Negro in New York: an Informal Social History.* New York, Oceana Publications, Inc., 1967. 328 p. $6.00.

1367 PATTERSON, Caleb Perry. *The Negro in Tennessee, 1790-1865.* Austin, University of Texas Press, 1922. 213 p.

1368 PEASE, William Henry and Jane H. Pease. *Black Utopia; Negro Communal Experiments in America.* Madison, State Historical Society of Wisconsin, 1963. 204 p.

1369 PHILLIPS, Ulrich Bonnell. *American Negro Slavery; a Survey of the Supply, Employment and Control of Negro Labor as Determined by the Plantation Regime.* Baton Rouge, Louisiana State University Press, 1966. 529 p. Paperback $2.95. Phillips viewed slaves from the outmoded standpoint of racial inferiority.

1370 PHILLIPS, Ulrich Bonnell. *Life and Labor in the Old South.* Boston, Little, Brown, 1963. 375 p. Paperback. Less emphasis on Negro inferiority than *American Negro Slavery.*

1371 PITT-RIVERS, George Henry Lane Fox. *The Clash of Culture and the Contact of Races.* London, Routledge & Sons, 1927. 312 p. Out of print.

1372 PITTS, Nathan Alvin. *The Cooperative Movement in Negro Communities of North Carolina.* Washington, Catholic University of America Press, 1950. 201 p.

1373 PLACE, Marian T. *Rifles and War Bonnets: Negro Cavalry of the West.* New York, Ives, Washburn, Inc., 1968. 151 p. $3.95.

1374 POPE, Liston. *The Kingdom Beyond Caste.* New York, Friendship Press, 1957. 170 p. Paperback $1.25.

1375 POWDERMAKER, Hortense. *After Freedom.* New York, 1939. Reprint by Russell and Russell. 408 p. $10.00.

1376 POWELL, Adam Clayton. *Marching Blacks: an Interpretive History of the Rise of the Black Common Man.* New York, Dial Press, 1945. Out of print.

1377 QUARLES, Benjamin. *Lincoln and the Negro.* New York, Oxford University Press, 1962. 275 p. $0.50.

1378 QUARLES, Benjamin. *The Negro in the American Revolution.* Chapel Hill, University of North Carolina Press, 1961. 231 p. $6.00. Paperback $1.95.

1379 QUARLES, Benjamin. *The Negro in the Civil War.* Boston, Little, Brown, 1953. 379 p.

1380 QUARLES, Benjamin. *The Negro in the Making of America.* New York, Collier Books, 1964. 288 p. Paperback $0.95.

1381 QUILLEN, Frank V. *The Color Line in Ohio.* Ann Arbor, George Wahr, 1913. 178 p.

1382 QUINT, Howard H. *Profile in Black and White.* Washington, D.C., Public Affairs Press, 1958. 214 p.

1383 RANDEL, William P. *The Ku Klux Klan: a Century of Infamy.* New York, Chilton Books, 1965. 300 p. $5.95.

1384 REDDING, Jay Saunders. *The Negro.* Washington, D.C., Potomac Books, 1967. 101 p. $3.75.

1385 REDDING, Jay Saunders. *They Came in Chains: Americans from Africa.* Philadelphia, J.B. Lippincott, 1950. 320 p. Out of print.

1386 ROGERS, Joel Augustus. *Africa's Gift to America; the Afro-American in the Making and Saving of the United States.* New York, 1959. 254 p. $6.00.

1387 ROSE, Arnold Marshall. *Assuring Freedom to the Free; a Century of Emancipation in the USA.* Detroit, Wayne State University Press, 1964. 306 p. $6.95.

1388 ROSE, Willie Lee. *Rehearsal for Reconstruction: the Port Royal Experiment.* Indianapolis, Bobbs-Merrill Co., 1964. 442 p. $6.50.

1389 ROUSSEVE, Charles Barthelemy. *The Negro in Louisiana; Aspects of His History and His Literature: New Orleans.* New Orleans, The

Xavier University Press, 1937. 212 p.

1390 RUBIN, Louis Decimus, ed. *Teach the Freeman: the Correspondence of Rutherford B. Hayes and the Slater Fund for Negro Education 1881-1887.* Baton Rouge, Louisiana State University Press, 1964. 2 vols.

1391 RUCHAMES, Louis. *The Abolitionists; a Collection of Their Writings.* New York, G.P. Putnam, 1963. 259 p. $5.00.

1392 SAUNDERS, Doris E., ed. *The Kennedy Years and the Negro; a Photographic Record.* Chicago, Johnson Pub. Co., 1964. 143 p. Paperback $2.00.

1393 SCARBOROUGH, Ruth. *The Opposition to Slavery in Georgia Prior to 1860.* Nashville, Tenn., George Peabody College for Teachers, 1933. 257 p.

1394 SCHEINER, Seth M. *Negro Mecca; a History of the Negro in New York City, 1865-1920.* New York, New York University Press, 1965. 246 p. $6.50.

1395 SEFTON, James E. *The United States Army and Reconstruction, 1865-1877.* Baton Rouge, Louisiana State University Press, 1967. 284 p. $8.00.

1396 SELLERS, James Benson. *Slavery in Alabama.* University, Ala., University of Alabama Press, 1950. 426 p.

1397 THE SEPIA SOCIALITE. *The Negro in Louisiana, Seventy-eight Years of Progress.* New Orleans, Sepia Socialite Pub. Co., 1942. 168 p.

1398 SEXTON, Patricia Cayo. *Spanish Harlem; an Anatomy of Poverty.* New York, Harper & Row, 1968 (c1965). $5.95. Paperback $1.45.

1399 SHENTON, James Patrick. *The Reconstruction: a Documentary History of the South After the War, 1865-1877.* New York, Putnam, 1963. 314 p. $5.95. One of the most difficult documentary histories to read.

1400 SIEBERT, Wilbur Henry. *The Underground Railroad from Slavery to Freedom.* Reprint of 1898 ed. New York, Russell and Russell, 1967. 478 p. $15.00.

1401 SIMKINS, Francis Butler and Robert H. Woody. *South Carolina During Reconstruction.* Chapel Hill, University of North Carolina Press, 1932. 610 p.

1402 SINGLETARY, Otis A. *Negro Militia and Reconstruction.* Austin, University of Texas Press, 1957. 181 p. $3.75. Paperback $2.25.

1403 SMITH, Elbert B. *The Death of Slavery: the United States, 1837-65.* Chicago and London, University of Chicago Press, 1967. 225 p. $5.00.

1404 SPANGLER, Earl. *The Negro in Minnesota.* Minneapolis, T.S. Denison and Company, 1961. 215 p.

1405 SPEAR, Allan H. *Black Chicago: the Making of a Negro Ghetto, 1890-1920.* Chicago and London, University of Chicago Press, 1967. 254 p. $7.50.

1406 SPENCER, Samuel R. *Booker T. Washington and the Negro's Place in American Life.* Boston, Little, Brown, 1955. 212 p.

1407 STAMPP, Kenneth Milton. *The Era of Reconstruction, 1865-1877.* New York, Alfred A. Knopf, 1965. 228 p. $4.95.

1408 STAMPP, Kenneth Milton. *The Peculiar Institution: Slavery in the Antebellum South.* New York, Alfred A. Knopf, 1956. 435 p. $6.00.

1409 STANTON, William Ragan. *The Leopard's Spots: Scientific Attitudes Toward Race in America, 1815-59.* Chicago, University of Chicago Press, 1960. 244 p.

1410 STEPHENSON, Clarence David. *The Impact of the Slavery Issue on Indiana County.* Marion Center, Pa., Malioning Mimeograph and Pamphlet Service, 1964. 155 p.

1411 STILL, William. *The Underground Railroad.* New York, Arno Press, Inc., 1968. $25.00. (Reprint of 1872 edition).

1412 STRICKLAND, Arvarh E. *History of the Chicago Urban League.* Urbana, Illinois, University of Illinois Press, 1966. 264 p. $7.50.

1413 STROTHER, Horatio T. *The Underground Railroad in Connecticut.* Middletown, Conn., Wesleyan University Press, 1962. 262 p. $5.00.

1414 SWINT, Henry Lee. *Dear Ones at Home: Letters from Contraband Camps.* Nashville, Vanderbilt University Press, 1966. 274 p. $6.95. Letters from Northern teachers of Negro freedmen.

1415 SWINT, Henry Lee. *The Northern Teacher in the South, 1862-1870.* Nashville, Tenn., Vanderbilt University Press, 1941. 221 p.

1416 TANNENBAUM, Frank. *Slave and Citizen: the Negro in the Americas.* New York, Alfred A. Knopf, 1947. 128 p. Paperback (Vintage). $1.45.

1417 TATE, Thaddeus W. *The Negro in Eighteenth-Century Williamsburg.* Williamsburg, Va., University Press of Virginia, 1965. 256 p.

1418 TAYLOR, Alrutheus Ambush. *The Negro in South Carolina During Reconstruction.* Washington, D.C., The Association for the Study of Negro Life and History, 1924. 341 p.

1419 TAYLOR, Alrutheus Ambush. *The Negro in the Reconstruction of Virginia.* Washington, D.C., The Association for the Study of Negro Life and History, 1926. 300 p. The best of the studies completed by Taylor and still the standard work on Virginia.

1420 TAYLOR, Joe Gray. *Negro Slavery in Louisiana.* Baton Rouge, Louisiana Historical Association, 1963. 260 p. $6.00.

1421 TEN BROECK, Jacobus. *Equal Under Law.* New enl. ed. New York, Collier Books, 1965. 352 p. Paperback $1.95.

1422 THORNBROUGH, Emma Lou. *The Negro in Indiana Before 1900.* Indianapolis, Indiana Historical Bureau, 1957. 412 p.

1423 THORPE, Earl E. *The Mind of the Negro: an Intellectual History of Afro-Americans.* Baton Rouge, La., Ortlieb Press, 1961. 562 p. $7.75.

1424 THORPE, Earl E. *Negro Historians in the United States.* Baton Rouge, La., Fraternal Press, 1958. 188 p.

1425 TINDALL, George Brown. *South Carolina Negroes: 1877-1900.* Baton Rouge, Louisiana State University Press, 1966. 336 p. $5.00. Paperback $1.95.

1426 TOPPIN, Edgar A., and Carol F. Drisko. *The Unfinished March: the*

*Negro in the United States, Reconstruction to World War I.* Garden City, N.Y., Doubleday, 1967. 118 p.

1427 TOWNSEND, William Henry. *Lincoln and the Blue Grass; Slavery and Civil War in Kentucky.* Lexington, University of Kentucky Press, 1955. 392 p.

1428 TURNER, Edward Raymond. *The Negro in Pennsylvania, 1619-1861.* Washington, D.C., American Historical Association, 1912. 314 p.

1429 U.S. CONGRESS. House. *Memphis Riots and Massacres.* 39th Congress, 1st Session, Report No. 101. Archives Serial No. 1274. Washington, D.C., U.S. Government Printing Office, 1867.

1430 U.S. CONGRESS. House. *New Orleans Riots Select Committee Report.* 39th Congress, 2d Session, House Document 57-70. Archives Serial No. 1292. Washington, D.C., Superintendent of Documents, U.S. Government Printing Office, 1867.

1431 U.S. CONGRESS. Joint Select Committee. *The Condition of Affairs in the Late Insurrectionary States.* 42d Congress, 2d Sess., Senate Report No. 41, pt. 1. Washington, D.C., U.S. Government Printing Office 1872. 13 vols. Binder title, Ku Klux Conspiracy.

1432 VAN DEUSEN, John G. *The Black Man in White America.* Washington, D.C., The Associated Publishers, Inc., 1944. 381 p. $4.00.

1433 VOEGELI, V. Jacque. *Free But Not Equal; the Midwest and the Negro During the Civil War.* Chicago, University of Chicago Press, 1967. 215 p. $4.95.

1434 WADE, Richard C., ed. *The Negro in American Life: Selected Readings.* Boston, Houghton Mifflin, 1965. 182 p. $1.40.

1435 WADE, Richard C. *Slavery in the Cities: the South 1820-1860.* New York, Oxford University Press, 1964. 340 p. $6.75.

1436 WAGANDT, Charles Lewis. *The Mighty Revolution; Negro Emancipation in Maryland, 1862-1864.* Baltimore, Johns Hopkins Press, 1964. 299 p. $6.50.

1437 WALKER, David. *David Walker's Appeal, in Four Articles, Together With a Preamble, to the Coloured Citizens of the World, but in*

*Particular, and Very Expressly, to Those of the United States of America.* Edited and With an Introduction by Charles M. Wiltse. New York, Hill and Wang, 1965. 78 p. Paperback $1.25.

1438 WALLACE, John. *Carpetbag Rule in Florida.* Jacksonville, Florida, De Costa Printing and Pub. House, 1888. Kennesaw, Ga., Continental Book Co., 1959. 444 p. A Florida Negro's view of Reconstruction.

1439 WARMOUTH, Henry Clay. *War, Politics and Reconstruction; Stormy Days in Louisiana.* New York, Macmillan Company, 1930. 285 p. A Reconstruction governor's memoirs.

1440 WARNER, Robert Austin. *New Haven Negroes, a Social History.* New Haven, Yale University Press, 1940. 309 p.

1441 WASHINGTON, Nathaniel Jason. *Historical Development of the Negro in Oklahoma.* Tulsa, Oklahoma, Dexter Publishing Co., 1948. 71 p.

1442 WESLEY, Charles Harris. *The History of the Prince Hall Grand Lodge of Free and Accepted Masons of the State of Ohio, 1849-1960; an Epoch in American Fraternalism.* Wilberforce, Ohio, Central State College Press, 1961. 457 p. $5.25.

1443 WESLEY, Charles Harris. *Neglected History; Essays in Negro History by a College President.* Wilberforce, Ohio, Central State College Press, 1965. 200 p.

1444 WESLEY, Charles Harris and Patricia W. Romero. *Negro Americans in the Civil War; From Slavery to Citizenship.* 2d ed. New York, Publishers Company, Inc., 1968. 291 p. Illustrations. (International Library of Negro Life and History).

1445 WESLEY, Charles Harris. *Ohio Negroes in the Civil War.* Columbus, Ohio State University Press, 1962. 46 p.

1446 WHARTON, Vernon Lane. *The Negro in Mississippi, 1865-1890.* Chapel Hill, University of North Carolina Press, 1947. 298 p.

1447 WHYTE, James Huntington. *The Uncivil War; Washington During the Reconstruction, 1865-1878.* New York, Twayne Publishers, 1958. 316 p. $5.00.

1448 WILEY, Bell Irwin. *Southern Negroes, 1861-1865.* New Haven, Yale University Press, 1965. 366 p. $5.00.

1449 WILLIAMS, George Washington. *History of the Negro Race in America from 1619-1880. Negroes as Slaves, as Soldiers and as Citizens.* New York, G.P. Putnam's Sons, 1883. 2 vols. Reprint, Arno Press. $34.50.

1450 WILLIAMS, George Washington. *A History of the Negro Troops in the War of the Rebellion: 1861-65.* New York, Bergman Publishers, 1968. 353 p. $22.50.

1451 WILLIAMSON, Joel. *After Slavery; the Negro in South Carolina During Reconstruction, 1861-1877.* Chapel Hill, University of North Carolina Press, 1965. 442 p. $7.50.

1452 WILSON, Charles H. *Education for Negroes in Mississippi Since 1910.* Boston, Meadow Publishing Company, 1947. 641 p.

1453 WISH, Harvey, ed. *The Negro Since Emancipation.* Englewood Cliffs, New Jersey, Prentice-Hall, 1964. 184 p. $4.95. Paperback $1.95.

1454 WISH, Harvey, ed. *Reconstruction in the South, 1865-1877: First-Hand Accounts of the American Southland After the Civil War, by Northerners and Southerners.* New York, Farrar, Straus and Giroux, 1965. 318 p. $5.95.

1455 WOOD, Forrest G. *Black Scare, the Racist Response to Emancipation and Reconstruction.* Berkeley, Calif., University of California Press, 1968. $6.50.

1456 WOODSON, Carter Godwin. *A Century of Negro Migration.* Washington, D.C., The Association for the Study of Negro Life and History, 1918. 221 p.

1457 WOODSON, Carter Godwin. *The Mind of the Negro as Reflected in Letters Written During the Crisis, 1800-1860.* Washington, D.C., The Association for the Study of Negro Life and History, Inc., 1926. 704 p. $10.00.

1458 WOODSON, Carter Godwin and Charles Harris Wesley. *The Negro in Our History.* 10th ed. Washington, D.C., Associated Publishers, 1962. 833 p. $6.50.

1459 WOODSON, Carter Godwin and Charles Harris Wesley. *Negro Makers of History.* Washington, D.C., The Associated Publishers, Inc., 1958. 406 p. $3.50.

1460 WOODSON, Carter Godwin. *Negro Orators and Their Orations.* Washington, D.C., The Associated Publishers Inc., 1925. 700 p. $5.25.

1461 WOODWARD, Comer Vann. *The Strange Career of Jim Crow.* New York, Oxford University Press, 1958. 183 p. Paperback $1.50.

1462 WRIGHT, James Martin. *The Free Negro in Maryland, 1634-1860.* New York, Columbia University Press, 1921. 362 p.

1463 WYNES, Charles E. *The Negro in the South Since 1865; Selected Essays in American Negro History.* University, Ala., University of Alabama Press, 1966. 253 p. $6.95.

1464 YOUNG, Donald. *American Minority Peoples.* New York, 1932. Out of print.

1465 ZILVERSMIT, Arthur. *The First Emancipation: the Abolition of Slavery.* Chicago and London, University of Chicago Press, 1967. 262 p. $6.95

## LAW

1466 ABRAHAM, Henry J. *Freedom and the Court; Civil Rights and Liberties in the United States.* New York, Oxford University Press, 1967. 335 p. $7.50. Paperback $2.75. "This book considers where a democratic society must draw the line between the rights of the individual and the rights of the community as a whole. It closely examines the role that the judiciary has played in the evolution and implementation of essential civil rights and liberties."

1467 ALEXANDER, Sadie Tanner, comp. *Who's Who Among Negro Lawyers.* n.p., National Bar Association, 1945. 38 p.

1468 BARTH, Alan. *The Price of Liberty.* New York, The Viking Press, 1961. 212 p. $4.50. Contains a few references to legal cases involving Negroes.

1469 BERGER, Morroe. *Equality by Statute; Legal Controls Over Group Discrimination.* With a Foreword by Robert M. MacIver. New York, Columbia University Press, 1952. 238 p. $3.25. "This book is a clear picture of the legal status and the welfare of minorities in this country since 1865, and the book undermines the popular notion that 'you can't legislate against prejudice'."

1470 CATTERALL, Helen Honor (Tunnicliff), ed. *Judicial Cases Concerning American Slavery and the Negro*. New York, Octagon Books, 1968. 51. Reprint of 1926 edition. vol. 1-4. "Under each state, the cases are set in chronological order."

1471 *THE CIVIL RIGHTS ACT OF 1964; What it Means to Employers, Businessmen, Unions, Employees, Minority Groups*. Text, Analysis, Legislative History. Washington, D.C., Published by BNA Inc., Operations Manual, 1964. 424 p. $9.50.

1472 CLARK, Mary T. *Discrimination Today; Guidelines for Civic Action*. Foreword by Bishop John J. Wright. New York, Hobbs, Dorman & Company, Inc., 1966. 372 p. $6.50. "This is a factual, hardhitting account of the place prejudice has in the United States."

1473 COLLINS, Charles Wallace. *The Fourteenth Amendment and the States; a Study of the Operation of the Restraint Clauses of Section One of the Fourteenth Amendment to the Constitution of the United States*. Boston, Little, Brown, and Company, 1912. 220 p.

1474 COUNTRYMAN, Vern, ed. *Discrimination and the Law*. Chicago and London, University of Chicago Press, 1965. 170 p. $5.00. "This volume is based on a conference held at the University of Chicago Law School concerning what the due processes of the law have achieved in the past ten years in four basic areas — employment, education, public accommodation, and housing."

1475 CURRY, Jesse E. and Glen D. King. *Race Tensions and the Police*. With a Foreword by George Eastman. Springfield, Ill., Thomas, 1962. 137 p.

1476 DAVIS, Warren Jefferson. *Law of the Land*. New York, Carlton Press, 1962. 180 p.

1477 FLEISHMAN, Stanley. and Sam Rosenwein. *The New Civil Rights Act: What it Means to You!* Los Angeles, Blackstone Book Company, 1964. 191 p. Paperback $0.95. "A layman's guide to this important Act; the full text of the law; recent court decisions analyzing the Act; etc."

1478 FRIEDMAN, Leon, ed. *The Civil Rights Reader; Basic Documents of the Civil Rights Movement*. Foreword by Martin Duberman. New York, Walker and Company, 1967. 348 p. $6.50. "Book collects together for the first time the basic documents of the Civil Rights struggle."

1479 GREENBERG, Jack. *Race Relations and American Law.* New York, Columbia University Press, 1959. 481 p. $10.00. "Book describes the legal doctrines that govern race relations in the United States. It shows the ways in which these doctrines have worked or failed to work in education, housing, employment, elections, the criminal law, public accommodations, interstate travel, domestic relations, and the armed forces."

1480 JOHNSON, Charles Spurgeon. *The Negro College Graduate.* Chapel Hill, University of North Carolina Press, 1938. 399 p. Chapter XXI is on the legal profession.

1481 JOHNSON, George Marion. *Integration of the Negro Lawyer Into the Legal Profession in the U.S.* Washington, D.C., Howard University, 1951. 17 p.

1482 JOHNSON, Ozie Harold. *Price of Freedom.* Printed in the United States of America, 1954. 177 p. "This is a true story which depicts events related principally to the progress and development of the School of Law of the Texas State University."

1483 KALVEN, Harry, Jr. *The Negro and the First Amendment.* Columbus, Ohio State University Press, 1965. 190 p. $4.75.

1484 KEPHART, William M. *Racial Factors and Urban Law Enforcement.* Philadelphia, University of Pennsylvania Press, 1957. 209 p.

1485 KING, Donald B., and Charles W Quick, eds. *Legal Aspects of the Civil Rights Movement.* With an Introduction by James M. Nabrit, Jr. Detroit, Wayne State University Press, 1965. 447 p. $12.50.

1486 KIRCHHEIMER, Otto. *Political Justice; the Use of Legal Procedure for Political Ends.* Princeton, N.J., Princeton University Press, 1961. 452 p.

1487 KOGER, Azzie Brisco. *The Negro Lawyer in Maryland.* Baltimore, Md., Clarke Press, 1948. 12 p.

1488 KUNSTLER, William Moses. *Deep in My Heart.* Forewords by James Forman and Martin Luther King, Jr. New York, Morrow, 1966. 384 p.

1489 MANGUM, Charles Staples. *The Legal Status of the Negro.* Chapel Hill, University of North Carolina Press, 1940. 436 p.

1490 *MISSISSIPPI BLACK PAPER; Fifty-seven Negro and White Citizens' Testimony of Police Brutality, the Breakdown of Law and Order and the Corruption of Justice in Mississippi.* Foreword by Reinhold Niebuhr. Introduction by Hodding Carter. New York, Random House, 1965. 92 p.

1491 MURRAY, Pauli, comp. and ed. *States' Laws on Race and Color and Appendices; Containing International Documents, Federal Laws and Regulations, Local Ordinances and Charts.* Cincinnati, Ohio, Woman's Division of Christian Service, 1950. 746 p. $4.00.

1492 NATIONAL ASSOCIATION FOR THE ADVANCEMENT OF COLORED PEOPLE. *Equal Justice Under Law.* New York, Legal Defense and Educational Fund, Inc., June 1948. 16 p.

1493 SNETHEN, Worthington Garrettson. *The Black Code of the District of Columbia, in Force September 1st, 1848.* New York, Published for the A. & F. Anti-Slavery Society, by W. Harned, 1848. 61 p. Contains the District of Columbia ordinances of the corporation and ordinances of the corporation of Georgetown.

1494 SOBEL, Lester A., ed. *Civil Rights 1960-66.* New York, Facts on File, Inc., 1967. 504 p. $3.95.

1495 SOVERN, Michael I. *Legal Restraints on Racial Discrimination in Employment.* New York, Twentieth Century Fund, 1966. 270 p.

1496 STEPHENSON, Gilbert Thomas. *Race Distinctions in American Law.* New York and London, D. Appleton and Company, 1910. 388 p.

1497 STYLES, Fitzhugh Lee. *The Negro Lawyers' Contribution to Seventy-one Years of Our Progress.* 71st Anniversary Celebration of Negro Progress. Philadelphia, Pa., The Summer Press, c1934. n.p. Portraits.

1498 STYLES, Fitzhugh Lee. *Negroes and the Law in the Race's Battle for Liberty, Equality and Justice Under the Constitution of the United States; With Causes Célèbres. A Manual of the Rights of the Race Under the Law.* Boston, The Christopher Publishing House, 1937. 320 p.

1499 TOWLER, Juby Earl. *The Police Role in Racial Conflicts.* Springfield, Ill., C.C. Thomas, 1964. 119 p.

1500 TUSSMAN, Joseph, ed. *The Supreme Court on Racial Discrimination.* New York, Oxford University Press, 1963. 393 p. $1.95.

1501 U.S. COMMISSION ON CIVIL RIGHTS. *Freedom to the Free: Century of Emancipation, 1863-1963; a Report to the President.* Washington, D.C. For sale by the Superintendent of Documents, U.S. Government Printing Office, 1963. 246 p.

1502 U.S. COMMISSION ON CIVIL RIGHTS. *Law Enforcement; a Report on Equal Protection in the South.* Washington, D.C. For sale by the Superintendent of Documents, U.S. Government Printing Office, 1965. 188 p.

1503 U.S. COMMISSION ON CIVIL RIGHTS. State Advisory Committees. *The 50 States Report.* Washington, D.C., U.S. Government Printing Office, 1961. 687 p.

1504 WILSON, Theodore Brantner. *The Black Codes of the South.* University, Ala., University of Alabama Press, 1965. 177 p.

## POLITICS

1505 AIKEN, Charles J. *The Negro Votes.* San Francisco, Chandler Publishing Company, 1962. 377 p. Paperback $2.50.

1506 AMERICAN FEDERATION OF LABOR AND CONGRESS OF INDUSTRIAL ORGANIZATIONS. Industrial Union Department. *Tent City, "Home of the Brave."* (Washington, D.C., 1961?) 22 p. Negroes in Fayette County, Tennessee and politics.

1507 AMERICAN NEGRO ACADEMY. *The Negro and the Elective Franchise,* edited by the American Negro Academy. Washington, D.C., The Academy, 1905. 85 p.

1508 BAILEY, Harry A., ed. *Negro Politics in America.* Columbus, Ohio, Charles E. Merrill Books, Inc., 1967. 455 p. $4.95. Essays covering the period of the 1950's and '60's.

1509 BANFIELD, Edward C. and James Q. Wilson. *City Politics.* Cambridge, Harvard University Press and MIT Press, 1963. 362 p. $6.95. Includes a chapter on the Negro.

1510 BANFIELD, Edward C. *Political Influence.* Glencoe, Ill., Free Press, 1961. 354 p. Includes a study of machine politics in a Negro ward in Chicago.

1511 BREWER, John Mason. *Negro Legislators of Texas and Their Descendants, a History of the Negro in Texas Politics from Reconstruction to Disfranchisement.* Dallas, Texas, Mathis Publishing Company, 1935. 134 p.

1512 BROGAN, Dennis W. *Politics in America.* New York, Harper, 1954. 467 p. $5.00.

1513 BROOKE, Edward W. *The Challenge of Change; Crisis in Our Two-Party System.* Boston, Little, Brown, 1966. 269 p. $5.95.

1514 BROWN, William Garrott. *The New Politics, and Other Papers.* Boston and New York, Houghton Mifflin Company, 1914. 234 p.

1515 BUNI, Andrew. *The Negro in Virginia Politics, 1902-1965.* Charlottesville, The University of Virginia Press, 1967. 296 p. $6.00.

1516 CLARKE, Jacquelyne Johnson. *These Rights They Seek; a Comparison of Goals and Techniques of Local Civil Rights Organizations.* Washington, Public Affairs Press, 1962. 85 p.

1517 CLAYTON, Edwart T. *The Negro Politician; His Success and Failure,* With an Introduction by Martin Luther King, Jr. Chicago, Johnson Publishing Company, 1964. 213 p. $4.95.

1518 COLE, Taylor, and John H. Hallowell, eds. *The Southern Political Scene, 1938-1948.* Gainesville, Florida, The Journal of Politics, Kallman Publishing Co., 1948. 567 p.

1519 CORNELL-TOMPKINS COUNTY COMMITTEE FOR FREE AND FAIR ELECTIONS IN FAYETTE COUNTY, TENNESSEE. *Step By Step; Evolution and Operation of the Cornell Students' Civil-Rights Project in Tennessee, Summer, 1964.* New York, Published for the Fayette County Fund by W.W. Norton, 1965. 128 p.

1520 COX, LaWanda and John H. *Politics, Principle, and Prejudice, 1865-1866; Dilemma of Reconstruction America.* New York, Free Press of Glencoe, 1963. 294 p. $6.00.

1521 DeSANTIS, Vincent P. *Republicans Face the Southern Question:*

*the New Departure Years, 1877-1897.* Baltimore, Johns Hopkins Press, 1959. 275 p.

1522 DuBOIS, William Edward Burghardt. *Black Reconstruction in America: an Essay Toward a History of the Part Which Black Folk Played in the Attempt to Reconstruct Democracy in America, 1860-1880.* Cleveland, The World Publishing Company, Meridian Books, 1964 (c1962). 746 p. Paperback $3.45.

1523 EDMONDS, Helen G. *The Negro and Fusion Politics in North Carolina, 1894-1901.* Chapel Hill, University of North Carolina Press, 1951. 260 p.

1524 FLEMING, George James. *An All-Negro Ticket in Baltimore.* New York, Holt, Rinehart and Winston, 1960. 16 p.

1525 GOSNELL, Harold F. *Negro Politicians; the Rise of Negro Politics in Chicago,* With an Introduction by James Q. Wilson. Chicago, University of Chicago Press, 1966, (c1935). 396 p. Paperback $2.95.

1526 HALL, Woodrow Wadsworth. *A Bibliography of the Tuskegee Gerrymander Protest; Pamphlets, Magazines and Newspaper Articles Chronologically Arranged.* Tuskegee, Alabama, Department of Records and Research, 1960. 54 p.

1527 HEARD, Alexander. *A Two-Party South?* Chapel Hill, University of North Carolina Press, 1952. 334 p.

1528 HIRSHSON, Stanley P. *Farewell to the Bloody Shirt; Northern Republicans and the Southern Negro, 1877-1893.* Introduction by David Donald. Bloomington, Indiana University Press, 1962. 334 p.

1529 JACKSON, Luther Porter. *Negro Office-holders in Virginia, 1865-1895.* Norfolk, Virginia. Guide Quality Press, 1945. 88 p.

1530 JARRETTE, Alfred Q. *Politics and the Negro.* Boston, Vinjano Educational Publishers, 1964. 54 p.

1531 JONES, Lewis W. and Stanley Smith. *Tuskegee, Alabama: Voting Rights and Economic Pressure.* New York, Anti-Defamation League, 1958.

1532 KEY, V.O., Jr. *Southern Politics in State and Nation.* New York, Knopf, 1949; Vintage Caravelle, 1963. 675 p. Classic.

1533 LADD, Everett. *Negro Political Leadership in the South*. Ithaca, N.Y., Cornell University Press, 1966. 348 p. $8.50.

1534 LEWINSON, Paul. *Race, Class and Party; a History of Negro Suffrage and White Politics in the South*. New York, Grosset and Dunlap, 1965 (c1921). 302 p. Paperback $1.95.

1535 LLOYD, Raymond Grann. *White Supremacy in the United States, an Analysis of its Historical Background, With Especial Reference to the Poll Tax*. Washington, D.C., Public Affairs Press, 1952. 23 p.

1536 LOGAN, Rayford W. *The Attitude of the Southern White Press Toward Negro Suffrage, 1932-1940*. With a Foreword by Charles H. Wesley. Washington, D.C., The Foundation Publishers, 1940. 115 p.

1537 MABRY, William Alexander. *The Negro in North Carolina Politics Since Reconstruction*. Durham, N.C., Duke University Press, 1940. 87 p. (Historical Papers of the Trinity College Historical Society, Ser. XXIII).

1538 MATTHEWS, Donald R. and J. W. Prothro. *Negroes and the New Southern Politics*. New York, Harcourt, Brace and World, 1966. 551 p. $12.50.

1539 MILLER, Loren. *The Petitioners: the Story of the Supreme Court of the United States and the Negro*. New York, Pantheon Books, 1966. 461 p. $8.95.

1540 MOON, Henry Lee. *Balance of Power; the Negro Vote*. Garden City, New York, Doubleday, 1948. 256 p. Out of print.

1541 MORTON, Richard Lee. *The Negro in Virginia Politics, 1865-1902*. Charlottesville, The University of Virginia, 1919. 199 p.

1542 MOSELEY, J.H. *Sixty Years in Congress and Twenty-Eight Out*. New York, Vantage Press, 1960. 99 p. $2.95. Discusses Negroes in Congress.

1543 NOLAN, William A. *Communism Versus the Negro*. Chicago, H. Regnery Company, 1951. 276 p.

1544 NOWLIN, William Felbert. *The Negro in American National Politics*. Boston, Mass., The Stratford Company, 1931. 148 p.

1545 OGDEN, Frederick D. *The Poll Tax in the South.* University, Ala., University of Alabama Press, 1958.

1546 OLBRICH, Emil. *The Development of Sentiment on Negro Suffrage to 1860.* Madison, Wisconsin, The University of Wisconsin Press, 1912. 135 p.

1547 PERRY, Jennings. *Democracy Begins at Home, the Tennessee Fight on the Poll Tax.* Philadelphia, New York, J.B. Lippincott Company, 1944. 280 p.

1548 PIKE, James Shepherd. *The Prostrate State: South Carolina Under Negro Government.* New York, D. Appleton and Company, 1874. 279 p.

1549 POSEY, Thomas Edward. *The Negro Citizen of West Virginia.* Institute, W.Va., Press of West Virginia State College, 1934. 119 p.

1550 PRICE, Hugh Douglas. *The Negro and Southern Politics; a Chapter of Florida History.* With an Introduction by William G. Carleton. New York, New York University Press, 1957. 133 p. $5.00.

1551 PRICE, Margaret. *The Negro and the Ballot in the South.* Atlanta, Southern Regional Council, 1959.

1552 PRICE, Margaret. *The Negro Voter in the South.* Atlanta, Southern Regional Council, 1958. 55 p.

1553 RECORD, Wilson. *Race and Radicalism: the NAACP and the Communist Party in Conflict.* Ithaca, New York, Cornell University Press, 1964. 237 p. $5.95. Paperback $1.95.

1554 RILEY, Jerome R. *The Philsosophy of Negro Suffrage.* Washington, D.C., 1897. 142 p.

1555 ROADY, Elston E. *The Negro's Role in American Society.* Tallahasse, Florida State University, 1958.

1556 RUSCO, Elmer R. *Voting Patterns of Racial Minorities in Nevada.* Reno, Bureau of Governmental Research, University of Nevada, 1966. 49 p.

1557 RUSSELL, Robert T. *Antebellum Studies in Slavery, Politics, and the Railroads.* Kalamazoo, Michigan, Western Michigan University, 1960. 98 p.

1558 SCHOLLIANOS, Alva. *New Frontiers; America's Problems and Opportunities.* New York, William-Frederick Press, 1961. 169 p.

1559 SMITH, Samuel Denny. *The Negro in Congress, 1870-1901.* Port Washington, New York, Kennikat Press, 1966 (c1940). 160 p. $6.00.

1560 STEPHENSON, Gilbert Thomas. *Race Distinction in American Law.* New York and London, D. Appleton and Company, 1910. 388 p.

1561 SUGARMAN, Tracy. *Stranger at the Gates; a Summer in Mississippi.* New York, Hill and Wang, 1966. 240 p. $5.95.

1562 TAPER, Bernard. *Gomillion Versus Lightfoot: the Tuskegee Gerrymander Case.* New York, McGraw-Hill, 1962. 118 p. Paperback $1.95.

1563 TATUM, Elbert L. *The Changed Political Thought of the Negro, 1915-1940.* With a Foreword by Lawrence A. Davis. New York, Exposition Press, 1951. 205 p. Out of print.

1564 U.S. COMMISSION ON CIVIL RIGHTS. *Hearings Before the United States Commission on Civil Rights. Hearings Held in New Orleans, Louisiana, September 27, 1960, September 28, 1960, May 5, 1961, May 6, 1961.* Washington, D.C., U.S. Government Printing Office, 1961. 848 p.

1565 U.S. COMMISSION ON CIVIL RIGHTS. *Voting in Mississippi; a Report.* Washington, D.C., U.S. Government Printing Office, 1965. 74 p.

1566 U.S. COMMISSION ON CIVIL RIGHTS. *The Voting Rights Act: the First Months.* Washington, D.C., 1965. 78 p.

1567 U.S. COMMISSION ON CIVIL RIGHTS. *The Voting Rights Act of 1965.* Washington, D.C., U.S. Government Printing Office, 1956. 16 p.

1568 WALLACE, Jesse Thomas. *A History of the Negroes of Mississippi from 1865 to 1890.* Clinton, Miss., 1927. 188 p.

1569 WARDLAW, Ralph Wilkinson. *Negro Suffrage in Georgia, 1867-1930.* Athens, Ga., 1932.

1570 WARING, James H.N. *Work of the Colored Law and Order League.* Baltimore, Maryland, Cheyney, Pa., Committee of Twelve for the Advancement of the Interests of the Negro Race, 1908. 29 p.

1571 WATTERS, Pat and Reese Cleghorn. *Climbing Jacob's Ladder: the Arrival of Negroes in Southern Politics.* New York, Harcourt, Brace and World, 1967. 389 p. $8.95.

1572 WEEKS, Stephen Beauregard. *The History of Negro Suffrage in the South.* Boston, Ginn & Company, 1894. 703 p.

1573 WIGHTMAN, Orrin Sage. *Early Days of Coastal Gerogia.* St. Simons Island, Georgia, Fort Frederica Association, 1955. 235 p.

1574 WILSON, James Q. *Negro Politics: the Search for Leadership.* Glencoe, Illinois, Free Press, 1960. 342 p. $5.95. Paperback $2.45.

## RACIAL DISSENT

### RACE RELATIONS AND CIVIL RIGHTS

1575 ABRAHAM, Henry Julian. *Freedom and the Court; Civil Rights and Liberties in the United States.* New York, Oxford University Press, 1967. 335 p. $7.50. Paperback $2.75.

1576 AMERICAN ACADEMY OF POLITICAL AND SOCIAL SCIENCE, Philadelphia. *The Negro Protest.* Special editor, Arnold M. Rose. Philadelphia, American Academy of Political and Social Science, 1965. 214 p. $3.00.

1577 BALDWIN, James. *Tell Me How Long the Train's Been Gone.* New York, Dial Press, 1968. 484 p. $5.95.

1578 BERNSTEIN, Abraham. *The Education of Urban Populations.* New York, Random House, 1967. 398 p. $3.95.

1579 BERSON, Lenora E. *Case Study of a Riot: the Philadelphia Story.* With commentaries by Alex Rosen and Kenneth B. Clark. New York, Institute of Human Relations Press, 1966. 71 p.

1580 BILLINGSLEY, Andrew. *Black Families in White America.* New Jersey, Prentice-Hall, 1968. $4.95. Paperback (Spectrum).

1581 BLAUSTEIN, Albert P., and Robert L. Zangrando, eds. *Civil Rights and the American Negro: a Documentary History.* New York, Trident Press, 1968. $7.95. Paperback, (Washington Square Press, 1968). $1.45. "Includes more than 100 major civil rights documents spanning more than 300 years. Included are legal briefs, court decisions, executive orders, editorials, manifestos and public addresses having to do with Negroes' quest for racial equality in voting, education, public accommodations, the armed forces, employment and housing.

1582 BOOKER, Simeon. *Black Man's America.* Englewood Cliffs, N.J., Prentice-Hall, 1964. 230 p. Out of print.

1583 BRINK, William and Louis Harris. *Black and White: a Study of U.S. Racial Attitudes Today.* New York, Simon and Schuster, 1967. 285 p.

1584 BRINK, William and Louis Harris. *The Negro Revolution in America; What Negroes Want, Why and How They are Fighting, Whom They Support, What Whites Think of Them and Their Demands.* New York, Simon & Schuster, 1964 (c1963). 249 p. $5.95. Paperback $1.45.

1585 BRODERICK, Francis L. and August Meier. *Negro Protest Thought in the Twentieth Century.* New York, Bobbs-Merrill Co., 1965. 444 p. $7.50. Paperback $3.25.

1586 BUDD, Edward C. *Inequality and Poverty.* New York, W.W. Norton & Co., Inc., 1967. 217 p. $6.00.

1587 BUNCHE, Ralph J. *A World View of Race.* Port Washington, N.Y., Kennikat Press, 1968 (c1936). 98 p. (Kennikat Series on Negro Culture & History). $5.00.

1588 BUREAU OF NATIONAL AFFAIRS. *The Civil Rights Act of 1964; Text, Analysis, Legislative History: What It Means to Employers, Businessmen, Unions, Employees, Minority Groups.* Washington, Bureau of National Affairs, 1964. 424 p. $9.50.

1589 BURNS, W. Haywood. *The Voices of Negro Protest in America.* London, New York, Oxford University Press, 1963. 88 p. Paperback $1.00.

1590 CARTER, Wilmoth Annette. *The Negro of the South; a Portrait of Movements and Leadership.* New York, Exposition Press, 1967. 58 p. $4.00.

1591 CHICAGO COMMISSION ON RACE RELATIONS. *The Negro in Chicago: a Study of Race Relations and a Race Riot.* Chicago, University of Chicago Press, 1922. 672 p.

1592 CLARK, Kenneth B. *The Negro Protest: James Baldwin, Malcolm X,*

*Martin Luther King Talk With Kenneth B. Clark.* Boston, Beacon Press, 1963. 56 p.

1593 CLARK, Mary T. *Discrimination Today; Guidelines for Civic Action.* New York, Hobbs, Dorman, 1966. 372 p. $6.50.

1594 CLEAVER, Eldridge. *Soul On Ice.* With an introduction by Maxwell Geismar. New York, McGraw-Hill Book Co., 1968. 210 p. $5.95. Examines and analyzes such topics in the life of the American Negro today as the Negro's stake in the Vietnam War, the effects of the death of Malcolm X, and James Baldwin's role as a literary spokesman.

1595 COMMAGER, Henry Steele. *The Struggle for Racial Equality; a Documentary Record.* New York, Harper and Row, 1967. 260 p. Paperback $2.75.

1596 CONGRESSIONAL QUARTERLY SERVICE, Washington, D.C. *Revolution in Civil Rights.* 3d ed. Washington, 1967. 120 p. $2.50.

1597 CONOT, Robert. *Rivers of Blood: Years of Darkness.* New York, Morrow, 1968. $6.95. Paperback (Bantam Books, Inc., 1967). 497 p. $0.85. The unforgettable classic account of the Watts riot.

1598 COUNTRYMAN, Vern, ed. *Discrimination and the Law.* Chicago, University of Chicago Press, 1965. 170 p. $5.00.

1599 CRAY, Ed. *The Big Blue Line: Police Power vs. Human Rights.* New York, Coward-McCann, Inc., 1967. 250 p. $5.95.

1600 CRUMP, Spencer. *Black Riot in Los Angeles; the Story of the Watts Tragedy.* Los Angeles, Trans-Anglo Books, 1966. 160 p.

1601 CRUSE, Harold. *Rebellion or Revolution.* New York, William Morrow and Company, 1968. 272 p. $6.95.

1602 DAMERELL, Reginald G. *Triumph in a White Suburb; the Dramatic Study of Teaneck, N.J., the First Town in the Nation to Vote for Integrated Schools.* New York, William Morrow & Co., 1968. 351 p. $6.50.

1603 DENTLER, Robert A., Bernard Mackley and Mary Ellen Warshaeur, eds. *The Urban R's; Race Relations as the Problem in Urban Education.* New York, Published for the Center for Urban Education. New York, Praeger, 1967. 304 p. $7.50. Paperback $2.50.

1604 DEXTER, Harriet Harmon. *What's Right With Race Relations.* New York, Harper, 1958. 248 p. Out of print.

1605 DORMAN, Michael. *We Shall Overcome.* New York, Delacorte Press, 1964. 340 p. Out of print.

1606 DOUGLAS, William O. *Mr. Lincoln and the Negroes; the Long Road to Equality.* New York, Atheneum Publishers, 1963. 237 p. $4.95.

1607 DOYLE, Bertram Wilbur. *The Etiquette of Race Relations in the South.* Port Washington, N.Y., Kennikat Press, 1968. 249 p. $8.50.

1608 DuBOIS, William Edward Burghardt. *The Philadelphia Negro; a Social Study.* Introduction by E. Digby Baltzell; together with a Special Report on Domestic Service, by Isabel Eaton. New York, Schoken, 1967. 550 p. $8.50. Paperback $2.95.

1609 EDWARDS, G. Franklin, ed., with Introduction. *E. Franklin Frazier on Race Relations.* Chicago, University of Chicago Press, 1968. $13.50.

1610 ELLI, Frank. *The Riot.* New York, Coward-McCann, 1967. 255 p. $4.95.

1611 ENDLEMEN, Shalom, ed. *Violence in the Streets.* Chicago, Quadrangle Books, Inc., 1968. $8.95.

1612 EVERETT, Robinson O., ed *Anti-Poverty Programs.* New York, Oceana Publications, 1966. 249 p. $6.00.

1613 FANON, Frantz. *Black Skin, White Masks.* New York, Grove Press, 1967. 232 p.

1614 FARMER, James. *Freedom When?* New York, Random House, 1966 (c1965). 197 p. $4.95.

1615 FIELDS, Uriah J. *The Montgomery Story, The Unhappy Effects of the Montgomery Bus Boycott.* New York, Exposition Press, 1959. 87 p. $2.75.

1616 FONTAINE, William Thomas. *Reflections on Segregation, Desegregation, Power and Morals.* Springfield, Ill., Thomas, 1967. 162 p. $6.75.

1617 FORMAN, James. *Sammy Younge, jr. The First Black College Student to Die in the Black Liberation Movement.* New York, Grove Press, 1968. $6.50.

1618 FRANKLIN, John Hope, ed. *Color and Race.* Boston, Houghton Mifflin Company, 1968. $6.00. A discussion of prejudice.

1619 FRANKLIN, John Hope, and Isidore Starr, eds. *The Negro in the Twentieth Century America: a Reader on the Struggle for Civil Rights.* New York, Vintage Books, 1967. 542 p. Paperback $2.45.

1620 FREEDOM OF INFORMATION CONFERENCE, 8th. University of Missouri, 1965. *Race and the News Media.* Edited by Paul L. Fisher and Ralph Lowenstein. New York, Praeger, 1967. 158 p. $1.95.

1621 FRIEDMAN, Leon, ed. *The Civil Rights Reader.* New York, Walker and Co., 1967. 348 p. $6.50.

1622 GILBERT, Ben W. *Ten Blocks from the White House. The Washington Riots of 1968.* New York, Frederick A. Praeger, 1968. 328 p. $6.50. Paperback $1.95.

1623 GOLDEN, Harry. *Mr. Kennedy and the Negroes.* Cleveland, World Publishing Co., 1964. 319 p. $4.95. Paperback $0.60. The history of the Negro struggle for equality and of John F. Kennedy's role in the Civil Rights Movement.

1624 GREENE, Constance McLaughlin. *The Secret City: a History of Race Relations in the Nation's Capital.* Princeton, N.J., Princeton University Press, 1967. 389 p. $8.50.

1625 GREGORY, Dick. *The Shadow that Scares Me.* Edited by James R. McGraw. New York, Doubleday & Co., Inc., 1968. 213 p. $4.50.

1626 GREGORY, Dick. *Write Me In.* Bantam, 1968. Paperback $0.95. 158 p. Humor in racial crises.

1627 GRIMKE, Francis James. *The Negro; His Rights and Wrongs, the Forces for Him and Against Him.* Washington, D.C., 1898. 100 p.

1628 GRIMKE, Francis James. *The Next Step in Racial Cooperation; a Discourse Delivered in the Fifteenth Street Presbyterian Church.* Washington, D.C., 1921. 11 p.

1629 GRIMKE, Francis James. *The Race Problem – Two Suggestions as to its Solution.* Washington, D.C., 1919. 8 p.

1630 HAMMOND, Lily (Hardy). *Southern Women and Racial Adjustment.* Lynchburg, Va., J.P. Bell Company, Inc., 1917. 32 p.

1631 HANSBERRY, Lorraine. *The Movement; Documentary of a Struggle for Equality.* New York, Simon and Schuster, 1964. 127 p. $4.95. Paperback $1.95.

1632 HARLAN, Louis R. *Separate and Unequal: Public School Campaigns and Racism in the Southern Seaboard States 1901-1915.* With a New Preface by Hugh Hawkins. New York, Atheneum, 1968. 290 p. $2.75. (Studies in American Negro Life, August Meier, General Editor). Paperback.

1633 HARRIS, Janet. *The Long Freedom Road; the Civil Rights Story.* Foreword by Whitney M. Young, Jr. New York, McGraw-Hill, 1967. 150 p.

1634 HEACOCK, Roland T. *Understanding the Negro Protest.* New York, Pageant Press, 1965. 138 p. $3.00.

1635 HESSLINK, George K. *Black Neighbors; Negroes in a Northern Rural Community.* Indianapolis, Bobbs-Merrill, 1968. 190 p. $6.00.

1636 HILL, Roy L., comp. *Rhetoric of Racial Revolt.* Denver, Golden Bell Press, 1964. 378 p. $5.50.

1637 HOLMES, S.J. *The Negro's Struggle for Survival.* Port Washington, New York, Kennikat Press, Inc., 1966 (c1965). 296 p. $9.00.

1638 HOLT, Len. *The Summer that Didn't End.* New York, Morrow, 1965. 351 p. $5.00.

1639 HOWLETT, Duncan. *No Greater Love; the James Reeb Story.* New York, Harper and Row, 1966. 242 p. $4.95.

1640 HUGHES, Langston. *Fight for Freedom; the Story of the NAACP.* New York, W.W. Norton Co., 1962. 224 p. $4.95.

1641 ILLINOIS. THE CHICAGO COMMISSION ON RACE RELATIONS. *The Negro in Chicago: a Study of Race Relations and a Race Riot.* Chicago, Ill., The University of Chicago Press, 1922. 672 p. $6.00.

1642 JACKSON, Joseph Harrison. *Unholy Shadows and Freedom's Holy Light.* Nashville, Townsend Press, 1967. 270 p. $5.00.

1643 JACKSON, Kenneth T. *The Ku Klux Klan in the City 1915-1930.* New York, Oxford Press, 1967. 326 p. $7.50.

1644 JACOBS, Paul, and Saul Landau. *The New Radicals; a Report with Documents.* New York, Random House, 1968. $6.95. Paperback (Vintage Books) $1.95.

1645 JACOBS, Paul. *Prelude to Riot; a View of Urban America from the Bottom.* New York, Random House, 1968 (c1967). 298 p.

1646 JONES, Leroi, and Larry Neal, eds. *Black Fire.* New York, Morrow, 1968. $7.50. "A naked indictment of American prejudice and a flaming prophecy of future turmoil are to be found in this anthology of Black writing."

1647 JORDAN, Winthrop D. *White Over Black; American Attitudes Toward the Negro, 1550-1812.* Chapel Hill, N.C., University of North Carolina Press, 1968. 651 p. $12.50.

1648 KELLOGG, Charles Flint. *NAACP: a History of the National Association for the Advancement of Colored People,* vol. 1, 1909-1920. Baltimore, Johns Hopkins Press, 1967. 332 p. $8.75.

1649 KILLIAN, Lewis Martin and Charles Grigg. *Racial Crisis in America; Leadership in Conflict.* Englewood Cliffs, N.J., Prentice-Hall, 1964. 144 p. $4.50. Paperback $1.95.

1650 KING, Martin Luther. *The Trumpet of Conscience.* New York, Harper & Row, 1968. $3.95. 78 p.

1651 KING, Martin Luther. *Where Do We Go From Here; Chaos or Community?* New York, Harper & Row, 1967. 209 p. $4.95.

1652 KING, Martin Luther. *Why We Can't Wait.* New York, Harper & Row, 1964. 178 p. $3.50. Paperback (Signet) $0.60.

1653 KONVITZ, Milton. *A Century of Civil Rights; With a Study of State Law Against Discrimination* by Theodore Leskes. New York, Columbia University Press, 1961. 293 p. $7.50. Paperback $2.25.

1654 LAVINE, Hannibal. *Call Me Anything But What I Am; the Conglomerate: the Negroes and Coloureds of North America.* Detroit, Mohawk Pub. Co., 1967. 79 p.

1655 LEWIS, Anthony, and the *New York Times. Portrait of a Decade; the Second American Revolution.* New York, Random House, 1964. 322 p. $6.95.

1656 LIGHTFOOT, Claude M. *Ghetto Rebellion to Black Liberation.* New York, International Publishers, 1968. $5.95. Paperback $1.95. "A leading Afro-American Communist outlines his views on black liberation, analyzing the ghetto uprisings, nationalism, armed self-defense and the present state of our society."

1657 LINCOLN, Charles Eric. *The Black Muslims in America.* Boston, Beacon Press, 1961. 276 p. $4.95.

1658 LINCOLN, Charles Eric. *My Face is Black.* Boston, Beacon Press, 1964. 137 p.

1659 LINCOLN, Charles Eric. *The Negro Pilgrimage in America.* New York, Bantam Pathfinder Editions, 1967. 184 p. Paperback $0.60.

1660 LINCOLN, Charles Eric. *Sounds of the Struggle; Persons and Perspectives in Civil Rights.* New York, William Morrow & Co., Inc., 1967. 252 p. $5.00.

1661 LOMAX, Louis E. *The Negro Revolt.* New York, Harper and Bros. 1962. 272 p. $4.50. Paperback (New York, New American Library, 1962). $0.95.

1662 LUBELL, Samuel. *White and Black; Test of a Nation.* New York, Harper and Row, 1964. 210 p. $4.95. Paperback $1.60.

1663 MARSHALL, Burke. *Federalism and Civil Rights.* New York, Columbia University Press, 1964. 85 p. $3.50.

1664 MARX, Gary T. *Protest and Prejudice: a Study of Belief in the Black Community.* New York, Harper & Row, 1967. 228 p. $8.95.

1665 MEIER, August and Elliott M. Rudwick. *The Making of Black America.* New York, Atheneum, 1968. $12.50. Paperback $5.95. A collection of essays on slavery and the free Negro from pre-Civil War days to the 20th Century.

1666 MENDELSOHN, Jack. *The Martyrs; Sixteen Who Gave Their Lives for Racial Justice.* New York, Harper & Row, 1966. 227 p. $5.00.

1667 MILLER, Kelly. *Race Adjustment; Essays on the Negro in America.* New York, Schocken Books, 1968. $6.50. Paperback $2.45. New title — *Radicals and Conservatives: and Other Essays in America.* Paperback $2.45.

1668 MOMBOISSE, Raymond M. *Riots, Revolts, and Insurrections.* Springfield, Ill., Thomas, 1967. 523 p. $6.50.

1669 NATIONAL ADVISORY COMMISSION. *Report of the National Advisory Commission on Civil Disorders.* With special Introduction by Tom Wicker of the *New York Times.* New York, Bantam Books, 1968. 608 p. Paperback $1.25.

1670 NATIONAL ADVISORY COMMISSION. *Report of the National Advisory Commission on Civil Disorders.* Washington, D.C., U.S. Government Printing Office, 1968. 425 p. $2.00.

1671 NATIONAL URBAN LEAGUE. *The Racial Gap, 1955-1965; 1965-1975 in Income, Unemployment, Education, Health and Housing,* by Sylvia Lauter. New York, 1967. 41 p.

1672 NEWBY, Idus A. *Challenge to the Court; Social Scientists and the Defense of Segregation, 1954-1966.* Baton Rouge, Louisiana State University Press, 1967. 239 p. $6.50.

1673 OLSEN, Jack. *Black Athletes in Revolt; the Myth of Integration in American Sports.* New York, Time-Life Books, 1968. $4.95.

1674 OSOFSKY, Gilbert. *The Burden of Race; a Documentary History of Negro-White Relations in America.* New York, Harper & Row, 1967. $7.95. 654 p.

1675 PECK, James. *Freedom Ride.* New York, Simon and Schuster, 1962. 160 p. Out of print.

1676 POOLE, Elijah (Elijah Muhammed). *Message to the Black Man in America.* Chicago, Muhammad Mosque of Islam No. 2, 1965. 355 p.

1677 PROCTOR, Samuel D. *The Young Negro in America, 1960-1980.* New York, Association Press, 1966. 160 p. $3.95.

1678 PROUDFOOT, Merrill. *Diary of a Sit-in.* Chapel Hill, University of North Carolina Press, 1962. 204 p. $5.00. Paperback $1.95. (New Haven, Conn., College and University Press, 1964).

1679 RAPER, Arthur F. *The Tragedy of Lynching.* Chapel Hill, University of North Carolina Press, 1933. 499 p.

1680 REUTER, Edward Byron. *The American Race Problem.* Rev. ed. New York, Thomas Y. Crowell Company, 1938. Out of print.

1681 ROMAN, Charles Victor. *A Knowledge of History is Conducive to Racial Solidarity, and Other Writings.* Nashville, Sunday-School Union Print, 1911. 54 p. Out of print.

1682 ROSE, Peter I. *The Subject is Race; Traditional Ideologies and the Teaching of Race Relations.* New York, Oxford University Press, 1968. 181 p. $4.95.

1683 RUDWICK, Elliott M. *W.E.B. DuBois, Propagandist of the Negro Protest.* With a New Preface by Louis R. Harlan and an Epilogue by the Author. New York, Atheneum, 1968. 390 p. $3.25. (Studies in American Negro Life, August Meier, General Editor). Paperback.

1684 RUDWICK, Elliott M. *Race Riot at East St. Louis, July 2, 1917.* Foreword by Oscar Handlin. Carbondale, Southern Illinois University Press, 1964. 300 p. $6.00.

1685 SALZMAN, Jack, ed. *Years of Protest.* New York, Pegasus, 1967. 488 p. $7.50.

1686 SAUTER, Van Gordon and Burleigh Hines. *Nightmare in Detroit.* Chicago, Henry Regnery Co., 1968. $4.95.

1687 SCHREIBER, Daniel, ed. *Profile of the School Dropout. A Reader of America's Major Educational Problem.* New York, Random House, 1968. $6.95. Paperback (Vintage Books) $1.95.

1688 SELBY, John. *Beyond Civil Rights.* Cleveland, World Pub. Co., 1965. 216 p. $6.95.

1689 SHOGAN, Robert and Tom Craig. *The Detroit Race Riot; a Study in Violence.* Philadelphia, Chilton Books, 1964. 199 p. $4.25.

1690 SILVER, James W. *Mississippi; the Closed Society.* New York, Harcourt, Brace and World, Inc., 1963. 250 p. $4.95.

1691 SMITH, Ed. *Where to, Black Man.* Chicago, Quandrangle Books, 1967. 221 p. $4.95.

1692 SOBEL, Lester A., ed. *Civil Rights, 1960-66.* New York, Facts on File, 1967. 504 p. Paperback $3.95.

1693 SPEAR, Allan H. *Black Chicago; the Making of a Negro Ghetto, 1890-1920.* Chicago, The University of Chicago Press, 1967. 254 p. $7.50.

1694 STAHL, David and others, eds. *The Community and Racial Crisis.* New York, Practicing Law Institute, 1966. 364 p. $7.50.

1695 STERLING, Dorothy. *Tear Down the Walls; a History of the American Civil Rights Movement.* Garden City, New York, Doubleday & Co., 1958. 259 p. $4.95.

1696 STOKES, Anson Phelps. *Negro Status and Race Relations in the United States, 1911-1946.* New York, Phelps-Stokes Fund, 1948. 219 p.

1697 STONE, Chuck. *Tell it Like it is.* New York, Trident Press, 1968. 211 p. $4.95.

1698 TEMPLEN, Ralph T. *Democracy and Nonviolence: the Role of the Individual in World Crisis.* Foreword by A.J. Muste. Introduction by James Farmer. Boston, Mass., Porter Sargent, 1968. 336 p. $4.00.

1699 U.S. COMMISSION ON CIVIL RIGHTS. *Freedom to the Free; Century of Emancipation, 1863-1963.* Washington, D.C., U.S. Government Printing Office, 1963. 246 p. $1.00.

1700 VAN DEN BERGHE, Pierre L. *Race and Racism; a Comparative Perspective.* New York, Wiley, 1967. 169 p.

1701 WARREN, Robert Penn. *Who Speaks for the Negro.* New York, Random House, 1965. 454 p. $5.95. Paperback $1.95.

1702 WASKOW, Arthur I. *From Race Riot to Sit-in, 1919 and the 1960's; a Study in the Connections Between Conflict and Violence.* Garden City, N.Y., Doubleday, 1967. 380 p. Paperback $1.45.

1703 WESTIN, Alan F., ed. *Freedom Now! The Civil-Rights Struggle in America.* New York, Basic Books, 1964. 346 p. $6.95.

1704 WHITE, Walter. *How Far the Promised Land.* New York, Viking Press, 1955. 244 p. Out of print.

1705 WOODWARD, Comer Vann. *The Strange Career of Jim Crow.* 2d rev. ed. New York, Oxford University Press, 1966. 205 p. $4.50. Paperback $1.50.

1706 WRIGHT, Nathan. *Ready to Riot.* New York, Holt, Rinehart and Winston, 1968. 148 p. $4.95.

1707 WYNES, Charles E. *Race Relations in Virginia, 1870-1902.* Charlottesville, University of Virginia Press, 1961. 164 p. $5.00.

1708 YOUNG, Whitney M. *To Be Equal.* New York, McGraw-Hill, 1964. 254 p. Paperback $1.95.

1709 ZINN, Howard. *SNCC, the New Abolitionists.* Boston, Beacon Press, 1964. 246 p. $4.95. Paperback $1.95. See also nos. 53, 55.

## BLACK POWER AND THE NEGRO REVOLUTION

1710 BARBOUR, Floyd Barrington, comp. *The Black Power Revolt; a Collection of Essays.* Boston, P. Sargent, 1968. 287 p. $5.95. Paperback $2.95

1711 BARNDT, Joseph R. *Why Black Power?* New York, Friendship Press, 1968. Paperback $0.95.

1712 BENNETT, Lerone. *Black Power USA. The Human Side of Reconstruction, 1867-1877.* Chicago, Ill., Johnson Publishing Co., 1968. 401 p. $6.95. Illustrations. Paperback (Penguin Books, Inc., 1968) $1.45.

1713 *BLACK POWER: Value Revolution Toward Community and Peace.* Minnesota, The Catechetical Guild, St. Paul, Minnesota, 1968. 84 p. Paperback $0.75. Book suggests that the black revolution cuts across race, party, class and age boundaries. Included in the paperback is a history of Afro-American contributions to our 'melting-pot' culture, a bibliography, a poetry section by John Beecher. Interspersed throughout are photographs, cartoons and caligraphic quotes from Teilhard de Chardin, Marshall McLuhan and Peter Maurin, among others.

1714 CARMICHAEL, Stokely and Charles V. Hamilton. *Black Power; the Politics of Liberation in America.* New York, Random House, 1967. 198 p. $4.95. Paperback (Vintage), $1.95. "Integration is not only 'unrealistic' but it is in fact, despicable'."

1715 CHAMBERS, Bradford. *Chronicles of Negro Protest; a Background Book for Young People Documenting the History of Black Power.* New York, Parents Magazine Press, 1968. 319 p. $4.50.

1716 FAGER, Charles E. *White Reflections on Black Power.* Grand Rapids, Michigan, William B. Eerdmans Publishing Co., 1967. 118 p. $3.50.

1717 FOLEY, Eugene P. *The Achieving Ghetto.* Washington, D.C., National Press, Inc., 1968. 156 p. $4.95. Paperback $2.45.

1718 GRANT, Joanne, ed. *Black Protest; History, Documents and Analysis from 1619 to the Present.* Greenwich, Conn., Fawcett Premier Original, 1968. 512 p. $0.95.

1719 HOUGH, Joseph C. *Black Power and White Protestants; a Christian Response to the New Negro Pluralism.* New York, Oxford University Press, 1968. 228 p. $5.75. Paperback $1.75.

1720 KILLIAN, Lewis Martin. *The Impossible Revolution: Black Power and the American Dream.* New York, Random House, 1968. 198 p. $5.95.

1721 LESTER, Julius. *Look Out, Whitey! Black Power's Gon' Get Your Mama!* New York, Dial, 1968. 152 p. $3.95. "The author is a spokesman for the militant version of Black Power and Nationalism now associated with SNCC."

1722 LIGHTFOOT, Claude M. *Ghetto Rebellion to Black Liberation.* New York, International, 1968. 192 p. $5.95. Paperback $1.95. The author, a member of the Communist National Committee, summarizes the Communist lessons for blacks he learned after visits to African countries, Soviet Republics, Cuba and India.

1723 MUSE, Benjamin. *The American Negro Revolution: From Non-violence to Black Power, 1963-1967.* Bloomington, Ind., Indiana University Press, 1968. 352 p. $6.95.

1724 POWLEDGE, Fred. *Black Power, White Resistance; Notes on the New Civil War.* Cleveland, World Publishing Co., 1967. 282 p.

1725 SCHUCHTER, Arnold. *White Power/Black Freedom.* Boston, Beacon Press, 1968. $11.50. An experienced city planner discusses the black community goals — self-determination and decision making — and the white power structure in new urban institutions.

1726 SHAFFER, H.B. *Negro Power Struggle.* Washington, D.C., Editorial Research Reports, 1968. 18 p. $2.00.

1727 STONE, Chuck. *Black Political Power in America.* Indianapolis, Bobbs-Merrill Co., Inc., 1968. $8.95.

1728 WRIGHT, Nathan. *Black Power and Urban Unrest; Creative Possibilities.* New York, Hawthorn Books, Inc., 1967. 200 p. $4.95.

1729 WRIGHT, Nathan. *Let's Work Together.* New York, Hawthorn Books, Inc., 1968. 271 p. $4.95. Paperback $1.95. Summary of the concepts of Black Consciousness and Black Power. Author's "vision" is not the destruction of America, but the fulfillment of its ideals under the leadership of its creative black minority.

## SCIENCE

1730 MARYLAND, Morgan State College, Baltimore. *The Negro in Science,* by the Calloway Hall Editorial Committee: Julius H. Taylor, editor and others. Baltimore, Morgan State College Press, 1955. 192 p.

## SOCIAL CONDITIONS

### RELIGION AND THE CHURCH

1731 AHMANN, Matthew, and Margaret Roach, eds. *Church and the Urban Racial Crisis.* Techny, Ill., Divine World, 1967. 262 p. $2.95. "The major addresses and background papers prepared for the August 1967 convention of the National Catholic Conference for Interracial Justice held at Rockhurst College in Kansas City, Mo."

1732 BROTZ, Howard. *The Black Jews of Harlem; Negro Nationalism and the Dilemmas of Negro Leadership.* New York, Free Press of Glencoe, 1964. 144 p. Out of print.

1733 CLARK, Elmer Talmage. *The Small Sects in America.* New York, Abingdon-Cokesbury Press, 1949. 256 p.

1734 CLARK, Henry. *The Church and Residential Desegregation; a Case*

*Study of an Open Housing Covenant Campaign.* New Haven, College & University Press, 1965. 254 p. $5.00.

1735 DuBOIS, William Edward Burghardt. *The Negro Church; Report of a Social Study Made under the Direction of Atlanta University...*Atlanta, Atlanta University Press, 1903. 212 p.

1736 ESSIEN-UDOM, E.U. *Black Nationalism: a Search for an Identity in America.* Chicago, University of Chicago Press, 1962. 367 p. $7.50. Paperback (Dell Publishing Company, 1962). 448 p. $0.75. A serious study of the Black Muslim movement.

1737 FAUSET, Arthur Huff. *Black Gods of the Metropolis; Negro Religious Cults of the Urban North.* Philadelphia, University of Pennsylvania Press, London, H. Milford. Oxford University Press, 1944. 126 p. Plates, portraits.

1738 FELTON, Ralph Almon. *These My Brethren; a Study of 570 Negro Churches and 1542 Negro Homes in the Rural South.* Madison, New Jersey, Department of Rural Church, Drew Theological Seminary, 1950. 102 p.

1739 FOLEY, Albert S. *God's Men of Color: the Colored Catholic Priests of the United States, 1854-1954.* New York, Farrar, Straus and Company, 1955. 322 p. Out of print.

1740 FRAZIER, E. Franklin. *The Negro Church in America.* New York, Schocken Books, 1964 (c1963). 92 p. $3.50. Paperback $1.45.

1741 GILLARD, John Thomas. *The Catholic Church and the American Negro; Being an Investigation of the Past and Present Activities of the Catholic Church in Behalf of the 12,000,000 Negroes in the United States, with an Examination of the Difficulties which affect the Work of the Colored Missions.* Baltimore, St. Joseph's Society Press, 1929. 324 p. Illustrations.

1742 GRIER, Eunice and George. *Privately Developed Interracial Housing; an Analysis of Experience.* Special Research Report to the Commission on Race and Housing. Berkeley, University of California Press, 1960. 264 p.

1743 HAYNES, Leonard. *The Negro Community Within American Protestantism, 1619-1844.* Boston, Christopher Publishing House, 1953. 264 p. Out of print.

1744 JOHNSTON, Ruby F. *The Development of Negro Religion.* New York, Philosophical Library, 1954. 202 p. Out of print.

1745 JONES, Howard O. *Shall We Overcome? A Challenge to Negro and White Christians.* Westwood, New Jersey, F.H. Revell Co., 1966. 146 p.

1746 JORDAN, Lewis Garnett. *Negro Baptist History, U.S.A. 1750-1930.* Nashville, Sunday School Publishing Board, N.B.C., 1930. 394 p. Portraits.

1747 KELSEY, George. *Racism and the Christian Understanding of Man.* New York, Scribner, 1965. 178 p. $4.50. Paperback $2.95.

1748 KING, Martin Luther, Jr. *The Measure of a Man.* Philadelphia, Pilgrim Press Books, 1968. $2.95. "Memorial edition of the earliest book of meditations and prayers by Dr. King."

1749 KING, Martin Luther, Jr. *Strength to Love.* New York, Harper and Row, 1963. 146 p. $3.50. Paperback (Pocket Books) $0.75.

1750 LINCOLN, Charles Eric. *The Black Muslims in America.* Boston, Beacon Press, 1961. 276 p. $4.95. Paperback $1.95.

1751 MAYS, Benjamin E. *The Negro's God as Reflected in His Literature.* Lithographs by James L. Wells. Boston, Chapman & Grimes, Inc., 1938. 269 p.

1752 MAYS, Benjamin E. and Joseph W. Nicholson. *The Negro's Church.* New York, Institute of Social and Religious Research, 1933. 231 p. Out of print.

1753 McAFEE, Sara Jane Regulus. *History of the Woman's Missionary Society in the Colored Methodist Episcopal Church, Comprising its Founders, Organizations, Pathfinders, Subsequent Developments and Present Status.* Revised Edition. Phenix City, Ala., Phenix City Herald, 1945. 468 p. Illustrated.

1754 PAYNE, Daniel Alexander. *History of the African Methodist Church.* Edited by Rev. C.S. Smith. Nashville, Publishing House of the A.M.E. Sunday School Union, 1891. 502 p. Portraits. Out of print.

1755 PELT, Owen C. and Ralph L. Smith. *The Story of the National Baptists.* New York, Vantage Press, 1960. 272 p. $3.75.

1756 PIPES, William Harrison. *Say Amen, Brother: Old-time Negro Preaching; a Study in American Frustration.* New York, William-Frederick Press, 1951. 210 p.

1757 POOLE, Elijah (Elijah Muhammad). *Message to the Black Man in America.* Chicago, Muhammad Mosque of Islam no. 2, 1965. 355 p. $5.00.

1758 RICHARDSON, Harry Van Buren. *Dark Glory, a picture of the Church Among Negroes in the Rural South.* New York, Published for Home Missions Council of North America and Phelps-Stokes Fund by Friendship Press, 1947. 209 p.

1759 SINGLETON, George A. *The Romance of the African Methodist Episcopal Church.* New York, Exposition Press, 1952. 251 p.

1760 SMITH, Charles Spencer. *A History of the African Methodist Episcopal Church,* being a Volume Supplemental to a History of the African Methodist Episcopal Church by Daniel Alexander Payne, Chronicling the Principal Events in the Advance of the African Methodist Episcopal Church from 1856 to 1922. Philadelphia Book Concern of the A.M.E. Church, 1922. 570 p. Out of print.

1761 THURMAN, Howard. *Disciplines of the Spirit.* New York, Harper and Row, 128 p. $3.00.

1762 TYMS, James D. *The Rise of Religious Education Among Negro Baptists:* a Historical Case Study. New York, Exposition Press, 1965. 355 p. $5.00.

1763 WASHINGTON, Joseph R. *Black Religion: the Negro and Christianity in the United States.* Boston, Beacon Press, 1964. 308 p. $5.00. Paperback $2.45.

1764 WASHINGTON, Joseph R. *The Politics of God.* Boston, Beacon Press, 1967. 234 p. $5.95.

1765 WEATHERFORD, Willis D. *American Churches and the Negro.* Boston, Christopher Publishing House, 1957. 310 p. $3.50.

1766 *WHY I BELIEVE THERE IS A GOD; an Anthology of Inspirational Essays.* With an Introduction by Dr. Howard Thurman. Chicago, Johnson Publishing Company, 1965. 120 p. $3.95.

1767 WOODSON, Carter G. *History of the Negro Church.* Washington, D.C., The Associated Publishers, Inc., 1921. 330 p. $3.25.

1768 WRIGHT, Richard R. *The Bishops of the African Methodist Episcopal Church.* Nashville, Tennessee, A.M.E. Sunday School Union, 1963. 389 p. $4.50.

1769 *YEAR BOOK OF NEGRO CHURCHES, with Statistics and Records of Achievements of Negroes in the United States, 1935/36.* Wilberforce, Ohio, Printed at Wilberforce University, 1936.

**HOUSING**

1770 ABRAMS, Charles. *The City is the Frontier.* New York, Harper & Row, 1965. 394 p. $6.50. Paperback $1.95.

1771 ABRAMS, Charles. *Forbidden Neighbors: a Study of Prejudice in Housing.* New York, Harper and Bros., 1955. 404 p. $5.00.

1772 ABRAMS, Charles. *Race Bias in Housing.* Sponsored Jointly by the American Civil Liberties Union, National Association for the Advancement of Colored People (and) American Council on Race Relations. New York, 1947. 31 p. Housing, segregation, and real covenants.

1773 ABRAMS, Charles. *The Segregation Threat in Housing.* In: Straus, Nathan. *Two-thirds of a Nation.* New York, 1952. pp. 135-210.

1774 AMERICAN FRIENDS SERVICE COMMITTEE. *Equal Opportunity in Housing.* A Report to the President. AFSC Experience and Recommendations. Re: Executive Order 11063. Philadelphia, 1967. 44 p.

1775 AMERICAN FRIENDS SERVICE COMMITTEE. *Fair Housing Handbook; a Practical Manual for Those Who Are Working to Create and Maintain Exclusive Communities.* Philadelphia, 1964. 42 p.

1776 AMERICAN JEWISH CONGRESS. *Civil Rights in the United States in 1951; a Balance Sheet of Group Relations.* New York, American Jewish Congress and National Association for the Advancement of Colored People, 1952. 128 p. Housing: pp. 70-83.

1777 ARTER, Rhetta Marie. *WINS Pilot Preview; Report of an Action-Research Demonstration Project on the Progress of Achieving Equal Housing Opportunities Women's Integrating Neighborhood Services;*

*Sponsored by the Educational Foundation of National Council of Negro Women, Inc.* 1st ed. New York, Research and Action Associates, c1961. 202 p. Housing in the New York metropolitan area.

1778 AVINS, Alfred. *Open Occupancy vs. Forced Housing Under the Fourteenth Amendment; a Symposium on Anti-Discrimination Legislation, Freedom of Choice, and Property Rights in Housing.* New York, Bookmailer, 1963. 316 p.

1779 BRANDEIS UNIVERSITY, WALTHAM, MASS. Florence Heller Graduate School for Advanced Studies in Social Welfare. *The Middle-Income Negro Family Faces Urban Renewal* (by Lewis G. Watts and others). A Study of Families During the Rehabilitation of a Boston Neighborhood by the Research Center for the Department of Commerce and Development, Commonwealth of Massachusetts, (n.p.), 1964. 112 p.

1780 *BUSINESS AND THE URBAN CRISIS,* a McGraw-Hill Special Report: Housing. 1968. pp. 10-13. Brief informative statement of the key problems and suggested solution.

1781 CLARK, Dennis. *The Ghetto Game; Racial Conflicts in the City.* New York, Sheed and Ward, 1962. 245 p. 1 vol. $4.00.

1782 CLARK, Henry. *The Church and Residential Desegregation; a Case Study of an Open Housing Covenant Campaign.* New Haven, College & University Press, 1965. 254 p. $5.00.

1783 COMMISSION ON RACE AND HOUSING. *Where Shall We Live? Report. Conclusions from a Three-year Study of Racial Discrimination in Housing...* Berkeley and Los Angeles, University of California Press, 1958. 77 p.

1784 DENTON, John H. *Race and Property.* Berkeley, California, Diablo Press, 1964. 159 p.

1785 DEUTSCH, Morton and Mary Evans Collins. *Interracial Housing; a Psychological Evaluation of a Social Experiment.* Minneapolis, University of Minnesota Press, 1951. 173 p. Reprinted by Russell and Russell, N.Y., 1968.

1786 DUNCAN, Otis Dudley and Beverly. *The Negro Population of*

*Chicago; a Study of Residential Succession.* Chicago, University of Chicago Press, 1957. 367 p.

1787 FAIR HOUSING COUNCIL OF METROPOLITAN WASHINGTON. *Negro Military Servicemen and Racial Discrimination in Housing.* Washington, Metropolitan Housing Program of the American Friends Service Committee, 1966. 12 p.

1788 FOOTE, Nelson N. *Housing Choices and Housing Constraints.* New York, McGraw-Hill, 1960. 450 p. $12.50.

1789 GLAZER, Nathan and Davis McEntire, eds. *Studies in Housing & Minority Groups.* With an introduction by Nathan Glazer. Special Research Report to the Commission on Race and Housing. Berkeley, University of California Press, 1960. 228 p.

1790 GREER, Scott. *Urban Renewal and American Cities: the Dilemma of Democratic Intervention.* Indianapolis, Bobbs-Merrill, 1965. 201 p. $5.95.

1791 GRIER, Eunice S. and George. *Discrimination in Housing: a Handbook of Fact.* New York, Anti-Defamation League of B'nai B'rith, 1960. 67 p.

1792 GRIER, Eunice S. and George. *Privately Developed Interracial Housing: an Analysis of Experience.* Berkeley, University of California Press, 1960. 264 p. $6.00.

1793 GRIER, George and Eunice S. *Equality and Beyond: Housing Segregation and the Goals of the Great Society.* Published in Cooperation with the Anti-Defamation League of B'nai B'rith. Chicago, Quadrangle Books, 1966. 115 p. $3.50.

1794 JOHNSON, Philip A. *Call Me Neighbor, Call Me Friend.* Garden City, N.Y., Doubleday, 1965. 184 p. $4.95.

1795 JONES, William H. *The Housing of Negroes in Washington, D.C.: A Study in Human Ecology.* Washington, D.C., Howard University Press, 1929. 191 p. Out of print.

1796 KRAUS, Henry. *In the City was a Garden: a Housing Project Chronicle.* New York, Renaissance Press, 1951. 255 p. Negroes and housing in San Pedro, California.

1797 LAURENTI, Luigi. *Property Values and Race; Studies in Seven*

Cities. *Special Research Report to the Commission on Race and Housing* (prepared under the direction of Davis McEntire). Berkeley, University of California Press, 1960. 256 p. $6.00.

1798 LAWYERS GUILD REVIEW. *Integration in Housing.* New York, National Lawyers Guild (Special issue: Spring, 1958). 1958. 47 p.

1799 LONG, Herman Hodge and Charles S. Johnson. *People vs. Property; Race Restrictive Covenants in Housing.* Nashville, Fisk University Press, 1947. 107 p.

1800 McENTIRE, Davis. *Residence and Race; Final and Comprehensive Report to the Commission on Race and Housing.* Berkeley, University of California Press, 1960. 409 p. $6.00.

1801 METHODIST CHURCH (United States). Department of Research and Survey. *The Church in a Racially Changing Community,* By Robert L. Wilson and James H. Davis. New York, Abington Press, 1966. 159 p.

1802 MEYERSON, Martin. *Housing, People, and Cities.* New York, McGraw-Hill, 1962. 386 p. $7.50.

1803 MEYERSON, Martin and Edward C. Banfield. *Politics, Planning, and the Public Interest: the Case of Public Housing in Chicago.* Glencoe, Ill., Free Press, 1955. 353 p.

1804 NATIONAL COMMITTEE AGAINST DISCRIMINATION IN HOUSING. *The Impact of Housing Patterns on Job Opportunities.* New York, NCADH, c1968. Preliminary study concerned with the movement of jobs from city to suburb and the relationship between access to housing and employment opportunities.

1805 NATIONAL COMMITTEE AGAINST DISCRIMINATION IN HOUSING BROTHERHOOD-IN-ACTION HOUSING CON-FERENCE. New York, 1965. *Affirmative Action to Achieve Integration; a Report Based on the NCDH Brotherhood-in-Action Housing Conference.* New York, NCDH, 1966. 40 p.

1806 NEEDHAM, Maurice d'Arlan. *Negro Orleanian; Status and Stake in a City's Economy and Housing.* New Orleans, Tulane Publications, 1962. 278 p.

1807 NOE, Kaye Sizer. *The Fair Housing Movement: an Overview and a Case Study.* College Park, Md., 1965. 172 p. Discrimination in housing.

1808 NORTHWOOD, Lawrence K. *Urban Desegregation; Negro Pioneers and Their White Neighbors.* Seattle, University of Washington, 1965. 131 p. Out of print.

1809 PASCAL, Anthony H. *Economics of Housing Segregation.* Santa Monica, Calif., Rand Corp., 1965. 28 p.

1810 POTOMAC INSTITUTE, Washington, D.C. *The Federal Role in Equal Housing Opportunity: an Affirmative Program to Implement Executive Order 11063.* Prepared by Arthur J. Levin, Staff Director. Washington, 1964. 28 p.

1811 RAPKIN, Chester and William G. Grigsby. *The Demand for Housing in Racially Mixed Areas: A Study of the Nature of Neighborhood Change.* Special Research Report to the Commission on Race and Housing in the Philadelphia Redevelopment Authority. Berkeley, University of California Press, 1960. 177 p.

1812 REID, Margaret G. *Housing and Income.* Chicago, University of Chicago Press, 1962. 415 p. $7.50.

1813 ROSEN, Harry M. *But Not Next Door.* New York, I. Oblensky, 1962. 175 p. Out of print.

1814 SCHORR, Alvin Louis. *Slums and Social Insecurity, an Appraisal of the Effectiveness of Housing Policies in Helping to Eliminate Poverty in the United States.* Washington, U.S. Government Printing Office, 1963. 168 p.

1815 *SOCIAL ACTION; Freedom of Residence.* In *Social Action,* Vol. 29, No. 9. May 1963. 36 p. (Entire issue on housing).

1816 *SOCIAL ACTION: Housing Without Racial Barrier.* In *Social Action,* Vol. 24, No. 3, Nov. 1957. 31 p. (Entire issue on housing).

1817 STERNLIEB, George. *The Tenement Landlord.* New Brunswick, N.J., Urban Studies Center, Rutgers, The State University, 1966. 269 p. (U.S. Housing and Urban Development. Demonstration Grant Program).

1818 TAEUBER, Karl E. and Alma F. *Negroes in Cities; Residential Segregation and Neighborhood Change.* Chicago, Aldine Pub. Co., 1965. 284 p. $9.75. (Population Research and Training Center Monographs).

1819 TILLMAN, James A. *Not by Prayer Alone; a Report on the Greater Minneapolis Interfaith Fair Housing Program*. Philadelphia, United Church Press, 1964. 223 p.

1820 TILLY, Charles, Wagner D. Jackson and Barry Kay. *Race and Residence in Wilmington, Delaware*. New York, Bureau of Publications, Teachers College, Columbia University, 1965. 145 p.

1821 U.S. BUREAU OF LABOR STATISTICS. *BLS Report No. 332*. Section V. Housing. 8 p. Data for 1966; a joint report of the Bureau of the Census and Bureau of Labor Statistics.

1822 U.S. COMMISSION ON CIVIL RIGHTS. *Civil Rights U.S.A.; Housing in Washington, D.C.* Washington, D.C., 1962. 45 p.

1823 U.S. COMMISSION ON CIVIL RIGHTS. *Housing in Washington; Hearings...* Washington, D.C., U.S. Government Printing Office, 1962. 478 p. Illustrations.

1824 U.S. COMMISSION ON CIVIL RIGHTS. *...One Nation Under God, Indivisible, with Liberty and Justice for All*. An Abridgment of the Report of the United States Commission on Civil Rights, 1959. Washington, D.C., U.S. Government Printing Office, 1959. 201 p.

1825 U.S. CONGRESS. Senate. Committee on Banking and Currency. *Fair Housing Act of 1967*. Hearings Before the Subcommittee on Housing and Urban Affairs of the United States Senate, 19th Cong., 1st Sess. on S. 1358. S. 2114, and S. 2280 Relating to Civil Rights and Housing. Washington, D.C., U.S. Government Printing Office, 1967. 508 p.

1826 U.S. HOUSING AND HOME FINANCE AGENCY. Intergroup Relations Service. *Fair Housing Laws: Summaries and Text of State and Municipal Laws*. Washington, D.C., Housing and Home Finance Agency Office of the Administrator; for sale by the Superintendent of Documents, U.S. Government Printing Office, 1965. 369 p.

1827 U.S. HOUSING AND HOME FINANCE AGENCY. Office of Program Policy. *Equal Opportunity in Housing; a Series of Case Studies* (prepared by) Office of Program Policy and Intergroup Relations Service. Washington, D.C., U.S. Government Printing Office, 1964. 89 p.

1828 U.S. HOUSING AND HOME FINANCE AGENCY. Office of Program Policy. *Our Non-White Population and Its Housing: the Changes Between 1950 and 1960.* Washington, D.C., U.S. Government Printing Office, 1963. 104 p. Tables.

1829 U.S. HOUSING AND HOME FINANCE AGENCY. Office of Program Policy. *Senior Citizens and How They Live; an Analysis of 1960 Census Data.* (Report prepared by the Statistical Reports Staff) Office of Program Policy. Washington, D.C., Housing and Home Finance Agency, Office of the Administrator, 1962-1963. 2 v.

1830 VOSE, Clement E. *Caucasians Only; the Supreme Court, the NAACP, and the Restrictive Covenant Cases.* Berkeley, University of California Press, 1959. 296 p. $6.00.

1831 WEAVER, Robert Clifton. *Dilemmas of Urban America.* Cambridge, Mass., Harvard University Press, 1965. 138 p. $3.50. Paperback $1.95. (New York, Atheneum Publishers, 1967).

1832 WEAVER, Robert Clifton. *Negro Ghetto.* New York, Russell & Russell Publishers, 1948. 404 p. $10.00.

1833 WEAVER, Robert Clifton. *The Urban Complex; Human Values in Urban Life.* Garden City, N.Y., Doubleday, 1964. 297 p. $4.95. Paperback $1.25.

1834 WELLER, Charles Frederick. *Neglected Neighbors; Stories of Life in the Alleys, Tenements and Shanties of the National Capital.* With a chapter by Eugenia Winston Weller. Philadelphia, John C. Winston Co., 1909. 342 p.

1835 WOLFF, Reinhold Paul. *Negro Housing in the Miami Area; Effects of the Postwar Building Boom.* Miami, Bureau of Business and Economic Research, University of Miami, 1951. 22 p. Illus., charts, map.

## MEDICINE AND HEALTH

1836 BENT, Michael J. and Ellen F. Greene. *Rural Negro Health. A Report on a Five-Year Experiment in Health in Tennessee for the Joint Health Education Committee.* Nashville, Tenn., Julius Rosenwald Fund, 1937. 83 p.

1837 CARR, Malcolm Wallace. *Dentistry; an Agency of Health Service.* New York, The Commonwealth Fund, 1946. 219 p.

1838 CHATMAN, J.A. *The Lone Star State Medical, Dental, and Pharmaceutical History.* Lubbock, Texas, Lone Star State Medical Association, 1959. 176 p. Pictorial.

1839 COBB, William Montague. *The First Negro Medical Society; a History of the Medico-Chirurgical Society of the District of Columbia, 1884-1939.* Washington, D.C., The Associated Publishers, Inc., 1939. 159 p.

1840 COBB, William Montague. *Medical Care and the Plight of the Negro.* New York, National Association for the Advancement of Colored People, 1947. 38 p.

1841 COBB, William Montague. *Progress and Portents for the Negro in Medicine.* New York, National Association for the Advancement of Colored People, 1948. 53 p.

1842 COGAN, Lee. *Negroes for Medicine.* Baltimore, Johns Hopkins Press, 1968. $4.95.

1843 CORNELY, Paul B. *Administration of Health Education and Health Supervision in Negro Colleges.* Reprinted from American Journal of Public Health, vol. 26, no. 9, Sept 1936. pp. 888-96.

1844 CORNELY, Paul B. and Stanley K. Bigman. *Cultural Considerations in Changing Health Attitudes.* Washington, D.C., U.S. Department of Health, Education, and Welfare, 1961. 3 vols.

1845 CORWIN, Edward Henry Lewinski and Gertrude E. Sturges. *Opportunities for the Medical Education of Negroes.* With an Introduction by Dr. Walter L. Niles and a Foreword by Walter White. New York, C. Scribner's Sons, 1936. 293 p.

1846 DuBOIS, William Edward Burghardt, ed. *The Health and Physique of the Negro American.* Report of a Social Study Made Under the Direction of Atlanta University; together with the Proceedings of the Eleventh Conference for the Study of the Negro Problems, held at Atlanta University, on May 29th, 1906. Atlanta, Ga., Atlanta University Press, 1906. 112 p.

1847 DUMMETT, Clifton Orrin. *The Growth and Development of the Negro in Dentistry in the United States.* National Dental Association, 1952. 124 p.

1848 GAFAFER, William McKinley, and C.T. Messner. *Results of a Dental Examination of 1,908 White and Colored Males at the Ohio State Reformatory.* Washington, D.C., U.S. Government Printing Office, 1936. 12 p.

1849 GLAZIER, Harlan E. *Keep 'em Alive; They're Useful; a Few Peeks and Pecks at Health Conditions for Negroes in the Capital of the Nation.* Washington, D.C., Inter-Racial Committee of the District of Columbia, n.d. 8 p.

1850 HAMPTON, VA. Normal and Agricultural Institute. *Patent Medicine and the Negro.* Issues for Teachers by the Nature Study Bureau. Hampton, Virginia, The Press of the Hampton Normal and Agricultural Institute, 1909. 18 p.

1851 HOLLAND, Jerome H., and William A. Gaines. *An Appraisal of the Health of the Delaware Negro, 1916-1955.* Dover, Del., Delaware State College Social Research Institute, 1958. 104 p. Out of print. Good statistical source. Bibliography excellent.

1852 HOWARD UNIVERSITY, Washington D.C. Center for Youth and Community Studies. *Health Aide Training Curriculum.* Washington, D.C., 1964. 14 p. (Its Training Reports, C.S. No. 5).

1853 HOWARD UNIVERSITY, Washington, D.C. College of Medicine. *Centennial Conference on the Health Status of the Negro Today and in the Future.* Sponsored by the Centennial Program Committee and the Department of Preventive Medicine and Public Health, Howard University, Washington, D.C., March 13-14, 1967. (n.p.) 1967. 91 p. 8 leaves.

1854 *THE JOURNAL OF NEGRO EDUCATION. The Health Status and Health Education of Negroes in the United States.* The Yearbook Number, XVIII. Washington, D.C., Published for the Bureau of Educational Research, Howard University, by the Howard University Press, Summer 1949. pp. 197-443.

1855 JULIUS ROSENWALD FUND. *Child Health Problems.* National Conference on Fundamental Problems in the Education of Negroes. Nashville, Julius Rosenwald Fund, 1934. 24 p.

1856 KENNEY, John Andrew. *The Negro in Medicine.* Nashville, Tennessee, Meharry Medical College, 1912. 60 p.

1857 LYNK, Miles Vandahurst. *Sixty Years of Medicine; or, The Life and Times of Dr. Miles V. Lynk, an Autobiography.* Memphis, Twentieth Century Press, 1951. 125 p.

1858 MANHATTAN MEDICAL SOCIETY. New York City. *Past, Present and Future Activities of the Manhattan Medical Society. A Brief Review of Major Events and a Forecast.* Approved and Adopted by the Society at the Regular Meeting on Oct. 2, 1935. 53 p.

1859 MAUND, Alfred. *The Untouchables.* New Orleans, Southern Conference Educational Fund, 1952. Unpaged. Negroes' health and hygiene.

1860 MORAIS, Herbert M. *The History of the Negro in Medicine.* New York, Publishers Company, 1967. 317 p. (International Library of Negro Life and History).

1861 NATHAN, Winfred Bertram. *Health Conditions in North Harlem, 1923-1927,* by Winfred B. Nathan, an abstract by Mary V. Dempsey. New York, National Tuberculosis Association, 1932. 68 p. (National Tuberculosis Association, Social Research Series No. 2).

1862 NATIONAL MEDICAL FELLOWSHIPS, INC. *Negroes in Medicine.* Chicago, National Medical Fellowships, Inc., 1946. 44 p.

1863 NATIONAL MEDICAL FELLOWSHIPS, INC. *New Opportunities for Negroes in Medicine.* Chicago, National Medical Fellowships, Inc., 1962. 34 p.

1864 NATIONAL TUBERCULOSIS ASSOCIATION. *Report of the Committee on Tuberculosis Among Negroes. A Five-Year Study and What it Has Accomplished.* New York, National Tuberculosis Association, 1937. 77 p.

1865 PLANNED PARENTHOOD FEDERATION OF AMERICA. Division of Negro Services. *Better Health for 13,000,000;* The Results of a Two-Year Experiment to Demonstrate That an Often Neglected but Fundamental Phase of Preventive Medicine Can be Made a Profitable Part of Every Public Health Program. New York, The Federation, 1943. 30 p.

1866 POSTELL, William Dosite. *The Health of Slaves on Southern Plantations.* Baton Rouge, Louisiana State University Press, 1951. 231 p.

1867 REITZES, Dietrich C. *Negroes and Medicine.* Cambridge, Published for the Commonwealth Fund by Harvard University Press, 1958. 400 p.

1868 ROBERT T. FREEMAN DENTAL SOCIETY. *50th Anniversary 1900-1950.* Washington, D.C., November 24-26, 1950. Washington, D.C., Robert T. Freeman Dental Society, 1950. 58 p. Portraits.

1869 ROMAN, Charles Victor. *Meharry Medical College, a History.* Nashville, Sunday School Publishing Board of the National Baptists Convention, 1934. 224 p.

1870 SECOND REGIONAL CONFERENCE OF COLLEGE HEALTH WORKERS. *Health Problems in the Negro Colleges.* Proceedings of the Second Regional Conference of College Health Workers. New York, National Tuberculosis Association, 1941. 78 p.

1871 SPENCER, Gerald Arthur. *Cosmetology in the Negro: a Guide to its Problems.* New York, The Arlain Printing Co., 1944. pp. 9-127.

1872 SPENCER, Gerald Arthur. *Medical Symphony; a Study of the Contributions of the Negro to Medical Progress in New York.* New York, 1947. 120 p.

1873 STEWARD, S. Maria. *Women in Medicine; a Paper Read before the National Association of Colored Women's Clubs at Wilberforce, Ohio, August 6, 1914.* Wilberforce, Ohio, S. Maria Steward. 1914. 24 p.

1874 *STUDIES ON TUBERCULOSIS.* Baltimore, The Johns Hopkins Press, 1941. 198 p. Contains numerous articles relating to the spread of tuberculosis in Negro families of Jamaica; a survey of tuberculosis infection in a rural area of east Alabama; and the fate of persons exposed to tuberculosis in white and Negro families in a rural area of east Alabama.

1875 TAGGART, Paul J. *Medical Facilities for the Colored in the District of Columbia.* Wilmington, Delaware, Press of William N. Cann, Inc., 1940. 55 p.

1876 WORK, Monroe Nathan. *The South and the Conservation of Negro Health.* Tuskegee Institute, Alabama, Tuskegee Institute, (n.d.) 11 p.

# SOCIAL CONDITIONS

## CRIME

1877 BAIN, Graham C.B. *Crime, the American Negro and the Urban Native in South Africa.* Pretoria, South Africa, The Carnegie Corporation Visitors' Grants Committee, 1938. 67 p.

1878 BONGER, Willem Adrian. *Race and Crime.* New York, Columbia University Press, 1943. 130 p.

1879 CHAMBERLAIN, Bernard Peyton. *The Negro and Crime in Virginia.* Charlottesville, University of Virginia, 1936. 132 p.

1880 COLLINS, Winfield Hazlitt. *The Truth About Lynching and the Negro in the South, in which the Author Pleads That the South Be Made Safe for the White Race.* New York, The Neal Publishing Company, 1918. 163 p.

1881 CURRY, J.E. and Glen D. King. *Race Tensions and the Police.* Springfield, Ill., Thomas, 1962. 137 p.

1882 DuBOIS, William Edward Burghardt. *Some Notes on Negro Crime, Particularly in Georgia.* Atlanta, Ga., The Atlanta University Press, 1957. 209 p.

1883 KEPHART, William M. *Racial Factors and Urban Law Enforcement.* Philadelphia, University of Pennsylvania Press, 1957. 209 p.

1884 LEMERT, Edwin McCarthy and Judy Roseberg. *The Administration of Justice to Minority Groups in Los Angeles County.* Berkeley, University of California Press, 1948. 27 p.

1885 LIGHTFOOT, Robert Mitchell. *Negro Crime in a Small Urban Community.* Charlottesville, University of Virginia, 1934. 85 p.

1886 McCORD, Charles Harvey. *The American Negro As a Dependent, Defective and Delinquent.* Nashville, Press of Benson Printing Company, 1914. 342 p.

1887 McCORMICK, Ken. *Spring: The Release of Willie Calloway.* New York, St. Martins, 1964.

1888 McGUIRE, Hunter, and G. Frank Lydston. *Sexual Crimes Among the Southern Negroes.* Louisville, Renz and Henry, n.d., 26 p.

1889 SMITH, D.B. *Two Years in the Slave Pen of Iowa.* Kansas City, H.H. Farey and Co., 1885. 205 p.

1890 SPIRER, Jesse. *Negro Crime*. Baltimore, Maryland, The Johns Hopkins Press, 1940. 64 p.

1891 TOWLER, Juby E. *The Police Role in Racial Conflicts*. Springfield, Ill., Charles C. Thomas, 1965. 119 p. $5.75. Handbook on the use of law as an instrument of repression.

1892 U.S. COMMISSION ON CIVIL RIGHTS. *Law Enforcement: a Report on Equal Protection in the South*. Washington, D.C., U.S. Government Printing Office, 1965. 188 p.

1893 WILCOX, Walter Francis. *Negro Criminality*. Boston, G.H. Ellis, 1899. 25 p.

## SPORTS AND RECREATION

1894 ADAMS, Caswell, ed. *Great American Sports Stories*. New York, Stamford House, 1947. 304 p. Includes Negro athletes.

1895 ARMSTRONG, Henry. *Gloves, Glory and God, an Autobiography*. Westwood, N.J., Revel, 1956. 256 p. $2.95. Out of print.

1896 ASHE, Arthur. *Advantage Ashe*. By Arthur Ashe as told to Clifford George Gewecke, Jr. New York, Coward-McCann, Inc., 1967. 192 p. $4.95.

1897 BASSEY, Hogan. *Bassey on Boxing*, by the Former World Featherweight Champion. London, New York, Nelson, 1963. 127 p. $2.50. Out of print.

1898 BONTEMPS, Arna Wendell. *Famous Negro Athletes*. New York, Dodd, Mead, 1964. 155 p. Short biographies.

1899 BROWN, James N. "Jimmy." *Off My Chest*, by Jimmy Brown, with Myron Cope. Garden City, New York, Doubleday, 1964. 230 p. $4.95. Out of print. The former fullback of the Cleveland Browns tells of his life as a professional and his private life.

1900 CAMPANELLA, Roy. *It's Good to be Alive*. Boston, Little, Brown, 1959. 306 p. $5.00

1901 COZENS, Frederick Warren and Florence Scovil Stumpf. *Sports in American Life*. Chicago, University of Chicago Press, 1953. 366 p. Out of print.

1902 DALEY, Arthur. *Times at Bat, a Half Century of Baseball.* New York, Random House, 1950. 306 p.

1903 DIXON, George. *A Lesson in Boxing, by George Dixon, Champion Featherweight of the World.* n.p., 1893. 15 p. Out of print.

1904 DURANT, John, and Edward Rice. *Come Out Fighting.* New York, Essential Books, Duel, Sloan, and Pearce, 1946. 245 p. Out of print.

1905 DURANT, John. *The Heavyweight Champions.* Foreword by P.F. Eagan. New York, Hastings House, 1960. 150 p. Out of print.

1906 DURANT, John, and Otto Bettman. *Pictorial History of American Sports From Colonial Times to the Present.* 2d rev. ed. New York, A.S. Barnes, 1962. 340 p.

1907 ESQUIRE. *Great Men and Moments in Sports.* New York, Harper and Brothers, 1962. 252 p. "Jersey" Joe Walcott, pp. 3-4. Joe Louis, pp. 12-18.

1908 FARR, Finis. *Black Champion: the Life and Times of Jack Johnson.* New York, Charles Scribner's Sons, 1964. 245 p. $4.95. Out of print.

1909 FLEISCHER, Nathaniel S. *Black Dynamite, the Story of the Negro in the Prize Ring From 1782 to 1938.* With numerous illustrations. New York, C.J. O'Brien, 1938. 4 vols.

1910 FLEISCHER, Nathaniel S. *The Heavyweight Championship, an Informal History of Heavyweight Boxing From 1719 to the Present Day.* New York, Putnam, 1949. 303 p. $4.50

1911 FLEISCHER, Nathaniel S., ed. *Nat Fleischer's All-Time Ring Record Book.* Norwalk, Conn., O'Brien Suburban Press, 1941. 316 p.

1912 FLEISCHER, Nathaniel S., and Sam Andre. *A Pictorial History of Boxing.* New York, Citadel, 1959. 316 p.

1913 FLETCHER, Tom. *One Hundred Years of the Negro in Show Business: The Tom Fletcher Story.* New York, Burdge & Co., Ltd., 1954. 337 p.

1914 GIBSON, Althea. *I Always Wanted to be Somebody.* New York, Harper, 1958. 176 p. Illustrations.

1915 GOLDING, Louis. *The Bare-Knuckle Breed.* New York, Barnes, 1954. 231 p.

1916 HENDERSON, Edwin B., and William A. Joiner, eds. *Inter-Scholastic Athletic Association of Middle Atlantic States.* New York, American Sports Publishing Co., 1911. 137 p. Illustrations. An illustrated handbook on Negro athletes and athletics on the Eastern Seaboard.

1917 HENDERSON, Edwin Bancroft. *The Negro in Sports.* New rev. ed. Washington, D.C., The Associated Publishers, Inc., 1949. 507 p. $4.00

1918 HIRSHBERG, Albert, and Joe McKenney. *Famous American Athletes of Today.* Boston, Page, 1947. 382 p.

1919 HOWARD, Elston. *Catching.* New York, Viking, 1966. 88 p. $2.95.

1920 JACKSON, Edward L. *Leisure-Time Activities of Negro Men, Ages Forty-Five Through Fifty-four.* Ann Arbor, University Microfilms, 1956. 171 p.

1921 JOHNSON, Jack. *Jack Johnson in the Ring and Out.* With introductory articles by "Tad," Ed W. Smith, Damon Runyon, and Mrs. Jack Johnson, special drawings by Edwin William Krauter. Chicago, National Sports Publishing Co., 1927. 259 p. $2.50. Out of print.

1922 JOHNSTON, Alexander. *Ten—and Out! The Complete Story of the Prize Ring in America.* With a Foreword by Jack Dempsey. Rev. and enl. ed. New York, Washburn, 1936. 371 p.

1923 KAESE, Harold. *Famous American Athletes of Today,* Sixth series by Harold Kaese and others. Foreword by William Bingham. Boston, Page, 1939. 407 p.

1924 KIERAN, John, and Arthur Daley. *The Story of the Olympic Games, 776 B.C.-1948 A.D.* Philadelphia, Lippincott, 1948. 406 p.

1925 LIEBLING, Abbott Joseph. *The Sweet Science.* New York, Viking, 1956. 306 p. On boxing.

1926 LISS, Howard. *The Willie Mays Album.* New York, Hawthorn Books, Inc., Publishers, 1966. 63 p. $2.95. Illustrations.

1927 LOUIS, Joe. *How to Box.* Edited by Edward J. Mallory. Philadelphia, David McKay Company, 1948. 64 p. $2.00. Illustrations.
Out of print.

1928 LOUIS, Joe. *The Joe Louis Story.* Written with the editorial aid of
Chester L. Washington and Haskell Cohen. New York, Grosset and
Dunlap, 1953. 197 p. Out of print.

1929 MANN, Arthur William. *Branch Rickey, American in Action.*
Boston, Houghton Mifflin, 1957. 312 p.

1930 MANN, Arthur William. *The Jackie Robinson Story.* New York,
Grosset, 1951. 120 p. $1.95.

1931 MARTIN, Fletcher, comp. and ed. *Our Great Americans, the Negro
Contribution to American Progress.* Chicago, 1953. 96 p.

1932 MAYS, Willie, and Charles Einstein. *Born to Play.* New York, G.P.
Putnam, 1955. 168 p. $3.29.

1933 MAYS, Willie. *My Secrets of Playing Baseball.* With Howard Liss.
Photographs by David Sutton. New York, Viking Press, 1967. 89 p.
$4.95. Illustrations.

1934 MAYS, Willie. *Willie Mays: My Life In and Out of Baseball,* as told
to Charles Einstein. New York, E.P. Dutton, 1966. 320 p. $4.95.
Illustrations.

1935 MEANY, Thomas. *Baseball's Greatest Players.* With a Foreword by
Ford C. Frick. New York, Grosset, 1953. 295 p.

1936 MENKS, Frank Grant, comp. *All-Sports Record Book.* New York,
Eastern Distributing Corp., 19-. v.

1937 MILLER, Margery. *Joe Louis: American.* New York, Hill and Wang,
1961. 198 p. $3.00.

1938 MOKRAY, William G. *Basketball Stars of 1961.* New York,
Pyramid, 1960. 160 p.

1939 MOORE, Archie. *The Archie Moore Story.* New York, McGraw-Hill
Book Company, Inc., 1960. 240 p. $4.95. Out of print.

1940 NEWCOMBE, Jack. *Floyd Patterson, Heavyweight King.* New York,

Bartholomew, 1961. 159 p. $0.60. Out of print.

1941 OLSEN, Jack. *The Black Athlete— A Shameful Story. Sports Illustrated,* 5 parts, July 1, 8, 15, 22, 29, 1968. 55 p. total. Illustrations. Very valuable, topical references.

1942 OLSEN, Jack. *Black Athletes in Revolt: the Myth of Integration in American Sport.* New York, Time-Life Books, 1968. 200 p. $4.95. "Based largely on a five-part series assigned by *Sports Illustrated, Black Athletes in Revolt* explodes the myth that American sports, professional and amateur, are truly integrated. The fact is, says author Jack Olsen, a senior editor of the magazine, the Negro athlete is discriminated against almost everywhere."

1943 OLSEN, Jack. *Black is Best; the Riddle of Cassius Clay.* New York, G.P. Putnam, 1967. 255 p. $4.95.

1944 PAIGE, Leroy, and David Lipman. *Maybe I'll Pitch Forever; a Great Baseball Player Tells the Hilarious Story Behind the Legend.* Garden City, New York, Doubleday, 1962. 285 p. $4.95.

1945 PATTERSON, Floyd. *Victory Over Myself.* With Milton Gross. New York, B. Geis Associates; Distributed by Random House, 1962. 244 p. $3.95. Paperback (Scholastic Books Service, 1962). $0.50. Floyd Patterson tells the story of his rise from a childhood of poverty, truancy, and petty thievery to his position as world heavyweight boxing champion.

1946 PAYNE, Effietee Martin. *Sport and Dance Films, a Descriptive Catalog of Selected 16 mm Films on Sports, Dance, and Recreation. With Appraisals, Purchase and Rental Sources.* New York, Educational Film Library Association, 1956. 125 p.

1947 PETERSON, Frank Loris. *Climbing High Mountains.* Illustrated by Harry Baerg. Washington, Review & Herald, 1962. 144 p. Out of print. Fascinating story. Good photos.

1948 POWERS, James Joseph Aloysius. *Baseball Personalities, the Most Colorful Figures of All Time.* New York, R. Field, 1949. 320 p. $3.00.

1949 RICE, Grantland. *The Tumult and the Shouting. My Life in Sport.* New York, Barnes, 1954. 368 p.

1950 ROBINSON, John Roosevelt, Charles Dexter, ed. *Baseball Has Done It.* Dexter. Philadelphia, J.B. Lippincott, 1964. 216 p. $3.50.

1951 ROBINSON, John Roosevelt. *Breakthrough to the Big League,* the Story of Jackie Robinson and Alfred Duckett. New York, Harper and Row, 1965. 178 p. $3.50.

1952 ROBINSON, John Roosevelt. *Jackie Robinson — My Own Story as told by Jackie Robinson to Wendell Smith of the Pittsburgh Courier and the Chicago Herald American.* New York, Greenberg Publishers, 1948. 170 p. $2.00. Out of print.

1953 ROBINSON, Louie. *Arthur Ashe, Tennis Champion.* 1st ed. Garden City, N.Y., Doubleday, 1967. 136 p. $2.95.

1954 ROEDER, Bill. *Jackie Robinson.* New York, A.S. Barnes & Co., 1950. 183 p. Photographs.

1955 ROWAN, Carl Thomas. *Wait Till Next Year; the Life of Jackie Robinson,* by Carl T. Rowan with Jackie Robinson. New York, Random House, 1960. 339 p. $4.95. Out of print. Biography of Jackie Robinson, first Negro in major league baseball, which traces his career in baseball to his success as a business executive.

1956 RUSSELL, William as told to William McSweeny. *Go Up for Glory.* New York, Coward-McCann, 1966. 217 p. $5.00.

1957 SATURDAY EVENING POST. *Sport U.S.A.: the Best From the Saturday Evening Post.* Edited by Harry T. Paxton. New York, Thomas Nelson and Sons, 1961. 463 p. Illustrations. "The truth about the Jackie Robinson case," pp. 381-91.

1958 SMITH, Robert Miller. *Baseball.* New York, Simon and Schuster, 1947. 362 p. Illustrations. Article on Negro — "Everytime I Wheel About," pp. 317-32.

1959 TUNNELL, Emlen with Bill Gleason. *Footsteps of a Giant.* Garden City, New York, Doubleday, 1966. 238 p. $4.95.

1960 WILLS, Maury, as told to Steve Gardner. *It Pays to Steal.* Englewood Cliffs, New Jersey, Prentice-Hall, Inc., 1963. 186 p. $3.95.

1961 YOUNG, Andrew Sturgeon Nash. *Great Negro Baseball Stars and*

*How They Made the Major Leagues.* New York, A.S. Barnes and Company, 1953. 248 p. $2.50. Out of print.

1962 YOUNG, Andrew Sturgeon Nash. *Negro Firsts in Sports.* Chicago, Johnson Publishing Company, 1963. 301 p. $4.00.

1963 YOUNG, Andrew Sturgeon Nash. *Sonny Liston: the Champ Nobody Wanted.* Chicago, Johnson Publishing Company, 1963. 224 p. $3.95. Paperback $0.95.

1964 ZIMMERMAN, Paul. *The Los Angeles Dodgers.* Preface by Walter Alston. Introduction by Mayor Norris Paulson. New York, Coward-McCann, Inc., 1960. 221 p. $3.95.

1965 ZINKOFF, Dave, with Edgar Williams. *Around the World With the Harlem Globetrotters.* Foreword by Abe Saperstein. Philadelphia, Macrae Smith Company, 1953. 218 p. $2.95. Illustrations. Out of print.

## CURRENT PERIODICALS

1966 *BLACK DIALOGUE, A Black Magazine for Black People.* 642 Laguna Street, San Francisco, California. Quarterly. $1.75.

1967 *BLACK THEATRE.* The New Lafayette Theatre, 200 W. 135th Street. New York, 10030. $1.50 per year. Six times a year.

1968 *CLA JOURNAL.* Official Publication of The College Language Association, Morgan State College, Baltimore, Maryland. Quarterly. $5.00 per year.

1969 *CRISIS,* Organ of the National Association for the Advancement of Colored People. The Crisis Publishing Company, Inc., 1790 Broadway, New York, New York, 10019. Monthly from October to May and Bi-monthly June-July, August-September. $1.50 per year.

1970 *EBONY.* Johnson Publishing Company, 1820 South Michigan Avenue, Chicago, Illinois, 60616. Monthly. $5.00 per year.

1971 *FREEDOMWAYS; A Quarterly Review of the Negro Freedom Movement.* Freedomway Associates, 799 Broadway, New York, New York, 10013. Quarterly. $3.50 per year.

1972 *HARVARD JOURNAL OF NEGRO AFFAIRS.* Organ of the

Association of African and Afro-American Students at Harvard and Radcliffe. Winthrop E-41, Harvard University, Cambridge, Massachusetts. Semi-annually. $2.00.

1973 *INTEGRATED EDUCATION.* Integrated Education Associates, 343 South Dearborn Street, Chicago, Illinois, 60604. Bi-monthly. $4.00 per year.

1974 *JET.* Johnson Publishing Company, 1820 South Michigan Avenue, Chicago, Illinois, 60616. Weekly, pocket-size. $7.00 per year.

1975 *JOURNAL OF BLACK POETRY.* 1308 Masonic Avenue No. 4, San Francisco, California, 94117. Quarterly. $3.80

1976 *JOURNAL OF HUMAN RELATIONS.* Central State College, Wilberforce, Ohio. Quarterly. $4.00 per year.

1977 *JOURNAL OF INTERGROUP RELATIONS.* National Association of Intergroup Relations Officials, 426 West 58th Street, New York, New York, 10019. Quarterly. $6.00 per year.

1978 *JOURNAL OF NEGRO EDUCATION.* Published for the Bureau of Educational Research by the Howard University Press, Washington, D.C., 20001. Quarterly. $5.00 per year.

1979 *JOURNAL OF NEGRO HISTORY.* The Association for the Study of Negro Life and History, Inc., 1538 Ninth Street, N.W., Washington, D.C., 20001. Quarterly. $6.00 per year.

1980 *JOURNAL OF RELIGIOUS THOUGHT.* The School of Religion, Howard University, Washington, D.C., 20001. Semi-annually. $3.00 per year.

1981 *JOURNAL OF THE NATIONAL MEDICAL ASSOCIATION.* The Association, 421 Hudson Street, New York, New York, 10014. Bi-monthly. $15.00 per year.

1982 *LIBERATOR.* Afro-American Research Institute, Inc., 244 East Street, New York, New York, 10017. Monthly. $3.00 per year.

1983 *MUHAMMAD SPEAKS.* Published by Muhammad's Mosque No. 2,634. E. 79th Street. Chicago, Ill., 60617. Weekly. $10.00 per year.

1984 *NEGRO-AMERICAN LITERATURE FORUM FOR SCHOOL AND*

*UNIVERSITY TEACHERS.* Terre Haute, Indiana, Indiana State University, 47809. Quarterly. $2.00 per year.

1985 *NEGRO DIGEST.* Johnson Publishing Company, 1820 South Michigan Avenue, Chicago, Illinois, 60616. Monthly. $4.00 per year.

1986 *NEGRO EDUCATIONAL REVIEW.* Florida Memorial College, St. Augustine, Florida. Quarterly. $5.00 per year.

1987 *NEGRO HERITAGE.* P.O. Box 1057, Washington, D.C., 20013. Monthly. $3.75 per year.

1988 *NEGRO HISTORY BULLETIN.* The Association for the Study of Negro Life and History, Inc., 1538 Ninth Street, N.W., Washington, D.C., 20001. Monthly except June, July, August and September. $3.00 per year.

1989 *NEW SOUTH.* Southern Regional Council, 5 Forsyth Street, N.W., Atlanta 3, Georgia. Quarterly. $3.00 per year.

1990 *PHYLON.* Atlanta University, Atlanta, Georgia. Quarterly. $3.00 per year.

1991 *QUARTERLY REVIEW OF HIGHER EDUCATION AMONG NEGROES.* Johnson C. Smith University, Charlotte, North Carolina. Quarterly. $2.00 per year.

1992 *RACE RELATIONS LAW REPORTER.* Vanderbilt University School of Law, 131 21st Avenue, South, Nashville, Tennessee, 37203. Quarterly. $5.00 per year.

1993 *RIGHTS AND REVIEWS, A Magazine of the Black Power Movement in America.* New York Chapter of CORE, 307 West 125th Street, New York, New York, 10027. Single copy $0.50.

1994 *SOULBOOK; the Quarterly Journal of Revolutionary Afro-America.* Berkeley, Calif. P.O. Box 1097. Quarterly $3.00. "Black Music, Economics, Black Poetry, Anti-imperialism."

1995 *SEPIA.* Sepia Publishing Company, 1220 Harding Street, Fort Worth, Texas, 76102. Monthly. $2.00 per year.

1996 *SOUTHERN PATRIOT.* Southern Conference Educational Fund, 3210 West Broadway, Louisville, Kentucky, 40211. Monthly except July. $3.00 per year.

# Author Index

Abbott, Martin. 1224
Abbott, Robert S. 415,926
Abraham, Henry J. 1466, 1575
Abrahams, Roger D. 974, 980
Abrams, Charles. 1770-1773
Adams, Caswell. 1894
Adams, Edward C.L. 981-983
Adams, Russell L. 235
Adger, Robert M. 1
Adler, Elmer. 537
Adoff, Arnold, 538
Ahmann, Matthew. 1731
Aiken, Charles J. 1505
Albert, Octavia Victoria Rogers. 304
Aldridge, Ira. 403, 583
Alexander, Albert A. 37
Alexander, Richard D. 1091, 1124
Alexander, Sadie Tanner. 1467
Allen, James Egert. 1225
Allen, James Stewart, 1043,1226
Allen, Richard. 404
Allen, Walter C. 305
Allen, William Francis. 932
Alston, Walter. 1964
American Academy of Political and Social
  Science, Philadelphia. 1576
American Council on Race Relations. 31
American Federation of Labor and Congress of
  Industrial Organization. 1506
American Friends Service Committee. 1774,
    1775
American Jewish Committee. 32
American Jewish Congress. 1776
The American Mercury. 539
American Negro Academy. 1507
American Oil Company. 158
Ames, William C. 1227
Amos, Preston E. 2
Anderson, Marian. 306,413,936
André, Sam. 1912
Andrews, Bennie. 538
Andrews, Sidney. 1228
Aptheker, Herbert. 307, 458, 1229-1234
Archibald, Helen A. 33
Armstrong, Henry. 1895
Arter, Rhetta Marie. 1777
*The Arts and the Black Revolution.* 507
Ashby, William Mobile. 715
Ashe, Arthur. 308, 1896, 1953
Ashmore, Harry S. 1163
Association for the Study of Negro Life and
  History. 1092
*At Work in Industry Today.* 1125
Atkins, James A. 309
Attaway, William. 716
*Aunt Sally; or, The Cross the Way to Freedom.*
  310
Austin, Frank Eugene. 1235
Avins, Alfred. 1236, 1778

Baerg, Harry. 1947
Bailey, Harry A. 1508
Bailey, Pearl. 311
Bain, Graham C.B. 1877
Bainbridge, Katherine. 948
Baker, Augusta. 34
Baker, Barbara. 88
Baker, O.J. 216
Baldwin, James. 51, 71, 112, 597, 598,
  717-720, 895, 896, 1577, 1592, 1594
Ball, Charles. 312, 313
Ball, Edward D. 1210
Ballagh, James C. 1237
Ballowe, Hewitt Leonard. 984
Baltimore/Afro-American 540
Baltzell, E. Digby. 1611
Banfield, Edward C. 1509, 1510, 1803
Bankett, Lelia W. 314
Banks, J.H. 315
Banneker, Benjamin. 361
Barbour, Floyd Barrington. 1710
Bardolph, Richard. 236, 1238
Barksdale, Gaynelle W. 206-210
Barndt, Joseph R. 1711
Barth, Alan. 1468
Bartlett, Irving H. 1239, 1240
Barton, Rebecca Chalmers. 237
Bassey, Hogan. 1897
Bates, Daisy. 316
Baugham, Lawrence E. Alan. 1241
Bayley, Solomon. 317
Beam, Lura. 1242
Beasley, Delilah L. 139, 1243
Becker, Gary S. 1044
Beech, Mollie L. 19
Beecher, John. 1713
Beechwood, Mary.
Belafonte, Harry. 490
Belasco, David. 435
Bell, James Madison. 621
Bell, William Kenan. 1045
Benet, Stephen. 708
Benford, Robert J. 79
Bennett, Elaine C. 137
Bennett, George 721
Bennett, John. 985
Bennett, Lerone. 238, 318, 897, 1244-1246,
  1712
Bent, Michael J. 1836
Berger, Morroe. 1247, 1469
Berman, Daniel M. 1164
Bernard, Jacqueline. 319
Bernstein, Abraham. 1165, 1578
Berson, Lenora B. 1579
Berthier, Denise. 488
Berthier, Michel. 488
Bethel, Elizabeth. 138
Bethune, Mary McLeod. 260, 375
Bettman, Otto. 1906

Bibb, Henry. 320
Bibliographic Survey: the Negro in Print. 4
Bicknell, Marguerite Elizabeth. 159
Bigman, Stanley K. 1844
Billingsley, Andrew. 1580
Billington, Ray Allen. 1248
Bingham, William. 1923
Bittle, William E. 1249
*The Black Book.* 222
*Black Dialogue.* 1966
*Black Power: Value Revolution Toward Community and Peace.* 1713
Black Theatre. 578, 1967
Blackburn, M.J. 986
Blair, Lewis Harvie. 1046
Bland, James. 338
Blanton, Lorenzo D. 573
Blaustein, Albert P. 1581
Blossom, Virgil T. 1166
Blythe, Legette. 334
Boas, Frank. 1015
Boles, Robert. 722
Bolivar, William Carl. 35
Bond, Frederick W. 574, 579
Bond, Horace Mann. 1167, 1168
Bone, Robert A. 508
Bonger, Willem Adriaan. 1878
Bontemps, Arna Wendell. 45, 54, 239, 240, 541, 542, 560, 723-728, 950, 1014, 1250, 1251, 1898
Booker, Simeon. 1582
*Books, Films, Recordings by and about the American Negro.* 36
Boris, Joseph J. 225, 226
Botkin, Benjamin Albert. 987, 1252
The Bowdoin College Museum of Art. 469
Bowers, Claude Gernade. 1253
Boyar, Burt. 341
Boyar, Jan. 341
Boykin, James H. 1254
Bradford, Perry. 933
Bradford, Roark. 602, 988, 989
Bradford, Sarah. 321
Bradley, Mary Hastings. 393
Bragg, George F. 241
Braithwaite, William Stanley Beaumont. 622, 623, 624
Branch, Hettye Wallace. 322
Branch, William Blackwell. 599
Brandeis University, Waltham, Mass. 1779
Brawley, Benjamin Griffith. 242, 243, 323, 509-511
Breitman, George. 324, 396
Breman, Paul. 543
Brewer, John Mason. 244, 990-994, 1511
Brickman, William W. 1169
Briggs, Vernon. 1142
Brink, William. 1093, 1583, 1584

Brock, William Ranulf. 1255
Broderick, Francis L. 325, 1585
Brogan, Dennis W. 1512
Bronz, Stephen H. 512
Brooke, Edward W. 1513
Brooks, Alexander D. 37
Brooks, Charlotte, 304
Brooks, Elaine C. 19
Brooks, Gwendolyn. 625-629, 729
Brooks, Hallie Beachem. 1177
Brooks, Maxwell R. 913
Broom, Leonard. 1256
Brotz, Howard. 1257, 1732
Brown, Claude. 326
Brown, Frank London. 730
Brown, H. Rap. 327
Brown, Hallie Quinn. 245
Brown, Hugh Victor. 1170
Brown, Ina Corinne. 1258
Brown, James N. 1899
Brown, John. 328, 347
Brown, Josephine. 329
Brown, Lloyd L. 731
Brown, Roscoe. 184
Brown, Sterling Allen. 513, 514, 544, 630
Brown, Warren. 38, 914
Brown, William Garrott. 1514
Brown, William Wells. 246, 247, 329, 330, 732
Browne, Robert T. 25
Bruce, John Edward. 248
Bryant, Lawrence Chesterfield. 934
Buckle, Richard. 491
Buckler, Helen. 331
Buckmaster, Henrietta. 1259, 1260
Budd, Edward C. 1586
Bullins, Ed. 563, 600
Bullock, Henry Allen. 1171
Bunche, Ralph J. 1587
Buni, Andrew. 1515
Burch, Charles Eaton. 149
Burckel, Christian. 230
Bureau of National Affairs. 1588
Burns, W. Haywood. 1589
Burroughs, Margaret T. 352
Business and the Urban Crisis. 1780
Butcher, Margaret Just. 515

Cade, John Brother. 332
Cain, Alfred E. 179, 1261
Caldwell, Ben. 601
Caldwell, Dista H. 1172
California Art Commission. 470
California. State Fair Employment Practice Commission. 1047
Caliver, Ambrose. 39, 40
Calloway, Willie. 1887
Calverton, Victor Francis. 545
Campanella, Roy. 1900

# INDEX

Campbell, Charles. 384
Campbell, James Edwin. 631
Cannon, David Wadsworth. 632
Carawan, Guy. 935
Carey, Elizabeth L. 41
Carleton, William G. 1550
Carmer, Carl. 987
Carmichael, Bennie. 1210
Carmichael, Stokely. 563, 1714
Carr, Malcolm Wallace. 1837
Carter, Hodding. 1490
Carter, Wilmoth Annette. 1094, 1590
Carver, George Washington. 60, 348, 374
Catterall, Helen Honor (Tunnicliff). 1470
Cayton, Horace R. 1051, 1126
*Celebrating Negro History and Brotherhood.* 471
Chamber of Commerce of the United States.
  1095, 1173
Chamberlain, Bernard Peyton. 1879
Chambers, Bradford. 1715
Chambers, H.A. 936
Chambers, Lucile Arcola. 1262
Chamerovzow, L.A. 328
Charters, Ann. 516
Charters, Samuel Barclay. 516, 937-939
Chastain, Thomas. 733
Chatman, J.A. 1838
Cherry, Gwendolyn. 249
Chesnutt, Charles Waddell. 140, 734, 735, 736,
  737, 738
Chesnutt, Helen M. 333
Chicago Commission on Race Relations. 1591
Christensen, Abigail M.H. 995
Cincinnati Public Schools. 1263
*The Civil Rights Act of 1964.* 1471
CLA Journal. 1968
Clark, Dennis. 1781
Clark, Edgar Rogie. 940
Clark, Elmer Talmage. 1733
Clark, Henry. 1734, 1782
Clark, Kenneth B. 182, 1048, 1579,
  1592
Clark, Mary T. 1472, 1593
Clark, Peter Wellington. 1264
Clark, Septima P. 334
Clark, Thomas D. 915
Clarke, Jacquelyne Johnson. 1516
Clarke, John Henrik. 546, 1049
Clay, Cassius. 1947
Clayton, Edward T. 1517
Cleaver, Eldridge. 335, 1594
Cleaves, Mary W. 3
Cleghorn, Reese. 1571
Clemons, Lulamae. 1265
Clift, Virgil A. 1174
Cluzel, Magdeleine. 492
Cobb, William Montague. 1839-1841
Cocke, Sarah Johnson. 996

Cogan, Lee. 1842
Cohen, Haskell. 1928
Cohen, Irving S. 1337
Cohn, David. 997
Cole, Carriebel B. 493
Cole, Taylor. 1518
Coleman, Edward Maceo. 566
Coleman, J. Winston. 1266
Coleman, James Samuel. 1175
Coles, Robert. 1176
Collier, Bert. 1212
Collins, Charles Wallace. 1473
Collins, Winfield Hazlett. 1880
Commager, Henry Steele. 1595
Commission on Race and Housing. 1783
Commons, John Rogers. 1127
Conference of Negro Writers. 1st, New York.
  517, 547
Conference on the Role of the Library in
  Improving Education in the South, Atlanta
  University, Atlanta, Georgia. 1177
Congressional Quarterly Service, Washington,
  D.C. 1596
Connecticut. Inter-racial Commission. 42
Connelly, Marcus Cook. 602, 953
Conot, Robert. 1597
Conrad, Earl. 336, 1267
Conroy, Jack. 239, 1250
Cooper, Sophia. 1083
Cope, Myron. 1902
Coppin, Levi Jenkins. 146
Cornell-Tompkins County Committee for Free
  and Fair Elections in Fayette County,
  Tennessee. 1519
Cornely, Paul B. 1843, 1844
Cornish, Dudley Taylor. 1268
Corwin, Edward-Henry Lewinski. 1845
Cotter, Joseph Seamon. 603, 633, 739
Couch, William. 587
Coulter, Ellis Merton. 1269
The Council on Human Relations. 43
Countryman, Vern. 1474, 1598
Courlander, Harold. 941, 998
Covarrubias, Miguel. 951
Cox, John H. 1520
Cox, LaWanda. 1520
Cozens, Frederick Warren. 1901
Craig, Tom. 1689
Crain, Robert L. 1178
Cray, Ed. 1599
*Crisis.* 1969
Crogman, William H. 166
Cromwell, John Wesley. 1270
Cromwell, Otelia. 548
Cronon, Edmund David. 337
Crosby, Muriel. 44
Crowe, Charles. 1271
Crum, Mason. 999

189

# INDEX

Eaton, Isabel. 1611
*Ebony*. 1970
Edmonds, Helen G. 1523
Edmonds, Randolph. 588, 589, 607, 608
*Education of the Colored Race in Industry*. 47
Edwards, G. Franklin. 524, 1054, 1609
Edwards, Harry Stillwell. 996
Edwards, Paul K. 1055
Edwin, Ed. 372
Eichner, Alfred S. 1303
Einstein, Charles. 1932, 1934
Elli, Frank. 1610
Elliott, Lawrence. 348
Ellis, Ethel M. Vaughan. 6, 204
Ellison, Ralph. 759, 903
Ellison, Virginia H. 37
Emanuel, James A. 349, 551
Embree, Edwin R. 260
Embry, James Crawford. 904
Emmett, Dan. 970
*Encyclopedia of the Negro*. 164
Endlemen, Shalom. 1611
Epps, Archie. 397
Eppse, Merl Raymond. 1287, 1288
Epstein, Lenore A. 1077
Errol, John. 609
*Esquire*. 1907
Essien-Udom, E.U. 1736
Evans, James C. 48
Evans, Lancelot O. 179
Evans, William McKee. 1289
Everett, Robinson. O. 1612
Evers, Charles. 924
Evers, Mrs. Medgar. 350
*The Evolution of Afro-American Artists*. 473

Faber, Doris. 261
Faber, Harold, 261
Fager, Charles E. 1716
Faggett, H.L. 540
Fahey, John Aloysius, 945
Fahey, William A. 287
Fair Housing Council of Metropolitan, Washington, 1787
Fanon, Frantz. 1613
Farbe, Michel. 49
Farmer, James. 1614, 1698
Farr, Finis. 351, 1908
Fauset, Arthur Huff. 262, 1737
Fauset, Jessie. 760-762
Federal Writers' Project. 552
Fien, Rashi. 1056
Feldman, Eugene P. Romayn. 50, 352
Feldman, Herman. 1057
Felton, Ralph Almon. 1738
Fenner, Thomas Putnam. 946
Ferguson, Blanche E. 353
Ferman, Louis A. 1128
Ferris, William Henry. 263

Fields, Uriah J. 1615
Filler, Louis. 7, 1290
Fischer, Russell G. 51
Fishel, Leslie H. 1291
Fisher, Miles Mark. 947
Fisher, Paul. 918, 1620
Fisher, Rudolph. 763, 764
Fisk University Nashville Tenn. 140, 211
Fisk University, Nashville. Social Science Institute. 264
Fitzgerald, Ed. 357
Fitzhugh, H. Naylor. 1110
Flanders, T. 52
Fleischer, Nathaniel S. 1909-1912
Fleishman, Stanley. 1477
Fleming, George James. 230, 1524
Fleming, Walter Lynwood. 1098, 1292
Fleming, William Henry. 1293
Fletcher, Tom. 1913
Foley, Albert S. 265, 354, 1739
Foley, Eugene P. 1058, 1717
Foner, Philip Sheldon. 355
Fontaine, William Thomas. 1616
Foote, Nelson N. 1788
Ford, Nick Aaron. 520
Foreman, Paul B. 8
Forman, James. 1617
Forten, Charlotte L. 1248
Forten, James.
Fortune, Amos. 400
Fortune, T. Thomas. 293
Foster, William Zebulon. 1294
Fountain, William A. 194
Fowler, Juby Earl. 1502
Fowler, Julian S. 145
Francis, Charles E. 1295
Frank, Waldo. 845
Franklin, Charles Lionel 1129
Franklin, John Hope. 1296-1299, 1618, 1619
Frazier, E. Franklin. 136, 1059, 1060, 1300, 1609, 1740
Frederick, John T. 576
Freedom of Information Conference. 1620
Freedomways, 1971
Freeman, Joseph. 554
Freeman, Walter E. 150
Frick, Ford C. 1935
Friedman, Leon. 1478, 1621
Friml, Rudolf. 948
Fuchs, Estelle. 1184
Furman, A.L. 844
Furness, William H. 421
*Further Reading on Student Movement*. 53

Gafafer, William McKinley. 1848
Gaines, William A. 1851
Gallagher, Buell Gordon. 1185
Gara, Larry. 1301
Gardiner, George L. 54

191

Gardner, Steve.
Garfinkel, Herbert. 1130
Garrison, Lucy McKim. 932
Garvey, A. Jacques. 356
Garvey, Marcus. 337, 356
Gates, Robbins L. 1186
Gay, Joseph R. 165, 181
Geis, Gilbert. 1249
Geismar, Maxwell. 335
Genovese, Eugene D. 1302
Gewecke, Clifford G. 308, 1896
Ghelderade, Michel de. 492
Gibson, Althea. 357, 1914
Gibson, John William. 166
Gilbert, Ben W. 1622
Gilbert, Olive. 358
Gillard, John Thomas. 1741
Gilmer, Gertrude Cordelia. 55
Ginzberg, Eli. 1061, 1099, 1100, 1131, 1134, 1187, 1303
Glazer, Nathan. 1289
Glazier, Harlan E. 1849
Gleason, William. 1959
Gloster, Hugh Morris. 521
Godrich, John.
Gold, Michael. 678
Golden, Harry. 334, 1623
Golden State Mutual Life Insurance Company. 474
Golding, Louis. 1915
Goldsborough, Edmund K. 1006
Golston, Robert. 1304
Gomillion, Charles G. 1562
Gonzales, Ambrose Elliott. 1007-1009
Gordon, Edmund W. 1188
Gore, George William, Jr. 919
Gorham, Thelma T. 917
Gosnell, Harold F. 1525
Gourlay, Jack G. 1132
Gow, James. 606
Graham, Hugh Davis. 920
Graham, Lorenz B. 765
Graham, Shirley. 359-361, 766, 767
Grant, Joanne. 1718
Grant, John Wesley. 768
Grauer, William. 959
Gray, Alma L.
Grayshon, Matthew Clifford. 56
Green, Elizabeth Lay. 522
Green, Ely. 362
Green, Jacob D. 363
Green, Paul. 620
Greenberg, Jack. 1479
Greenblat, Cathy S. 191
Greene, Constance McLaughlin. 1624
Greene, Ellen F. 1839
Greene, Harry Washington. 57, 266
Greene, Lorenzo Johnston. 1133, 1305
Greer, Scott. 1790
Gregory, Dick. 254, 364, 1625, 1626
Gregory, Montgomery. 593

Grier, Eunice S. 1742, 1791-1793
Grier, George. 1791, 1792
Griffin, Appleton Prentiss Clark. 28, 58
Grigg, Charles. 1649
Griggs, Sutton Elbert. 769-772
Grigsby, William G. 1811
Grimke, Angelina E. 277
Grimke, Angelina W. 610
Grimke, Francis James. 905, 906, 1627-1629
Grimke, Sarah. 276
Grinstead, Scott. 9
Gross, Milton. 1945
Gross, Seymour L. 523
Gross, Theodore L. 551
Gulledge, Ola Lee. 974
Gurin, Patricia. 1189
Gutman, Herbert G. 1157
Guttman, Egon. 1101, 1102
Guzman, Jessie Parkhurst. 59, 60, 193

Halasz, Nicholas. 1306
Haley, Alex. 395
Haley, James T. 167
Hall, Woodrow Wadsworth. 61, 1526
Hallowell, John H. 1518
Hamilton, Charles V. 1714
Hammon, Jupiter. 128
Hammond, Lily (Hardy). 1630
Hampton, Virginia. Normal and Agricultural Institute. Collis P. Huntington Library. 141, 1850
Hampton, Wade. 1319
Handlin, Oscar. 1307, 1684
Handy, James A. 267
Handy, William Christopher. 949-951
Hansberry, Lorraine. 611, 1631
Hardwick, Richard. 365
Hardy, John E. 523
Hare, Maud Cuney. 952
Harlan, Louis R. 168, 1308, 1632, 1683
Harmon Foundation. New York City. 475
Harmon, John H. 1092
Harper, Frances Ellen Watkins. 659-664, 773
Harrington, Ollie. 1034
Harris, Abram Lincoln. 1103, 1157
Harris, Janet. 1633
Harris, Joel Chandler. 953, 1010
Harris, Louis. 1586
Harris, Norman Dwight. 1309
Hartshorn, William Newton. 169, 268
Harvard Journal of Negro Affairs. 1972
Hatchcock, Louise. 1011
Hawkins, Hugh. 366, 1632
Hawkins, William George. 367
Hayden, Robert Earl. 552, 553, 665-668
Hayden, William. 368
Hayes, Rutherford B. 1390
Haynes, Elizabeth R. 269
Haynes, George Edmund. 1062
Haynes, Leonard. 1743

# INDEX

# INDEX

Lancaster, H. Carrington. 566
Landau, Saul. 1644
Lane, Isaac. 437
Lane, Lunsford. 367
Lanier, Betty. 94
Lanusse, Armand. 566
Larkin, John R. 1332
Larsen, Nella. 806, 807
Larsson, Cloyte M. 1071
Lash, John S. 72
Laurenti, Luigi. 1797
Lavine, Hannibal. 1654
Lawrence, Jacob. 679
Lawson, Elizabeth. 392
Lawson, Hilda Josephine. 73
Lawyers Guild Review. 1798
Leckie, William H. 1333
Lee, George Washington. 808, 809
Lee, Irvin H. 1139, 1334
Lee, Reba. 393
Lee, Ulysses. 544, 1140
Lehrer, Stanley. 1169
Leighton, Francis S. 418
Lemert, Edwin McCarthy. 1884
Lerner, Gerda. 276
Leskes, Theodore. 1653
Lester, Julius. 1721
Levene, Helen H. 1314
Levin, Arthur J. 1810
Lewinson, Paul. 147, 1534
Lewis, Anthony. 1655
Lewis, Claude. 394
Lewis, Edmonia. 473
Lewis, Edward Erwin. 1141
*Liberator.* 1982
Liebling, Abbott Joseph. 1925
Lightfoot, Claude M. 1656, 1722
Lightfoot, Philip M. 1562
Lightfoot, Robert Mitchell, 1885
Lincoln, Abraham. 1377, 1606
Lincoln, Charles Eric. 1657-1660, 1750
Lindsay, Arnett G. 1092
Lipman, David. 1944
Lipsyte, Robert. 364
Liss, Howard. 1926, 1933
Liston, Sonny. 1963
Little, Malcolm. 324, 395-397, 1592, 1594
Littlejohn, David. 528
Litwack, Leon F. 1335
Livingstone College. Salisbury, N.C.
  Carnegie Library.
Lloyd, Margaret. 498
Lloyd, Raymond Grann. 1535
Locke, Alain LeRoy. 12, 13, 77, 80, 237, 477,
  478, 529, 567, 593, 962
Lofton, John. 1336
Logan, Rayford W. 343, 384, 524, 923, 1337,
  1338, 1536
Loggins, Vernon. 74, 530

Loguen, Jermain Wesley. 398
Lomax, Alan. 935
Lomax, Louis E. 1661
Long, Herman Hodge. 1799
Long, Margaret. 75
Los Angeles Public Library. Municipal
  Reference Library. 76
Louis, Joe. 1927, 1928, 1937
Love, Nat. 399
Love, Rose Leary. 1020
Lowenstein, Ralph. 918
Lubell, Samuel. 1662
Lucas, John. 963, 964
Lumer, Hyman. 1072
Lyda, John W. 1339
Lyle, Jack. 172, 924
Lynch, John R. 927, 1340
Lynk, Miles Vandahurst. 1857
Lytle, Charlotte W. 197

Mabry, William Alexander. 1537
MacIver, Robert M. 1469
Mack, Raymond W. 1073
Mackley, Bernard. 1603
Madgett, Naomi Long. 695
Magdol, Edward. 1341
Magoun, F. Alexander. 400
Magriel, Paul David. 499
Mahoney, Jack. 965
Majors, Monroe Alphus. 277
Malcolm X See Little, Malcolm.
Mallalieu, Rev. Bishop Willard F. 304
Mallery, David. 1198
Mallory, Edward J. 1927
Malvin, John. 401
Mammy Pleasant. See Pleasant, Mary Ellen
Mangum, Charles Staples. 1489
Manhattan Medical Society, New York City.
  1858
Mann, Arthur William. 1929, 1930
Margetson, George Reginald. 696, 697, 698
Margolies, Edward. 50
Marsh, J.B.T. 966
Marshall, Albert Prince. 201
Marshall, Burke, 1663
Marshall, F. Ray. 1142-1144
Marshall, Herbert. 402, 582
Marshall, Paule 810
Martin, Fletcher. 1931
Martin, John Joseph. 500, 501
Martin, Robert E. 77
Marx, Barbara. 11
Marx, Gary T. 1664
Maryland, Morgan State College. 1730
Mason, Julian D. 709
Mather, Frank Lincoln. 231
Mathews, Marcia M. 403
Matlock, Lucius C. 320
Matthews, Brander. 688

Matthews, Donald R. 1538
Maund, Alfred. 1859
May, Samuel Joseph. 78, 421
Mayfield, Julian. 811-813
Mays, Benjamin E. 531, 1751, 1752
Mays, Willie. 1926, 1932-1934
Mazyck, Walter H. 1342
McAfee, Sara Jane Regulua. 1753
McCarthy, Agnes. 1343
McCauley, Patrick. 1210
McClellan, George Marion. 699
McCollum, Ruby. 382
McConnell, Roland C. 148
McCord, Charles Harvey. 1886
McCormick, Ken. 1887
McCulloch, Margeret C. 159
McEntire, Davis. 1800
McGee, Alice E. 573
McGinnis, Frederick A. 1199
McGrath, Earl James. 1200
McGraw, James R. 1625
McGuire, Hunter, 1888
McKay, George Frederick.
McKenney, Joe. 1918
McLin, Velma. E. 149
McManus, Edgar J. 1344
McMillan, Lewis K. 1201
McNamee, Lawrence F. 220
McPheeters, Annie L. 202
McPherson, James M. 1345, 1346
McSweeney, William. 1956
Meany, Thomas. 1935
Meier, August. 1347, 1348, 1350, 1665
Melbourn, Julius. 404
Melden, Charles. 167
Meltzer, Milton. 580, 1316, 1349, 1350
Mendelsohn, Jack. 1666
Menks, Frank Grant. 1936
Meredith, James H. 135, 1202
Merriam, Alan P. 79
Messner, C.T. 1848
Metcalf, George R. 278
Methodist Church (United States) Department
 of Research and Survey. 1801
Meyer, Howard N. 1312
Meyerson, Martin. 1802, 1803
Micheaux, Oscar. 814, 815
Michigan State University, East Lansing,
 Library. 150
Midgette, Lillian Avon. 80
Mikell, I. Jenkins. 1021
Miles, Louella. 14
Miller, Edward B. 208, 209
Miller, Elizabeth W. 15
Miller, Floyd. 405
Miller, Kelly. 1667
Miller, Loren. 1539
Miller, Margery. 1937

Miller, May. 594, 700, 701
Miller, Warren. 816
Miller, William Robert. 406
Mills, Clarence Harvey. 81
Minn, Joseph Karl. 1351
Mississippi Black Paper. 1490
Mitchell, George S. 1126
Mitchell, Glenford E. 910, 1352
Mitchell, James R. 1109
Mitchell, Joseph. 407
Mitchell, Lofton. 583, 616
Mokray, William G. 1938
Momboisse, Raymond M. 1668
Montgomery, David. 1353
Moon, Bucklin. 532, 568
Moon, Henry Lee. 1540
Moore, Archie. 1939
Morais, Herbert M. 170, 1860
Morgan, Albert Talmon. 1354
Morrow, Everett Frederick. 408
Morsbach, Mabel. 1263, 1355
Morton, Lena Beatrice. 409
Morton, Richard Lee. 1541
Moseley, J.H. 1542
Mossell, Gertrude E.H. Bustill. 279
Motley, Willard 817-820
Moton, Robert Russa. 166, 381, 410
Mott, Abigail F. 280
Muelder, Hermann Richard. 1356
Muhammed, Elijah See Poole, Elijah
Muhammed Speaks. 1983
Mulzac, Hugh. 411
Murphy, Beatrice M. 569, 570
Murray, Daniel Alexander Payne. 16
Murray, Florence. 173-176
Murray, Freeman Henry Morris. 479
Murray, Pauli. 412, 1491
Muse, Benjamin. 1203, 1357, 1723
Muste, A.J. 1698
Myrdal, Gunnar. 924, 1074

Nabrit, James M. Jr. 1485
Nashville, Tennessee. State Department of
 Education Division of School Libraries.
Nathan, Hans. 967
Nathan, Winfred B. 1861
National Advisory Commission. 1669, 1670
National Association for the Advancement of
 Colored People. 82, 1145, 1492
National Clearinghouse for Mental Health.
 Information Office of Communications. 83
NCDH Brotherhood in Action Housing Con-
 ference. 1805
National Committee against Discrimination in
 Housing. 1804
National Conference on Equal Employment
 Opportunity, Washington, D.C. 1146
National Conference on Small Business. 1110

# INDEX